THE
COMPLETE
Gone With the Wind
TRIVIA BOOK

THE COMPLETE Gone With the Wind TRIVIA BOOK

THE MOVIE AND MORE

second edition

Pauline Bartel

TAYLOR TRADE PUBLISHING
Lanham • Boulder • New York • Toronto • Plymouth, UK

Published by Taylor Trade Publishing
An imprint of Rowman & Littlefield
4501 Forbes Boulevard, Suite 200, Lanham, Maryland 20706
www.rowman.com

10 Thornbury Road, Plymouth PL6 7PP, United Kingdom

Distributed by NATIONAL BOOK NETWORK

British Library Cataloguing in Publication Information Available

Library of Congress Cataloging-in-Publication Data
Bartel, Pauline C.
  The complete Gone with the wind trivia book : the movie and more /
Pauline Bartel. — Second edition.
      pages cm
  Includes bibliographical references and index.
  ISBN 978-1-58979-820-5 (pbk. : alk. paper) — ISBN 978-1-58979-821-2
(electronic) 1. Gone with the wind (Motion picture) 2. United States—
History—Civil War, 1861–1865—Motion pictures and the war. 3. O'Hara,
Scarlett (Fictitious character) I. Title.
  PN1997.G59B37 2014
  791.43'72—dc23
                                                              2014007097

∞™ The paper used in this publication meets the minimum requirements
of American National Standard for Information Sciences—Permanence of
Paper for Printed Library Materials, ANSI/NISO Z39.48-1992.

Printed in the United States of America

Again, for George

Contents

CONTENTS

Acknowledgments

I thank the members of the Arnold Madison Writing Group for the support and encouragement they have shown me through the years, especially Joyce Bouyea, Jackie Craven, David Drotar, the late Kate Kunz, Joanne McFadden, Jane Streiff, and Donna Tomb.

I appreciate the special assistance provided by Karen DeMartino, Peter Michael Franzese, Barbara Ann Heegan, Jane Eskridge Thomas, and the Waterford Public Library. I am grateful to the wonderful staff at Rowman & Littlefield / Taylor Trade Publishing, especially Candace Johnson, Kalen Landow, Rick Rinehart, Jehanne Schweitzer, and Karie Simpson.

I remain eternally grateful to my mother, who talked a reluctant teenage daughter into seeing *Gone With the Wind* with her on a cold, snowy December afternoon. That changed everything. Thanks, Mom.

Introduction

"There has never been a picture like David O. Selznick's *Gone With the Wind*."

So wrote Kate Cameron, a *Daily News* movie critic, in her four-star review of the film's premiere in New York City on December 19, 1939. Her colleague at the paper, Wanda Hale, also awarded four stars to *Gone With the Wind*. And millions still agree. Today, this Academy Award–winning, box-office champion remains one of the most popular, best-loved movies in history.

Gone With the Wind celebrates its seventy-fifth anniversary in 2014. In honor of this cinematic milestone, I offer an updated edition of this book that will surprise and entertain any *GWTW* fan. *The Complete* Gone With the Wind *Trivia Book: The Movie and More* proves that *GWTW* is more than a film: it is a phenomenon. And the wonder of *GWTW* continues to the present day:

- The novel has sold more than thirty million copies in more than forty languages and still sells more than 75,000 copies in print and electronic formats every year.
- A recent Harris Poll ranked *GWTW* America's second-favorite book, behind the Bible, and America's #1 favorite movie of all time.

- The film holds its #1 spot on the list of all-time movie moneymakers with $1.64 billion in adjusted gross income.
- *GWTW* also remains #1 on the list of all-time ticket sales with more than 202 million tickets sold in North America.
- The American Film Institute ranked *GWTW* in the top ten on its "100 Years . . . 100 Movies" tenth anniversary list.

Through the updated edition of *The Complete* Gone With the Wind *Trivia Book*, you can explore the *GWTW* phenomenon from the writing and publishing of Margaret Mitchell's novel through the Hollywood frenzy of transforming the book into film. You can guess who spoke quotable quotes from the movie and the television miniseries, and you can experience the country's reactions as *GWTW* and *Scarlett* swept across America. The book takes you right up to present day, when appetites of fans have been whetted by the novel's seventy-fifth birthday and the seventy-fifth anniversary of the film.

In this new edition, you'll learn all about:

- The film's fiftieth anniversary celebration in 1989, reuniting eleven original cast members for Atlanta celebrations and the world premiere of a digitally remastered version of *Gone With the Wind*.
- The publication of *Scarlett*, the long-anticipated sequel to the novel, which earned praise as one of the fastest-selling books and scorn as one of the year's worst reads.
- The drama of the two-year, worldwide search for an actress to play Scarlett in the 1994 television miniseries, trouble on the set during filming, and the sneak-peek fiasco that brought laughter—and boos— from television critics.
- The discovery and publication of *Lost Laysen*—a South Pacific romance containing the literary seeds of *Gone with the Wind*—written by a sixteen-year-old Margaret Mitchell, given as a gift to a suitor, and forgotten about for nearly eighty years.
- The saga of the second sequel to *Gone with the Wind*: the first writer was fired, the second writer nixed the deal, and the third writer finally delivered the goods.
- Atlanta's Margaret Mitchell House and Museum, the apartment building where the author gave birth to Scarlett O'Hara; its Phoenix-

like rise after two suspicious fires; and its designation as a national "Literary Landmark."

- The reconstruction and opening of Clark Gable's birthplace in Cadiz, Ohio, as a landmark and as a site for annual celebrations of the actor's birth.
- The bombshell news that Loretta Young, who auditioned for the role of Scarlett, confirmed before her death that her adopted daughter was her biological child by Clark Gable.
- The legal battle over the publication of *The Wind Done Gone*, a novel reinterpreting Margaret Mitchell's story from the point of view of Scarlett's mixed-race half sister.
- The discovery of the typescript of the last four chapters of Margaret Mitchell's novel thought to have been destroyed after the author's death.
- The after–*Gone With the Wind* lives of the film's remaining cast members.
- The restoration work on three original *Gone With the Wind* costumes in time for the film's seventy-fifth anniversary; and much, much more.

What makes me such a *GWTW* expert? I was blown away by *The Wind* at the age of sixteen when, during Christmas vacation from school, I accompanied my mother to see the film's latest reissue. On that afternoon in 1968, I fell in love with this spectacular story of indomitable will and indestructible spirit. And so began my dream of one day visiting Margaret Mitchell's hometown. But little did I imagine the manner in which that dream would come true twenty-one years later.

On December 9, 1989, my Delta flight arrived at Hartsfield International Airport. I was thrilled to be in Atlanta, but I wasn't there as just a tourist. As the author of the first edition of *The Complete* Gone With the Wind *Trivia Book*, I was part of the weeklong celebration of the movie's fiftieth anniversary.

Turner Broadcasting Systems Inc. and a host of sponsors offered special events guaranteed to gladden the hearts of the thousands of "Windies" who packed Atlanta's hotels. Tours and exhibits as well as lectures on Margaret Mitchell and the making of the film were part of my *GWTW* immersion. I visited Jonesboro, the literary location of the fictional Tara; and I made a pilgrimage to the Crescent Apartments site where Margaret Mitchell wrote most of her novel.

At the Hyatt Regency, on December 12, I cheered the winners of the Scarlett and Rhett Look-Alike Contest, then later sipped Scarlett O'Hara cocktails at the Polaris, the hotel's revolving rooftop restaurant. At Rich's downtown, on December 13, I practically swooned meeting *GWTW*'s stars at the elegant, special-invitation Cast Reunion Party.

Hoopskirts and hoopla reigned at *Gone With the Wind*'s Fiftieth Anniversary Ball on the evening of the fourteenth. There at the Georgia International Convention and Trade Center, I was one of the 1,500 costumed guests who nibbled on lavish hors d'oeuvres and danced to the Ray Bloch Orchestra. On the dais, ten members of *GWTW*'s cast were introduced to the adoring attendees.

All the excitement of *GWTW*'s 1939 debut was re-created on Friday, December 15, with the re-premiere of the film at the fabulous Fox Theatre. The theater's façade was decorated with white columns, and a portrait of Scarlett and Rhett hung high above street level. Searchlights sweeping the scene and a band playing "Dixie" and "Tara's Theme" welcomed the cast members, who arrived in white limousines for the pre-film party.

At 7:30 p.m., I moved with nearly four thousand other partygoers into the main theater for the welcoming ceremony. Am I really here, I wondered, pinching myself to confirm that it was true—in Atlanta—at the re-premiere of *Gone With the Wind*?

Master of ceremonies Larry King, well-known radio and television host, introduced the cast members and Ted Turner. Then the houselights dimmed, a hush fell over the audience, and *GWTW*'s music filled the theater. For the next four hours, I watched Scarlett O'Hara win hearts with a toss of her dark curls, flash her willful green eyes at disaster, and vow to think of some way to get Rhett back. And I loved *GWTW* all over again.

As the curtain closed, the audience rose as one, applauding wildly. Later, while I followed the crowd to the post-premiere champagne brunch, I reflected with amazement and disbelief on all that had happened to me that week. My book had debuted in the city Margaret Mitchell had called home. I had met the remaining members of the movie's cast and the younger son of producer David O. Selznick. I had autographed copies of my book for them, and they had accepted me as part of *GWTW*'s family. My dream of visiting Atlanta had come true at last but better than I had ever imagined.

The updated edition of *The Complete* Gone With the Wind *Trivia Book: The Movie and More* is a true labor of love. The book is my seventy-fifth anniversary tribute to Margaret Mitchell, David O. Selznick, Vivien

Leigh, Clark Gable, Olivia de Havilland, Leslie Howard, and the countless others who were responsible for making *Gone With the Wind*, in the words of *Daily News* movie critic Wanda Hale, "the most magnificent motion picture of all time."

You could "think about it tomorrow," but why wait? Turn the page today and start exploring *The Complete* Gone With the Wind *Trivia Book: The Movie and More.*

ONE

Author! Author!

DID YOU KNOW THAT MARGARET MITCHELL . . .

- Was born, raised, and lived her life in Atlanta, Georgia?
- Enjoyed listening to Civil War stories told to her by Southern veterans, family, and friends?
- Was married twice? She married Berrien "Red" Upshaw in 1922. Her second husband, whom she married in 1925, was John R. Marsh. He had served as best man at her first wedding.
- Kept her birth name after marriage: Margaret Munnerlyn Mitchell?
- Published only one magazine piece, "Matrimonial Bonds," which appeared in a local periodical, the *Open Door*, in 1925?
- Worked for the *Atlanta Journal Sunday Magazine* as a reporter at a salary of twenty-five dollars a week? Her most famous interview was with Rudolph Valentino.
- Resigned in 1926 and filled her time researching information on the "War Between the States"?
- Was confined to her apartment by an injured ankle and began writing a Civil War novel?
- Wrote her book using a Remington portable typewriter and yellow copy paper?

- Wrote the last chapter of *Gone with the Wind* (*GWTW*) first?
- Kept completed chapters of *GWTW* in manila envelopes that she stacked on the floor of her apartment?
- Originally called her heroine Pansy O'Hara?
- Originally called Tara Fontenoy Hall?
- Originally called Melanie Permalia?
- Reported to friends that "It stinks" when they asked how her book was going?
- Received a $500 advance from Macmillan for the novel?
- Used *Another Day* as the working title for her book? Other titles she considered were *Milestones*, *Jettison*, *Ba! Ba! Black Sheep*, *Not in Our Stars*, and *Bugles Sang True*.
- Found the actual title for her novel in the first line of the third stanza of Ernest Dowson's poem "Non sum qualis eram bonae sub regno Cynarae" ("I have forgot much, Cynara! Gone with the wind")? When Margaret submitted her title to Macmillan, she correctly used the lowercase "w" in "with": *Gone with the Wind*. During Hollywood's transformation of the novel to film, the word "with" inexplicably gained an uppercase initial letter: *Gone With the Wind*.
- Suffered from eye hemorrhages after constant work preparing the manuscript for publication?
- Asked her attorney father, Eugene Mitchell, to review the manuscript for historical accuracy?
- Dedicated the book to her husband: "To J.R.M."?
- Never wrote another book after *GWTW* was published?

Margaret Mitchell began writing *Gone with the Wind* in 1926 and continued working on it on and off for ten years. Being a private person, Margaret told only a few close friends about her novel. One of those friends, Lois Cole, had become an associate editor at the Macmillan Company and told Macmillan vice president Harold Latham about Margaret's novel.

"No one has read it except her husband," Lois Cole told him, "but if she can write the way she talks, it should be a honey of a book."

In April 1935, Latham launched a three-month literary tour through the United States in search of new authors. His starting point was Georgia. He met Margaret at a luncheon in his honor at the Atlanta Athletic Club. Remembering Lois Cole's recommendation, Latham asked if Margaret would let him read her manuscript. Margaret was flattered but knew the awful shape her manuscript was in. The yellow paper had faded, and the typed pages contained many penciled corrections. She had different versions of some chapters, and she hadn't even written an opening chapter. Feeling embarrassed, Margaret denied she had anything to show him.

Latham gave Margaret other opportunities to share her manuscript, at a lunch the following day for local writers and at a tea the day after that. Each time, she refused to discuss her work. She did promise, though, that Latham would be the first to look at her manuscript when she was ready to show it. Margaret, however, thought that this was an unlikely possibility. But something happened after the tea that changed Margaret's mind—and her life—forever.

During the ride home, Margaret and a number of aspiring authors chatted about the evening's events, and someone asked Margaret why she hadn't given her book to Mr. Latham. Margaret admitted that the writing wasn't any good and that she was ashamed of it. One of the writers who was surprised to learn of Margaret's book remarked that she didn't think Margaret took life seriously enough to be a successful novelist. She even found fault with the fact that Margaret's manuscript had never been rejected by a publisher.

"*I've* been refused by the very best publishers. But my book is grand," she told Margaret. "Everybody says it will win the Pulitzer Prize. But, Peggy, I think you are wasting your time trying. You really aren't the type."

At that, Margaret became angry, and she remained angry when she arrived home.

"I was so mad still that I grabbed up what manuscript I could lay hands on," Margaret said, "forgetting entirely that I hadn't included the envelopes that were under the bed or the ones in the pot-and-pan closet, and I posted down to the hotel and caught Latham just as he was about to catch the train. My idea was that at least I could brag that I had been refused by the very best publisher." Margaret gave the large pile of envelopes to Latham and hurried home. Since Latham had no room in his bags, he bought an extra suitcase to carry the manuscript with him.

By the time Margaret cooled down, she realized what she had done. But it was too late. Harold Latham, on a train bound for New Orleans, was thoroughly engrossed in Margaret's manuscript. And the result of Margaret's impulsive act? Three months later, the Macmillan Company offered her a book contract.

PARALLELS BETWEEN
SCARLETT O'HARA AND MARGARET MITCHELL

Scarlett O'Hara

1. Married Lieutenant Charles Hamilton, who died of measles complications shortly after the Civil War began.
2. Shocked Atlanta society by dancing with Rhett Butler while in mourning.
3. Experienced the pain and confusion of the populace fleeing Atlanta after the burning of the depot warehouses.
4. Returned to Tara from Atlanta to find her mother, Ellen O'Hara, dead of typhoid. She had worn herself out nursing others.
5. Had three husbands: Charles Hamilton, Frank Kennedy, and Rhett Butler.

Margaret Mitchell

1. Was engaged to Lieutenant Clifford Henry, who was killed on a battlefield in France during World War I.
2. Shocked Atlanta society by performing a French Apache dance at a Junior League ball.
3. Experienced the panic and confusion that took place during the 1917 Atlanta fire.
4. Was called home to Atlanta from Smith College in Northhampton, Massachusetts, after her mother was stricken with Spanish influenza. Mrs. Mitchell, weak from nursing others during the epidemic, died before Margaret reached home.
5. Committed herself to three men: Clifford Henry, Berrien "Red" Upshaw, and John Marsh.

GWTW: A NOVEL QUIZ

1. Why did Margaret's character Gerald O'Hara leave Ireland?
2. Gerald was sent to his brothers, who were successful Savannah merchants. What were their names?

3. How did Gerald obtain both his valet and his plantation?
4. What was the name of Gerald's valet?
5. Who was raised in the bedroom of Ellen O'Hara's mother?
6. What was Ellen O'Hara's maiden name?
7. With what cousin was Ellen passionately in love?
8. Under what circumstances was he killed?
9. How old is Scarlett when the novel opens?
10. What was Scarlett's first name?
11. What fragrance did Scarlett always associate with her mother?
12. Where did Scarlett receive her education?
13. What were the given names of Scarlett's sisters, Suellen and Carreen?
14. How many brothers did Scarlett have?
15. Who was Suellen's beau?
16. Whom did Carreen love?
17. Why did Gerald O'Hara visit Twelve Oaks the day before the barbecue?
18. Who was the stepdaughter of Gerald's valet?
19. Who were Ashley Wilkes's sisters?
20. Who were the beaux of the Wilkes girls?
21. What was Mrs. Tarleton's first name?
22. What business did Mrs. Tarleton manage?
23. What was the identifying characteristic of Mrs. Tarleton's daughters?
24. Who were the Tarleton sons?
25. Who was the body servant for the Tarleton twins?
26. According to his neighbors, what was Hugh Calvert's big mistake?
27. How did Hugh Calvert's daughter follow in his footsteps?
28. Who were Scarlett's three children?
29. Why had the city of Atlanta always interested Scarlett?
30. What was Aunt Pittypat's real name?
31. Who was Aunt Pittypat's house servant?
32. Who was Aunt Pittypat's brother?
33. How much did Gerald O'Hara lose to Rhett Butler while playing cards?
34. What was Rhett Butler's middle initial?
35. When Ashley was reported missing, who discovered his whereabouts?

36. Where was Ashley held as a prisoner of war?
37. Which member of the Home Guard was Scarlett shocked to see marching to the battle near Kennesaw Mountain?
38. On what date was Melanie's son born?
39. After her return to Tara, Scarlett walked to Twelve Oaks looking for food. What did she eat there?
40. Scarlett rode on horseback to visit the Fontaine family. What was the name of their plantation?
41. When the Yankees returned to Tara, where did Scarlett hide the wallet taken from the deserter she had killed?
42. Which of Tara's rooms did the Yankees set on fire before they left?
43. Who was the one-legged Confederate soldier who stayed to take care of Tara?
44. Whom did he marry?
45. Why was Rhett in jail in Atlanta?
46. Who killed Jonas Wilkerson?
47. What became of Scarlett's youngest sister?
48. Who protected Scarlett on her rounds to the mills?
49. What did Bonnie Butler name her pony?
50. By the end of the novel, how old is Scarlett?

GWTW HITS THE BOOKSTORES

- Macmillan's spring 1936 catalog devoted a full page to announcing *GWTW*'s debut.
- A typographical error escaped the eyes of Macmillan's catalog proof-readers. The catalog's inside front cover referred to the book as *Come with the Wind*.
- Macmillan initially placed a print order for 10,000 copies of *GWTW* and planned to release the novel formally on May 5, 1936.
- The Book-of-the-Month Club named *GWTW* its feature selection for July 1936.
- Because of the book-club sale, Macmillan delayed the formal release date for *GWTW* to June 30, 1936. The publisher still shipped copies of the novel to bookstores in May.

- The prepublication price of *GWTW* was set at $2.75. But after considering typesetting and printing costs for the 1,037-page novel, Macmillan raised the publication price to $3.00.
- Word-of-mouth news about *GWTW* accelerated the public's demand for the new book. Macmillan ordered three subsequent printings during the month of June.
- Before the official release date had even arrived, a total of 100,000 copies of *GWTW* were in print.
- First-edition book collectors were confused! Copies of *GWTW* purchased at publication bore "Published in June" on the copyright page, yet earlier copies carried "Published in May." Collectors flooded Macmillan with requests for clarification. As a result, Macmillan was compelled to send out form letters explaining that copies of the novel with the May publication date were the real first editions.
- Bookstores were unable to keep *GWTW* on the shelves or in their window displays. Proprietors complained that bookstore windows were broken and that thieves were making off with copies of the novel.
- One month after publication, 201,000 copies of *GWTW* were in print. By September 1936, with 370,000 copies in print, *GWTW* was declared the fastest-selling book in history.
- The one-millionth copy of *GWTW* was printed on December 15, 1936. Macmillan made this most significant volume a gift to Margaret Mitchell.

GWTW: THE CRITICS' CHOICE

"This book has been waiting to be written for many years."

—Henry Seidel Canby, Book-of-the-Month Club

"The story, told with such sincerity and passion illuminated by such understanding, woven of the stuff of history and of disciplined imagination, is endlessly interesting."

—Henry Steele Commager,
New York Herald Tribune Books

"This is beyond doubt one of the most remarkable first novels produced by an American writer. It is also one of the best. . . . Although this is not a great novel, not one with any profound reading of life, it is nevertheless a book of uncommon quality, a superb piece of storytelling which nobody who finds pleasure in the art of fiction can afford to neglect. . . . In sheer readability, it is surpassed by nothing in American fiction."

—J. Donald Adams, *New York Times Book Review*

". . . one of the great novels of our time."

—*Chicago Daily News*

"It will be hailed as The Great American Novel, and it will deserve all the praise that it receives."

—*Boston Herald*

". . . more than a novel, perhaps a whole library in itself."

—*New Yorker*

". . . this book contains a literary experience rare as a roc's egg: the full realization of characters."

—*Newsweek*

"*Gone with the Wind* is very possibly the greatest American novel."

—*Publishers' Weekly*

"There ought to be a law that hangs anyone who writes a novel over 350 pages long. But I fell into this one as into a swimming pool. I don't know whether *Gone with the Wind* is a true picture of the South in those days. But I do know it is a true picture of the picture of those days that I got as a child from listening to aging, graying relations and friends of their youth."

—Mildred Seydell, *Atlanta Georgian*

"The history of criticism is strewn with the wrecks of commentators who have spoken out too largely, but we are ready to stand or fall by the assertion that this novel has the strongest claim of any novel on the American scene to be bracketed with the work of the great from abroad—Tolstoi, Hardy, Dickens. . . ."

—Edwin Granberry, *New York Sun*

". . . an unforgettable picture . . . a torrent of narrative . . . an extraordinary book."

—Harry Hansen, *World Telegram*

"It is an overwhelmingly fine novel . . . a broad canvas that throbs with color and life."

—Charles Hanson Towne, *American*

IT'S ONLY A RUMOR

Margaret Mitchell was not your average celebrity. She was a private person who shunned the spotlight, avoided interviews, and steered clear of public appearances. As a result, people who were hungry for information about her willingly believed the most outrageous rumors.

Rumors began flying almost as soon as *GWTW* was published. And there was no stopping them. Some of the more colorful ones claimed that Margaret Mitchell:

- Was coached in writing *GWTW* by the editors at Macmillan.
- Wrote *GWTW* on company time when she was a file clerk for an Atlanta insurance company.
- Was turned down by many publishers before Macmillan bought the novel.
- Paid Sinclair Lewis to write the book for her.
- Talked her brother into writing *GWTW*.
- Copied her novel directly from her grandmother's diary.
- Sold the novel to Macmillan for a paltry $250.

- Received so much money from Macmillan that she was able to purchase a large Long Island estate.
- Was in hiding on an Alaskan mink farm.
- Occupied a suite of rooms at an Atlanta hotel for weeks, during which time she was drunk and threw her money away.
- Supplied Macmillan with an additional chapter that revealed whether or not Scarlett got Rhett back. The chapter could be had by sending one dollar to the publisher.
- Used a rubber stamp to autograph copies of her book.
- Was insane, or dying from leukemia, or going blind, or had a wooden leg.
- Would only write by the light of an oil lamp.
- Sold articles to women's magazines for millions of dollars.
- Refused to come to the breakfast table until her husband had placed two dozen American Beauty roses at her place.
- Was in Reno divorcing her husband.
- Purchased and restored an antebellum mansion so that Selznick would have a background setting for the film.
- Was in charge of selecting the entire cast of *GWTW*.
- Was secretly taking acting lessons at Selznick's studio so she could play Scarlett.
- Had definitely been selected to play Melanie.
- Was behind the camera directing the film.
- Received a blank check from Louis B. Mayer to write a sequel to *GWTW*.

Such fanciful tales were the price of fame for Margaret Mitchell. She was amused by some and hurt by others. And as a result she spent a good deal of time trying to debunk the myths by telling people, "It's only a rumor."

AN AWARD-WINNING NOVELIST

Two important awards were bestowed upon Margaret Mitchell in the spring of 1937. The first was the annual award of the American Booksellers Association (now the National Book Awards). The second was the prestigious Pulitzer Prize.

On the recommendation of the Pulitzer School of Journalism's advisory board, the trustees of Columbia University named *Gone with the Wind* "the most distinguished novel of the last year."

Margaret's Pulitzer Prize of a thousand dollars caused a sensation in Atlanta. When the news hit the Associated Press wires, local newspaper reporters sought out the author for a statement. But Margaret Mitchell was unaware that she had won. When the congratulatory telegram arrived from the Columbia trustees, she was having dinner with visiting Macmillan vice president Harold Latham. Reporters scoured the city for her.

Lamar Q. Ball, city editor of the *Atlanta Constitution*, finally tracked her down by telephone at her father's Peachtree Street home. Not taking any chances with the publicity-shy Mitchell, Ball then hurried from his office with a photographer (even though the paper was on deadline) to the Mitchell residence to cover the story himself.

"I don't know which impressed me most," Margaret later quipped, "winning the Pulitzer Prize or having the city editor of the *Constitution* leave his desk."

In 1938 Margaret's two previous honors were joined by a third. The Southeastern Library Association bestowed upon her the Carl Bohnenberger Memorial Medal. The award was given for "the most outstanding contribution to Southern literature" in the previous two years. No doubt about it: Margaret was clearly an award-winning novelist.

HOW *GWTW* WAS SOLD TO THE MOVIES

In 1936, Annie Laurie Williams, an agent for Macmillan, sent copies of *GWTW* to movie studios that might be interested in obtaining film rights. Katherine "Kay" Brown, story editor for the New York office of Selznick International, read the book and could barely contain her excitement. She immediately wired her boss, David O. Selznick, and begged him to read the long synopsis of *GWTW* she was sending to him.

Selznick read the synopsis and winced. Another Civil War story! Selznick knew that, with the exception of D. W. Griffith's 1915 film *The Birth of a Nation*, movies about the Civil War were bad news at the box office. Paramount's *So Red the Rose* had proved that just the year before with its dismal ticket sales. Selznick also had no major actress under contract who could undertake the lead. So reluctantly, Selznick wired Kay Brown, "Most sorry to have to say no in face of your enthusiasm for this story."

But then Selznick rethought his decision and sent a follow-up wire to Kay Brown: "I have thought further about 'Gone With the Wind' and the more I think about it, the more I feel there is [an] excellent picture in it." Selznick suggested that Brown bring *GWTW* to the attention of the executives of Pioneer Pictures, the Technicolor division of Selznick International. Brown did just that and sent the synopsis to John Hay "Jock" Whitney, the president of Pioneer and chairman of the board of Selznick International. After reading the synopsis, Whitney wired Selznick that he would buy the film rights if Selznick didn't.

That was all Selznick needed to hear. On July 7, 1936, only one week after the book's official publication date, Selznick cabled Kay Brown and instructed her to close the deal for the film rights to *GWTW* for $50,000—a record amount for a first novel by an unknown author. Selznick then left on a vacation cruise to Hawaii accompanied by his wife and a copy of *GWTW*. While reading the book during the long days at sea, Selznick realized for the first time the monumental task ahead of him: translating the 1,037 pages of the novel into a workable movie script.

THE MOVIE MOGULS SELZNICK
BESTED WITH HIS *GWTW* BUY

Other film studios had the opportunity to buy the film rights to *GWTW*, but Selznick International was the first one to make the best offer to Macmillan. To see who David O. bested with his *GWTW* buy, match the movie mogul in the first column to the studio with which he was associated in the second column.

1. Pandro S. Berman   a. Warner Bros. Pictures
2. Harry Cohn   b. Paramount Pictures
3. Louis B. Mayer   c. Twentieth Century Fox
4. Jack L. Warner   d. Metro-Goldwyn-Mayer
5. Darryl Zanuck   e. RKO
6. Adolph Zukor   f. Columbia Pictures

TWO

Gable Grumbles
and Selznick Searches

ACTORS WHO WERE
CONSIDERED FOR RHETT BUTLER

Warner Baxter
Humphrey Bogart
Ronald Colman
Gary Cooper
Melvyn Douglas
Errol Flynn
Joel McCrea
Fredric March
Ray Milland
Vincent Price
Basil Rathbone
Franchot Tone

HOW SELZNICK GOT HIS RHETT BUTLER

When the news broke that Selznick International would be making *GWTW* into a movie, the public flooded the studio's offices with mail. Fans of the novel all across the country wrote to Selznick stating their choices for the casting of the major roles.

For the role of Rhett Butler, stars such as Ronald Colman and Fredric March had their supporters, but the name of Clark Gable dominated the pack from the very beginning. Soon movie magazines even got into the act with "The Great Casting Battle of *Gone with the Wind*." The October 1937 issue of *Photoplay*, for example, featured a portrait of Gable as Rhett Butler dressed in a black antebellum coat and characterized him in the role as "cool, impertinent, utterly charming." The magazine admitted, "We like all the other handsome actors mentioned as Rhett—only we don't want them as Rhett. We want Gable."

Selznick wanted Gable, too. He was number one on Selznick's list of actors for the role, followed by Gary Cooper and Errol Flynn. But one obstacle stood in the way of offering the part to Gable: Louis B. Mayer, Selznick's father-in-law and the head of Metro-Goldwyn-Mayer (MGM). Mayer had Gable under exclusive contract, and Selznick knew that L. B. would demand a heavy price for Gable's services. So despite the overwhelming public clamor for Gable, Selznick decided to look elsewhere for his male star.

For months, Selznick worked hard to secure Gary Cooper for the role. Cooper, though, was under contract to Sam Goldwyn, a friend of Selznick's. Friend or no friend, Goldwyn was unwilling to lend his hot property to another producer.

When Warner Bros. learned of Selznick's interest in their star Errol Flynn, Jack L. Warner offered Selznick a package deal. Besides Flynn for the role of Rhett Butler, Warner agreed to lend Bette Davis for the role of Scarlett and Olivia de Havilland for the role of Melanie. Davis, however, refused to play opposite Flynn, and the offer fell through. Selznick, now back to square one, knew he had to deal with Mayer.

The terms of the deal were dear. Louis B. Mayer, after all, didn't have just the ace that Selznick needed; Mayer held the whole deck. As part of the contract, MGM agreed to lend Gable to Selznick and to contribute $1.25 million toward the film's estimated $2.5 million production costs. In return, MGM obtained exclusive distribution rights to *GWTW* plus 50 percent of the film's profits. MGM's parent company, Loew's Inc., was entitled to 15 percent of the film's gross receipts for handling physical distribution. Selznick had no choice but to agree. Unexpectedly, though, a hitch occurred that even Selznick could not have anticipated. Gable wanted nothing to do with the role of Rhett Butler.

Why Gable Hated the Role He Was Born to Play

"I don't want the part for money, chalk, or marbles," Gable told Selznick. Why would Gable resist taking on the role he was born to play, the role the public demanded he play?

"I was scared when I discovered that I had been cast by the public," Gable explained. "I felt that every reader would have a different idea as to how Rhett should be played on the screen, and I didn't see how I could please everybody."

Gable had always been plagued by insecurities about his acting talent. That was why MGM had sought similar roles for him in all his films, lots of rough-and-tumble action but not much emotion.

The exception to this was *Parnell*. Gable was still smarting from his portrayal of the Irish Nationalist. A costume drama, *Parnell* was a disaster with fans and critics alike. That made Gable leery of making another historical picture.

Additionally, MGM had always teamed Gable up with directors who supported and guided Gable's masculine image. But that wouldn't be the case with *GWTW*. Portraying Rhett Butler would make demands on Gable he did not think he could meet, and Selznick had tapped George Cukor as the director of the film. Gable knew Cukor's reputation in Hollywood as a "woman's director." He feared that Cukor would view *GWTW* as Scarlett's story and focus greater attention on Leigh's performances, leaving Gable adrift in the role of Rhett.

Gable was determined not to do the film for love or money. But in the end, he did it for both.

Love and Money Change Gable's Mind

Clark Gable was a married man in love. Although legally separated, he was married to Ria Langham Gable, his second wife. However, he was in love with Carole Lombard, the gifted actress known for her roles in screwball comedies. Gable had sought a divorce, but his wife, who was seventeen years his senior, had refused. She was convinced the affair would soon blow over. But the Gable-Lombard romance flourished under the tolerant eye of the movie industry.

Why was Gable so in love with Lombard? She was sexy, funny, and young—age thirty to Gable's thirty-seven. He found in her an extraordinary companion, far different from the two middle-aged women he had married. Lombard had a joyously unrestrained personality, and Gable never knew what she would do next. She might send him a ham with his picture on it or "indulge" his love of cars with a junkyard jalopy painted red and white for Valentine's Day. A selfless, caring person, she anticipated his needs and even shed her glamour-girl image to hunt, fish, and ride with him. Lombard was a heady intoxicant to Gable, and her high-spiritedness was a perfect counterpoint to his serious nature. They loved each other passionately, and their romance was electric with that passion.

One who watched the affair with particular interest was Gable's boss, Louis B. Mayer. All studio bosses were concerned with the public images of their stars, but Mayer had a more important reason for monitoring Gable's love life. Mayer wanted his studio to play a part in *GWTW*'s production, but he had already heard Gable's grumblings concerning the Rhett Butler role. If Gable refused the role, Mayer could suspend him; that was in Gable's contract. What Mayer needed was a bargaining chip to ensure that Gable would not turn down the role. He found that bargaining chip in Ria Gable.

Mrs. Gable saw, via the newspapers, the deepening love between Gable and the beautiful, blonde Carole Lombard. Gossip was rampant in the Hollywood tabloids that the lovers were planning to marry. Eventually, Ria Gable accepted the fact that she would never get her husband back. And that's what Louis B. Mayer had been waiting to hear. He then secretly encouraged Mrs. Gable to ask for an exorbitant divorce settlement. Mayer believed that if Gable were desperate for money, he wouldn't dare risk suspension by refusing the Rhett Butler role.

The divorce would cost Gable plenty: $286,000 plus income taxes on the settlement. A frugal man by nature, Gable probably howled when he learned the terms of the divorce. But he would do anything to marry Lombard, the woman who had captured his heart. Mayer generously offered Gable a signing bonus to sweeten the Rhett Butler deal, and Gable had no choice. Love and money had changed his mind.

In late August 1938, Gable forced a smile as L. B. Mayer, with David O. Selznick looking on, signed the contracts that lent Gable to Selznick International for *GWTW*.

STAR TRACKS: CLARK GABLE

- Born on February 1, 1901, in Cadiz, Ohio.
- Parents: William H. Gable, a wildcatter in the oil-drilling business, and Adeline (Addie) Hershelman Gable, a farmer's daughter who died nine months and thirteen days after her son was born. In April 1903, Will Gable married Jennie Dunlap, a milliner and dressmaker from Hopedale, Ohio.
- Dropped out of Edinburgh High School at age sixteen and moved to Akron, where he found jobs in the tire and rubber industry.
- Decided to become an actor after being mesmerized by the play *The Bird of Paradise*, a shocking melodrama performed by the Ed Clark Lilley–Pauline McLean Players at the Akron Music Hall.
- Became an unpaid gofer for the Lilley-McLean Players and eventually had a brief walk-on part in one of its productions that cemented his desire to become an actor.
- Worked his way west and joined a Portland, Oregon, stock company, the Astoria Players, in 1922.
- Studied acting with drama coach Josephine Dillon, whom he married in 1924.
- Moved to Hollywood and found work as a movie extra in *Forbidden Paradise* (1924), *The Merry Widow* (1925), and *The Pacemakers* (1925).
- Attracted the attention of filmmakers with his stage work as "Killer" Mears in the 1930 Los Angeles production of *The Last Mile*.
- Earned his first screen credit in the 1931 William Boyd Western *The Painted Desert*.
- After appearing in 1931's *The Easiest Way* for Metro-Goldwyn-Mayer, Gable signed a short-term contract with the studio and had minor roles in a succession of films.
- Caused a sensation in 1931's *A Free Soul* when, as Ace Wilfong, he manhandled his leading lady, Norma Shearer. The public reacted by sending Gable thousands of fan letters. The *Hollywood Reporter* declared: "A star in the making has been made."
- Appeared in his first starring role in 1931's *Sporting Blood* with Madge Evans.

- After renewing Gable's contract, MGM featured him opposite many of the screen's most desirable women, including Joan Crawford, Greta Garbo, Jean Harlow, Marion Davies, and Myrna Loy.
- Married his second wife, Maria Franklin Prentiss Lucas Langham—a wealthy Texas socialite—in June 1931.
- First met Carole Lombard, the love of his life, when they worked together on the film *No Man of Her Own* in 1932.
- Was lent out to Columbia Pictures for the screwball comedy *It Happened One Night*. Gable, in one scene, unbuttoned his shirt and revealed that he was not wearing an undershirt. Taking Gable's cue, millions of American men apparently believed it was manlier not to wear an undershirt. Within a year, sales of undershirts plummeted by 75 percent, and garment executives blasted Gable for causing the near ruination of the undershirt industry.
- Won the 1934 Academy Award as Best Actor for *It Happened One Night*.
- Was reluctant to play Fletcher Christian in 1935's *Mutiny on the Bounty* because he feared audiences would think he was a sissy in knickers and a pigtail.
- Was nominated for but lost the Academy Award for Best Actor for *Mutiny on the Bounty*.
- Was officially elected "the King of Hollywood" in a contest conducted by Ed Sullivan, entertainment columnist for the *Chicago Tribune-New York Daily News* syndicate, in 1937. The public cast more than twenty million votes.
- Was signed to play Rhett Butler in *GWTW* in August 1938.

PROBLEMS ON TOP OF PROBLEMS

In 1936, when Selznick bought the rights to *GWTW*, he realized he would be foolhardy to rush into production. Millions were currently reading the novel; characters and scenes were fresh in readers' minds.

Given the novel's monumental size, Selznick knew that translating the story to manageable film footage would involve lengthy cuts. But Selznick also knew the woe that could befall a producer who eliminated a favorite scene or a memorable line of dialogue. Readers would remember and would never forgive him for tampering with Margaret Mitchell's epic. Selznick's plan was to allow a healthy dose of time to dim readers' memories of the book's characters and events.

A circumstance that further delayed production was the deal for Gable. As part of that arrangement, MGM had exclusive distribution rights to *GWTW*. But Selznick had a contract with United Artists to release his films through the end of 1938. That meant Selznick couldn't begin filming *GWTW* until early 1939.

How could Selznick possibly hold the public's interest in *GWTW* for the three years it would take to get the film into the movie houses? To compound the problem, he also had to find a leading lady equal to the task of portraying the fiery Scarlett. But David O. Selznick was a genius; he decided to kill two birds with one stone.

HUMDINGER OF A HOAX:
THE SEARCH FOR SCARLETT

Selznick's solution to his dilemma was pure genius and pure hype. His idea was to launch a nationwide search for an unknown actress to play Scarlett O'Hara.

Selznick had no illusions that the search would actually discover a suitable actress. His only aim was publicity and lots of it. What better way to keep the country's attention on *GWTW* than by offering America's secretaries, store clerks, and hope-filled starlets the chance to audition for the most coveted role in Tinseltown. What better way to keep reporters and columnists turning out copy about the movie than by providing the media with material for a potential Cinderella story.

Selznick had the perfect accomplice for his hoax. Russell "Bird" Birdwell, Selznick's publicity director, was a master at dreaming up publicity stunts that turned into front-page news for the studio. For the release of *The Garden of Allah*, for example, Birdwell convinced the book's author, Robert Hichens, to invite the recently abdicated King Edward VIII and Wallis Simpson to spend their honeymoon at his Egyptian villa, the Garden of Allah. Newspapers reported that story as a sidebar to the ongoing coverage of the abdication.

In orchestrating the bogus search for Scarlett, Birdwell lost no time in heralding the news. He arranged a press conference to make the announcement and then dispatched three talent scouts to scour the country. Oscar Serlin covered the north and east, Maxwell Arnow headed south with director George Cukor, and Charles Morrison went west.

And while all of America went into a Scarlett frenzy, Selznick turned his attention to the real search: finding his Scarlett among Hollywood's established stars.

ACTRESSES WHO
WERE CONSIDERED FOR SCARLETT

Jean Arthur
Lucille Ball
Tallulah Bankhead
Joan Bennett
Claudette Colbert
Joan Crawford
Bette Davis
Irene Dunne
Joan Fontaine
Paulette Goddard
Jean Harlow
Susan Hayward
Katharine Hepburn
Miriam Hopkins
Carole Lombard
Norma Shearer
Ann Sheridan
Margaret Sullavan
Lana Turner
Loretta Young

Moments to Remember in the Search for Scarlett

- Selznick was forced to hire extra security personnel when would-be Scarletts began crashing the studio gates and applying for the role in person.

- On Christmas morning 1937, Selznick discovered a gaily wrapped and beribboned seven-foot-high box outside his front door. When he tore the paper from this supersized surprise, he found a dust-jacketed replica of the *GWTW* novel. Out of the book stepped a young woman dressed in a hoopskirted gown who announced, "Merry Christmas, Mr. Selznick! I am your Scarlett O'Hara."

- While in Atlanta on a talent scouting expedition, director George Cukor's train was attacked by a bevy of costumed belles all demanding movie contracts. One of the belles, known as Honey Chile, was particularly persistent. She raced through the train's corridors opening stateroom doors in search of the director. In her wake, she managed to disturb honeymooning couples, sleeping children, and gentlemen who were relaxing sans their trousers. Cukor was hiding on the train during the uproar. His assistant, John Darrow, caught up with the agitated actress when she left the sleeping cars to search the platform. With some fast talking, he convinced her that Cukor had gone on to New Orleans by car and that it was futile to pursue him. He detained her until the whistle blew and the train began pulling out of the station. Then he leapt aboard and rejoined Cukor for the next leg of their journey.

The Brightest Stars Vied for Scarlett

Selznick could choose his Scarlett from the brightest stars in the Hollywood firmament. Here's how the major contenders fared:

Bette Davis: Ms. Davis pulled in 40 percent of the public's write-in vote as the actress to play Scarlett. Warner Bros. offered Selznick a package deal of Davis as Scarlett and Errol Flynn as Rhett Butler. But Davis refused to star with the dashing swashbuckler. Warner Bros. would not substitute another actor for Flynn, the deal fell through, and Davis's chances to play Scarlett ended. However, that did not stop Davis from playing *another* Southern vixen.

Tallulah Bankhead: The Alabama-born Tallulah Bankhead was better known for her work on the London and Broadway stages than for her work in films. But she was a former inamorata of Jock Whitney, and she became the first actress Selznick tested for the role of Scarlett.

Selznick was not impressed with the thirty-four-year-old actress's portrayal of the youthful Scarlett, but the flamboyant, husky-voiced Bankhead was convincing as the more mature Scarlett. Characterizing her tests as "very promising indeed," Selznick told Bankhead that although he considered her "a definite possibility," he wanted to leave his decision open for the time being.

Louella Parsons used her column to warn Selznick about Bankhead's unpopularity: "George Cukor, her friend, is going to direct [the film]. Jock Whitney, another friend, is backing it. So I'm afraid she'll get the part. If she does I personally will go home and weep because she is not Scarlett O'Hara in my language, and if David O. Selznick gives her the part he will have to answer to every man, woman and child in America."

Parsons needn't have worried. Selznick eventually decided that Bankhead was not his Scarlett. He did think, though, that she would make a perfect Belle Watling. Since he had rejected her for the lead, however, he was afraid to approach the explosive Bankhead with his latest inspiration. This task he delegated to Kay Brown. But he cautioned her: "For God's sake, don't mention my name in connection with it, simply saying that it is an idea of your own that you haven't yet taken up with me." But Brown considered it the better part of valor not to mention the idea at all to Bankhead.

Miriam Hopkins: Like Bankhead, Miriam Hopkins was a daughter of the South. Hopkins had recently played the title role in *Becky Sharp*, and her characterization of Thackeray's willful heroine drew Selznick's attention. Instead of testing Hopkins, Selznick screened *Becky Sharp*, and he had Hopkins read for the role of Scarlett. Her intensity in the reading impressed Selznick, but she wasn't quite what he was looking for.

Norma Shearer: The thirty-seven-year-old widow of Irving Thalberg was eager for the part, but Selznick thought her too mature to play sixteen-year-old Scarlett. Nonetheless, her legions of fans equaled box-office draw and a force Selznick could not afford to ignore. So Selznick decided to test the waters. He leaked to columnist Walter Winchell that Shearer was being considered for the role. When Winchell announced the news to his radio audience, pandemonium ensued! Shearer's fans responded in outraged letters that castigated Selznick for even thinking of asking the gentle, dignified Shearer to play the impetuous, fiery Scarlett. Shortly thereafter, Shearer withdrew her name from consideration for the role.

Katharine Hepburn: When she read the novel, Hepburn knew she was Scarlett O'Hara. Unfortunately, RKO turned down the opportunity to buy the film rights because they felt that part was not right for her. When she learned that Selznick had acquired the film rights and that Cukor would be directing, Hepburn felt she still had a shot at it. She had worked successfully with both Selznick and Cukor in 1932 in *A Bill of Divorcement*.

Cukor, however, was not convinced Hepburn was the right choice. Selznick was more direct in his reaction to her candidacy: "I can't imagine Rhett Butler chasing you for ten years." But Hepburn was tenacious. She offered herself as a standby in case Selznick's search for Scarlett turned up empty.

Later Cukor changed his mind about Hepburn. He had just finished working with her on the film *Holiday* and extolled her acting gifts to Selznick. Selznick ordered a test of her in the role of Scarlett, but Hepburn refused. She insisted that by now Selznick knew if she could act or not. Unfortunately, Selznick was also aware of Hepburn's current unpopularity among film distributors. In 1938, after a series of commercial flops such as *Mary of Scotland*, *A Woman Rebels*, and *Quality Street*, Hepburn was tagged box office poison. Despite this, Selznick felt he couldn't eliminate Hepburn from the running just yet.

Paulette Goddard: Ms. Goddard was Selznick's strongest contender for the role of Scarlett. In her test she personified Selznick's image of Scarlett: a dark beauty with a bold and fiery personality. But Goddard was inexperienced as an actress. Selznick signed Goddard to a five-year contract, hired a coach to refine her talents, and sent her for training to develop a Southern accent. Another test confirmed to Selznick just how good Goddard was, and it seemed as if she had the role wrapped up. Columnist Louella Parsons even began referring to her as "Scarlett O'Goddard." But a hitch developed.

Goddard was the protégée of Charles Chaplin. She had costarred in his film *Modern Times* and was currently starring in the role of the third Mrs. Chaplin. Although the pair lived together, there was widespread disbelief about their married status. When women's clubs across the country learned that Goddard was about to be signed for the role of Scarlett, Selznick was deluged with letters of protest. The public was not only furious over a suspected immoral liaison but provoked as well by the left-wing views Chaplin had exhibited in *Modern Times*.

Goddard assured Selznick that she and Chaplin had been married aboard a yacht anchored in the Singapore harbor during a cruise to the Orient. Selznick demanded to see the marriage license. Goddard countered that the yacht had been attacked by guerrillas and all the records destroyed.

Rather than risk censure—and boycott—of his film by an outraged public, Selznick decided to continue looking for his Scarlett.

Jean Arthur: Charmingly original at thirty-three years of age, Jean Arthur was a sentimental favorite for Selznick. He and Arthur had been a Hollywood item before he married Louis B. Mayer's daughter Irene. Arthur's early readings had a magic quality, and although she clearly was not a Southern belle, Selznick seriously considered her for the role.

Joan Bennett: Ms. Bennett had been a rising star with lovely blonde looks and a fine performance in *Little Women* to her credit. After she wore a black wig for her role in *Trade Winds*, her stunning appearance convinced her to remain a brunette and to audition for Scarlett. Selznick was equally impressed with the new Bennett. He offered her an opportunity to read for the role of Scarlett, but she insisted on a screen test. After he viewed the test, Selznick decided Bennett was a serious contender for the role.

Lesser Luminaries Also Had a Chance to Shine

Other rising stars in the Hollywood galaxy had the opportunity to read and test for Scarlett O'Hara. They included:

Lana Turner: "Sweater Girl" Lana was one of the newest sex symbols when she tested for Scarlett. She had played a Southern girl in Warner's *They Won't Forget*, a 1937 film people were still talking about. Turner's Scarlett screen test had her paired with Melvyn Douglas playing Ashley. But Selznick found her "completely inadequate, too young to have a grasp of the part."

Susan Hayward: According to Hollywood legend, Irene Mayer Selznick spotted attractive, redheaded, nineteen-year-old Edythe Marrener modeling hats in a New York fashion show. Marrener traveled to Hollywood and tested for Scarlett. Although her performance was stiff and unprofessional, Selznick gave her a six-month contract. He used her as a Scarlett stand-in during tests for other roles. At the end of her contract period, Selznick dismissed Marrener. Undaunted, Marrener changed her name to Susan Hayward, won a contract from Paramount, and enjoyed a successful Hollywood film career.

Ann Sheridan: Selznick had heard fabulous things about Ann Sheridan. A relative newcomer, she had an amazing string of hits at Warner Bros., and Selznick was worried about passing up an actress with great potential.

Under close scrutiny, though, Sheridan's talents failed to impress the producer.

Lucille Ball: To leave no stone unturned, Selznick offered Scarlett tryouts to actresses under contract to other studios. RKO rounded up eight of its stock girls, handed them scripts containing three scenes from *GWTW*, and told them to be ready for auditions in three weeks. One of the stock girls, redheaded Lucille Ball, knew she could never be Scarlett O'Hara. But rather than balk and risk losing her RKO contract, she memorized her lines.

On her way to the afternoon audition, Ball was caught in a freak cloudburst. She arrived at Selznick's office thoroughly soaked. Selznick had not yet arrived, so the bedraggled Ball was ushered into the producer's office and told to wait. She knelt in front of the blazing fireplace to dry herself and decided to practice her lines.

Moments later she was startled at the sound of Selznick's voice complimenting her on her reading. She was aghast at his finding her rehearsing, but he urged her to continue. Summoning all her strength, she completed her scenes. Selznick said he enjoyed her reading, thanked her for coming, and then helped her to her feet. Only then did Ball realize she had auditioned for the Scarlett O'Hara role on her knees.

Lucille Ball made a name for herself as a madcap comedienne in the years that followed her disastrous audition. When she and her husband Desi Arnaz were looking for a location to produce their *I Love Lucy* television series, they bought the old Selznick studio. And which office did Ball choose for herself? Selznick's old one.

THREE

Casting Call

MARGARET MITCHELL: AN INNOCENT
BYSTANDER IN THE *GWTW* CASTING BATTLE

Margaret Mitchell was emphatic. She wanted absolutely, positively nothing to do with the casting of *GWTW*, and she made this perfectly clear when she sold the film rights to Selznick. The only problem was nobody listened to her. And during the two years it took Selznick to select his stars, Margaret found herself involved, to her great consternation, in the *GWTW* casting battle.

People stopped her on the street, phoned her, wrote to her. When that didn't work, they appeared at her apartment to voice their opinion about the casting of the major roles or to beg for a part in the film. One woman conned Margaret into letting her into her apartment. Once inside, the woman announced she was an actress, smeared dark makeup on her face, and began portraying Mammy in the middle of Margaret's living room.

Margaret probably pulled her hair out when she read Louella Parsons's October 23, 1936, column. In the column, Parsons wrote: "These rumors of a cast for 'Gone With the Wind' are gradually getting David Selznick down. . . . No one has yet been chosen and will not be until the author, Margaret Mitchell, is consulted."

That prompted a lengthy letter to Parsons from Margaret. "Everybody in the world reads your column and that is why I am appealing to you for assistance," Margaret wrote. She begged the columnist to publish a notice stating that Margaret had nothing at all to do with the casting. Parsons came to Margaret's rescue in her November 8 column, in which she quoted Margaret's letter at length. The disturbances to Margaret's private life subsided, at least for a while.

Another incident that dragged Margaret into the fray occurred in October 1938. Mrs. Ogden Reid, vice president of the *New York Herald Tribune*, phoned Margaret and invited her to the Eighth Annual Women's Forum on Current Problems that was being held in New York. Because of family illness, Margaret declined. Mrs. Reid mentioned that Katharine Hepburn was to be the guest speaker and asked Margaret's opinion of the actress. Margaret commented that she had enjoyed Hepburn's performance in *Little Women* and thought she looked attractive in hoopskirts. Little did she realize how those innocent words would be twisted.

At the forum, Mrs. Reid introduced Hepburn as "my candidate for Scarlett O'Hara in *Gone With the Wind*" and added that the actress also had Margaret Mitchell's endorsement. The three thousand women in attendance erupted into a standing ovation.

In Atlanta, Margaret was besieged with phone calls from reporters all over the country asking for a statement about her endorsement of Katharine Hepburn. Margaret, stunned at the misinterpretation of her comments, told all who called, "I have never expressed a preference, and I never will."

The press was still not satisfied and hounded Margaret whenever a new contender for Scarlett was announced in Hollywood. She lamented to Kay Brown, "Life has been awful since I sold the movie rights!" Margaret was convinced her quiet, peaceful life was permanently gone with the wind.

MARGARET MITCHELL'S *GWTW* CHOICES

As much as she sought to avoid entering the Great Casting Battle, it appears that Margaret did express her casting preferences, once and *only* once. In a July 1936 letter to Macmillan editor Lois Cole, Margaret noted that "Miriam Hopkins has been my choice for Scarlett from the beginning." For Melanie, she liked Elizabeth Allan, who was known for her recent film portrayal of David Copperfield's mother. "I wish Charles Boyer didn't have a French accent for he's my choice for Rhett," Margaret added. "Next to him, Jack Holt [a Western actor] is the only person I can think of."

WARNER BROTHERS' *JEZEBEL* REVENGE

In the vernacular, a "jezebel" is a shameless woman. In Selznick's mind, *Jezebel*, the 1938 Warner Bros. film starring Bette Davis, was a shameless imitation of *GWTW*. And Selznick was furious.

After the deal fell through to have Bette Davis portray Scarlett, Warner Bros. bought the rights to the 1933 play *Jezebel*. Set in pre–Civil War years, the drama concerned the machinations of a strong-willed Southern vixen very much in character like Scarlett O'Hara. Years earlier, Davis had encouraged her employers to make the purchase when the play was appearing on Broadway. But the production turned out to be a dismal failure, and no studio was interested in the movie rights. However, now that *GWTW* was the talk of the country, Warner Bros. snapped up *Jezebel* and rushed the film into production.

Bette Davis played New Orleans belle Julie Marsden, whose headstrong actions destroy the love of Preston Dillard (Henry Fonda), and the film was shot in less than eight weeks. During the filming, vice president in charge of production Jack L. Warner called the press's attention to the similarities between his studio's film and *GWTW*. Warner noted that on the set Davis was known as "Scarlett." In interviews Davis commented on the parallels between the characters.

This was enough to set off Selznick. After previewing *Jezebel*, he sent a telegram to Warner warning that "it would be a very great pity indeed . . . if so distinguished and costly a picture as *Jezebel* should be damned as an imitation by the millions of readers and lovers of *Gone with the Wind*."

Selznick noted that *Jezebel* was "permeated with characterizations, attitudes, and scenes that unfortunately resemble *Gone With the Wind*." He cited one scene in which men, gathered around a dinner table, discuss the threat of war and the North's military advantages over the South. "This scene is lifted practically bodily out of *Gone With the Wind*," Selznick charged. The scene was later dropped from *Jezebel*.

In closing, Selznick stated that he thought it was important "that the success which your picture deserves should not be marred by any appearance of an attempt to capitalize on a work for which the American public has demonstrated such a great love."

The American public that loved *GWTW* also loved *Jezebel*. The film was wildly successful. And almost a year before *GWTW* made its film debut, Davis's memorable performance in *Jezebel* won her an Academy Award, her second. To say the least, Selznick was not pleased.

THE BOGUS SEARCH PAYS OFF

By the time the two-year search for Scarlett ended, the stunt had cost Selznick nearly $92,000. Nearly 149,000 feet of black-and-white film and 13,000 feet of Technicolor film had been shot in tests of 1,400 aspiring Scarletts. And the resulting national publicity was all that Selznick had hoped for.

Surprisingly, though, the search did uncover three actresses, all Southern belles, who captured secondary roles in *GWTW*. Marcella Martin from Shreveport, Louisiana, won the role of Cathleen Calvert; Mary Anderson from Birmingham, Alabama, was selected for Maybelle Merriwether; and Alicia Rhett from Charleston, South Carolina, was chosen to play India Wilkes.

DETERMINED DE HAVILLAND
CAPTURES THE ROLE OF MELANIE

RKO actress Joan Fontaine received a message that George Cukor wanted her to read for *GWTW*. Oh, what she wouldn't give to play Scarlett! But when she arrived for her appointment, she discovered that the director had her in mind for Melanie. Since that role held no interest for her, she suggested that Cukor test her sister, Olivia de Havilland.

De Havilland was hungry for Melanie. And she knew that her competition was stiff: Elizabeth Allan, Andrea Leeds, Anne Shirley, and Frances Dee had tested for the role. She read for the part at Cukor's office, and he suggested that she read for Selznick.

Several days later, de Havilland replayed the same scene in Selznick's house with Cukor taking the role of Scarlett. When de Havilland finished, Selznick decided that she *was* Melanie and offered her the role on the spot. She was joyous, but then her emotions crashed to the floor. Jack L. Warner would never let her accept the part.

De Havilland was a contract player at Warner Bros. When her career began there in the 1930s, she was cast opposite handsome Errol Flynn. The combination worked. Dashing Flynn and doe-eyed de Havilland starred in a string of hero-rescues-damsel-in-distress films from *Captain Blood* to *Robin Hood*. But as Flynn's career soared, de Havilland's seemed permanently grounded.

Under her contract, de Havilland had to appear in any film to which she was assigned. If she refused any role, she could be immediately suspended without pay. And under the studio system, which indentured its stars to multiyear contracts, suspension was professional suicide.

Also against her was Warner's star system that favored male actors such as Cagney, Robinson, and Bogart. Plus, the reigning queen of the lot, Bette Davis, was not easily dethroned. So there really was no place for de Havilland's career to go unless she sought roles outside the studio. And this, according to Jack L. Warner, was verboten.

True to his dictates, Warner's response was a resounding no when de Havilland approached him about taking on the role. He also feared that once de Havilland had a taste of freedom she would be unwilling to return to the shackles of the studio system.

But Warner underestimated demure de Havilland. Rather than accept Warner's verdict as the final word, this iron-willed magnolia decided to appeal to someone who could change her boss's mind: his wife.

De Havilland invited Ann Page Warner for tea at the Beverly Hills Brown Derby and poured out the details of her plight. Mrs. Warner, a former actress, was sympathetic and pledged to do what she could. With such a powerful force at work, Jack L. Warner soon capitulated.

As part of the deal for de Havilland, Selznick agreed to lend new star James Stewart for use in Warner's film *No Time for Comedy*. Warner thought he would profit from the deal, but the price he eventually paid for lending out de Havilland was incalculable.

Warner was right that de Havilland would be difficult to work with after she found stardom outside the studio. What he could not have anticipated was her leading a rebellion when she returned to the Warner lot. Her challenge to Jack L. Warner's authority moved from the lot, through the California court system, and ended with the destruction of the very studio system he controlled.

STAR TRACKS: OLIVIA DE HAVILLAND

- Born on July 1, 1916, in Tokyo, Japan.
- Parents: Walter and Lillian Ruse de Havilland. Walter was a professor of law at Waseda University in Tokyo. Their marriage broke up after the birth of a second child, Joan, in 1917. Afterward, Lillian returned to America, settled with her daughters in California, and later married George Fontaine.
- Original career goal was to become a teacher.
- Portrayed Puck in a 1934 local production of *A Midsummer Night's Dream*, which caught the eye of a talent scout. The talent scout represented producer Max Reinhardt, who was planning to begin a national tour of the play at the Hollywood Bowl. De Havilland traveled to Hollywood to audition and was selected as second understudy to the actress playing Hermia. Before opening night, the actress and her first understudy were called to make a motion picture, leaving de Havilland to undertake the role. In front of a star-studded audience, de Havilland triumphed.
- Her opening-night performance was seen by a producer at Warner Bros., who convinced Jack L. Warner to fly out from New York to see de Havilland. Warner Bros. was planning a film version of the play. Warner attended the last night of the performance, was impressed with de Havilland, and offered her a long-term contract.
- Was cast in some forgettable productions for Warner Bros., including *Alibi Ike*, *The Irish in Us*, and *Hard to Get*.
- Began playing opposite newcomer Errol Flynn in films such as *Captain Blood* and *Charge of the Light Brigade*. She became infatuated with the handsome but reckless actor.
- Was cast as Angela opposite Fredric March in the title role in *Anthony Adverse* (1936).
- Used her iron will and determination to capture the role of Melanie in *GWTW* after Jack L. Warner refused to lend her to Selznick International.

THE WINNING OVER OF LESLIE HOWARD

For Selznick, Leslie Howard was the perfect Ashley Wilkes. Howard was known for his portrayals of intelligent, introspective, and idealistic characters in films such as *Of Human Bondage*, *The Petrified Forest*, and *Pygmalion*.

For Howard, playing Ashley was perfect nonsense. "I haven't the slightest intention of playing another weak, watery character such as Ashley Wilkes," he told Selznick. "I've played enough ineffectual characters already."

Howard's refusal stunned Selznick. Any one of the actresses he was considering for Scarlett could handle that role, but finding another actor to play Ashley was impossible. Howard *was* Ashley.

In the light of Howard's refusal, Selznick tested Melvyn Douglas and found him "much too beefy physically" for the delicate Ashley. At his wife Irene's suggestion, Selznick tested Ray Milland. Milland, however, couldn't quite master the Southern accent. For a while, Selznick even considered newcomer Jeffrey Lynn, but he was rejected as well.

"I think it extremely unlikely that we will find any Ashley that will be as satisfactory to me, or that any of the Ashleys that we are testing will prove on film to be as right as Leslie Howard seems to be in my imagination," Selznick confided to an associate.

Howard was adamant, though. At forty-five, he felt uncomfortable playing the youthful Ashley. He also felt that accepting the role would continue the typecasting he had grown to hate.

Selznick was now faced with the task of winning over Leslie Howard. Unlike Gable, Howard could not be seduced by money. But Selznick knew of Howard's longing to produce or direct films; what might appeal to Howard, then, would be the chance to escape to behind the camera. Selznick decided to make the actor an enticing offer. If Howard would accept the role of Ashley, Selznick would give him the opportunity to star in and be the associate producer of Selznick's next film, *Intermezzo*. The prospect was utterly irresistible, and Howard signed on the dotted line.

STAR TRACKS: LESLIE HOWARD

- Born Leslie Howard Steiner on April 3, 1893, in London, England.
- Parents: Ferdinand and Lilian Blumberg Steiner. His father was an office worker and stockbroker. The family changed its name to "Stainer" at the time of the First World War.

- Encouraged by his mother to write plays and to act. He did so while completing his education, but his father discouraged him from entering the acting profession. Howard worked as a banker until World War I interrupted his career.
- Married Ruth Martin in 1916.
- Enlisted in the British army and was sent to the front lines in France. A year later, he was sent home suffering from shell shock.
- Disillusioned with banking, he decided to become an actor. Most stage actors were at this time fighting in the war, so it was relatively easy for him to find work. He began his career on the London stage and used his first and middle names as his stage name. He toured in *Peg O' My Heart* and *Charley's Aunt*.
- Promised his wife in 1917 that if he wasn't successful as an actor in five years, he would quit and become a businessman.
- His son, Ronald, was born in 1918.
- Left London for America in late 1920 to accept a role in the Broadway play *Just Suppose*.
- His daughter, Leslie Ruth, was born in 1924.
- Found success in other American plays: *Outward Bound*, *The Green Hat*, and *Her Cardboard Lover*.
- After his debut in *Her Cardboard Lover* in 1926, the *New York Daily News* proclaimed, "Cardboard Lover Belongs to Howard." His star finally shone—nine years after the promise he made to his wife.
- Traveled to Hollywood in 1930 to make his first film—*Outward Bound*—for Warner Bros.
- Signed a contract with MGM to make three films in 1931: *Never the Twain Shall Meet*, *Five and Ten*, and *A Free Soul*, which featured Norma Shearer and Clark Gable.
- Signed a three-year, three-pictures-a-year contract with Warner Bros. in 1933.
- Other films: *Of Human Bondage* (1934); *The Scarlet Pimpernel* (1935); *The Petrified Forest* (1936); *Romeo and Juliet* (1936).
- Originally played in *The Petrified Forest* on Broadway with newcomer Humphrey Bogart in the role of gangster Duke Mantee. When Warner Bros. was casting the film version, Howard was asked to re-create his role, but the studio wanted Edward G. Robinson to take the Bogart part. Howard told Warner Bros. that he would not make the film unless Bogart could re-create his role as

well. The brothers Warner gave in, and Bogart got the role that launched his career.

- Academy Award nominations: Howard was nominated for Best Actor of 1932–1933 for his role of Peter Standish in the film *Berkeley Square*; nominated for Best Actor of 1938 for his role of Professor Henry Higgins in the screen version of *Pygmalion*. He lost both times.
- Signed for the role of Ashley Wilkes in January 1939.

SMALLER ROLES

Gerald O'Hara

Versatile character actor Thomas Mitchell was the only serious contender for the role of Scarlett's father. Mitchell had originally followed in his father's footsteps into a newspaper career, but he soon began writing plays in his spare time and dreamed of becoming an actor. His dream became reality in 1916 when he debuted on Broadway in the original play *Under Sentence*. For years, he had a triple stage career acting, directing, and writing.

A contract from Columbia Pictures lured Mitchell to Hollywood in 1936. His early credits included *Craig's Wife*, *Theodora Goes Wild*, and *When You're in Love*. In 1937, Mitchell appeared in Frank Capra's *Lost Horizon* and John Ford's *The Hurricane*; both brought him important attention. For his work in *The Hurricane*, he was nominated for an Academy Award as Best Supporting Actor. That led to three roles that would crown the year 1939 for Mitchell: Doc Boone in Ford's *Stagecoach*, "Diz" Moore in *Mr. Smith Goes to Washington*, and Gerald O'Hara in *GWTW*.

Ellen O'Hara

Selznick had few choices for the role of Scarlett's mother. He first offered the part to Lillian Gish, but she turned it down. He was considering Cornelia Otis Skinner when he decided on Barbara O'Neil.

O'Neil began her career on stage when she joined a summer stock company, University Players, which is where she met her future husband, director Joshua Logan. She made her Broadway debut in 1933 in *Carrie Nation*.

Deciding to try films, O'Neil headed for Hollywood and in 1937 debuted as the warm second wife in *Stella Dallas*. She and Thomas Mitchell played husband and wife in 1938's *Love, Honor and Behave*, and her casting as Scarlett's mother in 1939 renewed their working relationship.

Suellen O'Hara

Evelyn Keyes, a native of Port Arthur, Texas, was raised in Atlanta, Georgia. As a teenager, she left Margaret Mitchell's hometown for Hollywood and a film career. Cecil B. DeMille offered her a contract, and she won roles in his films *The Buccaneer* and *Union Pacific*.

When casting *GWTW*, Selznick wrote to a staff member, "I don't know anything about Evelyn Keyes and will be interested to see her." He met her, liked what he saw in the attractive blonde actress, and immediately attempted to lure her to the infamous casting couch. Keyes eluded the pursuing Selznick by running around his large mahogany desk until he had to stop to catch his breath. Then she escaped. But Selznick didn't hold her rebuff against her; he offered her the role of Suellen O'Hara.

Carreen O'Hara

Selznick originally wanted Judy Garland for the role of Scarlett's youngest sister. But Garland accepted the role of Dorothy in *The Wizard of Oz*, which put her out of the running for the small role of Carreen O'Hara. Instead, Selznick turned to Andy Hardy's girlfriend.

Canadian-born Ann Rutherford began her career in radio. She moved on to small roles in films, and then in 1937 she was offered a contract by MGM. In 1938, she played the Spirit of Christmas Past in *A Christmas Carol*. She is best known for the twelve Andy Hardy movies she made in which she played Mickey Rooney's girlfriend, Polly Benedict.

Rutherford almost *didn't* get the part of Carreen. Louis B. Mayer refused to lend her for the role because, as he told her when he summoned her to his office, "it's a nothing part." Rutherford begged for the role because "I knew it was going to be a film for the ages." But she couldn't persuade Mayer. Then she did something she had never done before in front of the studio head: she burst into tears. That did it. He relented, and she won the part.

Stuart Tarleton

Max Arnow, Selznick's casting director, discovered handsome George Bessolo acting in a play at the Pasadena Playhouse in Southern California. Bessolo was signed to play one of Scarlett's beaux, Stuart Tarleton. A confusing name game ensued. After signing Bessolo, Selznick contracted him out to Warner Bros., where he adopted the professional name George Reeves. That name was used on the screen credits for *GWTW*, but he was mistakenly identified as Brent Tarleton.

Brent Tarleton

New Orleans native Herman Frederick Crane had no intention of trying out for *GWTW* when he accompanied his cousin (the daughter of silent-screen siren Leatrice Joy) to Selznick International Pictures for her audition for the role of Suellen O'Hara. Noticing Crane's handsome looks and hearing his mellifluous voice and Southern drawl, the casting director insisted that the aspiring actor meet George Cukor. The director declared Crane's voice "just perfect" and, in turn, introduced him to David O. Selznick. Crane's script reading of the film's opening scene with Vivien Leigh so impressed the producer, he signed Crane to a thirteen-week contract for fifty dollars a week.

As Brent Tarleton, Crane spoke the first lines of *GWTW*: "What do we care if we *were* expelled from college, Scarlett? The war's going to start any day now, so we'd have left college anyhow!" But he was misidentified as Stuart Tarleton in the screen credits. By the time the error was caught, it was too late and would have been too costly to correct.

Mammy

Selznick read that Elizabeth McDuffie, Mrs. Franklin D. Roosevelt's maid, was the star of the White House servants' amateur theater troupe. With Mrs. Roosevelt's permission, Selznick tested McDuffie for the role of Mammy and reaped a harvest of national publicity. More seriously, Selznick tested Hattie Noel and Louise Beavers for the role before he selected Hattie McDaniel.

McDaniel's career began when she worked as a singer with Professor George Morrison's Orchestra, a black band that toured the country. She was the first African American woman to sing on network radio. In 1931, she arrived in Hollywood to seek a film career and began as an extra before capturing larger parts. She is remembered for her roles in *Show Boat*, *Saratoga* (especially for the scene in which she sang with Clark Gable), and *China Seas*. During times when work in films was not available, she hired herself out as a domestic or a cook.

Her portrayal of Mammy in *GWTW* brought her fame as well as unexpected criticism. Thereafter, she came under fire for continually accepting movie roles as a stereotypical domestic. But McDaniel pointed to the domestic work she had done during the lean years. Comparing the differences in salaries between working as a domestic and portraying one, McDaniel said she much preferred the film work.

Prissy

Selznick was certain he had a winner with his selection of squeaky-voiced Butterfly McQueen to play Scarlett's addlebrained maid, Prissy.

In 1935, Thelma McQueen moved from her hometown of Tampa, Florida, to New York City, where she joined a Harlem acting group. She adopted the name Butterfly after dancing the "Butterfly Ballet" in the group's production of *A Midsummer Night's Dream*. She debuted on Broadway in 1937 in *Brown Sugar*. Her first film role was Lulu in 1939's *The Women*.

When she was in Philadelphia touring with the play *What a Life!*, she learned that David O. Selznick had chosen her for the role of Prissy. The news surprised McQueen. She had been previously rejected for the part by a talent scout that had deemed her too plump for the role.

Jonas Wilkerson

Robert Gleckler began the role of Jonas Wilkerson, but the actor died of uremic poisoning during production. He was replaced by Victor Jory.

Born in the Yukon Territory of Canada to American parents, Jory was a champion boxer and wrestler during his military service in the United States Coast Guard before he turned his attention to acting. His first film in 1930, *Renegades*, led to others in which he was usually cast as a villain. He played Injun Joe in the 1938 Selznick production *The Adventures of Tom Sawyer*.

India Wilkes

When Selznick's story editor Kay Brown first saw her in Charleston, South Carolina, local thespian Alicia Rhett was auditioning for the role of Melanie. "She gave a lovely reading of Melanie, insofar as any amateur can read Melanie," Brown reported to Selznick in December 1936. Impressed with the auburn-haired actress's poise and presence, Brown mentioned Rhett to George Cukor, who was in the South scouting talent for *GWTW*. Rhett auditioned and Cukor was captivated.

Cukor offered screen tests to the Savannah native, after which he determined that "Alicia Rhett has charm and the ideal looks and quality for Melanie. . . . Rhett has a reality about her that is very engaging." Yet he worried that her inexperience in front of a camera combined with the challenges of the role would make it too daunting for Rhett. Instead, Cukor offered her the part of Melanie's sister-in-law, India Wilkes.

During principal filming, Rhett, a talented artist, sketched members of *GWTW*'s cast. She shared her behind-the-scenes portraits with the stars and also offered the sketches to Charleston's *News & Courier*.

Charles Hamilton

The role of Scarlett's first husband was won by Rand Brooks, an MGM contract player, who had made his screen debut in 1938's *Love Finds Andy Hardy*, starring Mickey Rooney, Judy Garland, and Ann Rutherford. (Sharp-eyed viewers will spot Brooks as the uncredited Young Man on Bandstand.) That same year, Rand had a supporting role in *Dramatic School*, which also featured Rutherford. In 1939, he had parts in *The Old Maid*, *Thunder Afloat*, *Babes in Arms*, and *Dancing Co-Ed* before being cast as the hapless Charles Hamilton.

Frank Kennedy

The role of Scarlett's second husband went to Carroll Nye, who began his career in the 1925 silent film *Three Wise Crooks*. His most noteworthy role before *GWTW* was the romantic lead in 1928's *While the City Sleeps*. Despite Nye's twenty-two-film resume, stardom eluded him for the next ten years. But when the spotlight of *GWTW* shone upon him, he hoped that playing Frank Kennedy would be his break to the big time.

Aunt Pittypat Hamilton

Billie Burke was desperate for the role of Aunt Pittypat. Although Selznick thought she was too young and slim for the part, he agreed to a screen test.

Her costume was stuffed with pounds of padding. Makeup artists fattened her features with a fake double chin and piled cotton stuffing into her cheeks. She waddled onto the set and began her test. Her overabundant padding and the oppressive studio lights conspired against her: she almost keeled over from the heat. Several days after this disastrous test, Selznick signed the more robust Laura Hope Crews for the role.

Crews began acting at the age of four. Her career as a child actress was interrupted by her education, but after high school she left her native San Francisco for the lights of Broadway. She debuted in *Merely Mary Ann* in 1903. During the 1920s, she appeared in numerous plays, including *Mr. Pim Passes By*, *Merry Wives of Gotham*, and *Hay Fever* (which she directed). Following her outstanding performance in *The Silver Cord* in 1926, she was offered the opportunity to travel to Hollywood to coach film stars making the transition from silent films to the talkies.

Her own film career, which had begun in 1915 with the silent film *The Fighting Hope*, moved into sound films with 1929's *Charming Sinners* and then blossomed in the 1930s. Highlights included reprising her stage role of Mrs. Phelps in the film *The Silver Cord*, playing Prudence in *Camille*, and landing Aunt Pittypat in *Gone With the Wind*.

Uncle Peter

Selznick originally tested Eddie Anderson for the role of Pork, the O'Haras' house servant, but gravel-voiced Anderson was signed to play the Hamiltons' majordomo, Uncle Peter.

Anderson acquired his distinctive voice after he damaged his vocal cords as a twelve-year-old newspaper hawker on the streets of San Francisco. He soon abandoned that career to join vaudeville and tour in a song-and-dance duo with his brother and later as a solo act.

In Hollywood, he found small parts in movies, but his real claim to fame came from radio. His portrayal of the wisecracking valet Rochester Van Jones on *The Jack Benny Show* in 1937 kept listeners in stitches.

Anderson appeared in *The Green Pastures* (1936), *You Can't Take It with You* (1938), and *You Can't Cheat an Honest Man* (1939). Even though

Anderson landed a role in *Jezebel*, Selznick obviously forgave him and used his talents in *GWTW*.

Dr. Meade

Selznick decided on Lionel Barrymore for the role of Dr. Meade in 1937. But by the time *GWTW* was ready for shooting, Barrymore had been stricken with crippling arthritis and was confined to a wheelchair. Lewis Stone, who was known for his role as Andy Hardy's father, was also considered, but Selznick decided on veteran actor Harry Davenport.

Davenport was born in New York City to a theatrical family. So it was not unusual for Davenport's career debut to be on the Philadelphia stage when he was only five in the 1871 play *Damon and Pythias*. As a teenager, he performed in Shakespearean productions for stock companies, and at the age of twenty-eight he made his Broadway debut in the musical comedy *The Voyage of Suzette*.

From his vast work in theater he moved on to motion pictures in 1913 and debuted in the silent short *Kenton's Heir*. He starred in and directed silent shorts and feature films until 1921, when he returned to the stage.

After being widowed in 1934, Davenport returned to Hollywood and, at the age of sixty-nine, quickly established himself as a character actor, recruited for films by all the major studios. His pre-*GWTW* work included roles in *The Life of Emile Zola* (1937) and *You Can't Take It with You* (1938).

Belle Watling

Selznick had wanted to test Tallulah Bankhead, a rejected Scarlett, for the role of Atlanta's madam. But the suggestion was diplomatically ignored. Selznick fleetingly thought Mae West "might be glad to do it as a stunt." He tested Joan Blondell, Loretta Young, and Gladys George, but then he saw Ona Munson.

Munson had entered the world of vaudeville in 1922 as a singer and dancer. She toured in the starring role of *No, No, Nanette*, then played the role in the Broadway production. Other productions such as *Manhattan Mary* and *Hold Everything* followed. In the latter, she introduced the song "You're the Cream in My Coffee."

The year 1931 found her breaking into films in Hollywood. She had a role in *Five Star Final*, an Edward G. Robinson film that was nominated for an Academy Award as Outstanding Production, a category later called Best Picture. She continued her work on Broadway during the 1930s and even took her musical and dramatic talents to radio. She played Lorelei Kilbourne in the *Big Town* radio series.

The scene chosen for Munson's *GWTW* test was Belle's encounter with Melanie outside the Atlanta church-turned-hospital. Munson's performance was superb, and Selznick signed her immediately.

FOUR

Selznick "Finds" His Scarlett

THE CONTINUING SAGA OF TRANSFORMING
GWTW INTO A SCRIPT, PART ONE

Since Margaret Mitchell refused to have anything to do with turning her novel into a movie script, Selznick had to find a writer equal to the task. He found that someone in Sidney Howard.

Howard, a Pulitzer Prize winner and one of America's leading playwrights, had a reputation for excellence. Not only did he write for the stage (*They Knew What They Wanted, The Silver Cord, Yellow Jacket*, and *Dodsworth*), he also wrote for the screen (*Bulldog Drummond, Raffles*, and *Arrowsmith*).

Howard began working on *GWTW*'s script in mid-December 1936, using a fifty-page treatment he had prepared from initial readings of the novel and from feedback on the treatment from Selznick. The producer was not happy that Howard preferred to work on the East Coast. "I never had much success with leaving a writer alone to do a script, without almost daily collaboration with myself and usually the director," Selznick complained in a memo to Kay Brown, who had negotiated the deal for Howard.

Howard wrote at a breakneck sixteen-hour-a-day pace and completed the script—all four hundred pages of it—in eight weeks. He had condensed pages of narration into manageable scenes; eliminated minor characters; and had cut, cut, cut without losing any of the flavor that Margaret Mitchell had imparted.

Selznick was pleased with Howard's work. But the script had a playing time of nearly six hours. For a while, Selznick considered making the film as two pictures, but he changed his mind when he was advised that the format would be unpopular with audiences. So together in California in the spring and summer of 1937, Selznick and Howard hammered out subsequent drafts of the script, the two of them discussing the story line and Howard doing the actual writing. Howard, feeling that his work was finished, then returned home. But Selznick called him back, and Howard did further script revisions from January to February 1938.

Selznick, ever the perfectionist, was still not completely satisfied with the script. He put it on a shelf but browsed through it occasionally during the next few months, making notes on areas for revision.

In October 1938, Selznick tried to coax Howard to accompany him on a trip to Bermuda so they could work on the script again. But Howard, the owner of a seven-hundred-acre cattle farm in Tyringham, Massachusetts, refused: "I have a cow with calf. I'm not about to leave at this time."

By the end of October, three months before the official date of shooting, Selznick had put Howard's script aside and began thinking about getting another writer to handle the project. (*To be continued . . .*)

THE LONG AND THE SHORT OF FILMING *GWTW*

According to calculations worked out by Selznick's studio, filming *GWTW* exactly as Margaret Mitchell wrote it would yield a picture 168 hours long. Moviegoers would certainly have had sore bottoms. At that length, it would take a week of straight twenty-four-hour-a-day viewing to see the entire film. Thankfully, Selznick was thinking in realistic terms. He envisioned the film running between two-and-a-half and three hours.

STAR TRACKS: VIVIEN LEIGH

- Born Vivian Mary Hartley on November 5, 1913, in Darjeeling, India.

- Parents: Ernest Richard Hartley and Gertrude Robinson Yackje. Ernest worked in the brokerage house of Piggott Chapman and Company.
- Received her education in English, French, and Italian convent schools. As a child, she knew she wanted to be an actress. After completing her formal education, she attended London's Royal Academy of Dramatic Art.
- Married Herbert Leigh Holman (called Leigh), an English barrister, in 1932 and welcomed a daughter, Suzanne, the following year.
- First films: Played an extra in *Things Are Looking Up* and had the second female lead role in *The Village Squire*, two 1935 British films.
- Adopted the professional name Vivien Leigh by slightly changing the spelling of her given name and borrowing her husband's middle name.
- Caused a sensation in London with her role in the stage production *The Mask of Virtue* (1935) and attracted the attention of Alexander Korda, who signed her to a contract with London Films.
- Fell in love with Laurence Olivier after seeing him in the play *Theatre Royal*.
- Acted for the first time with Olivier in the film *Fire Over England* (1937). The two were lovers by this time.
- Broke her ankle while skiing in Austria in 1936 and recuperated by reading a recently published novel titled *Gone with the Wind*.
- Had the second female lead as an unfaithful wife in the 1938 MGM film *A Yank at Oxford*. She played Elsa Craddock, whose flirtatious behavior nearly gets star Robert Taylor expelled from Oxford.
- Played an East London pickpocket in 1938's *St. Martin's Lane* with Charles Laughton and Rex Harrison. The film was retitled *The Streets of London* for its American release.
- Captured the coveted role of Scarlett O'Hara in *GWTW*.

SELZNICK DISCOVERS HIS SCARLETT

The Official Story

By December 1938, Selznick had still not found his Scarlett. And time was running out. Selznick had to put Gable to work soon, which meant production could not be delayed any longer. Filming *GWTW* had to begin with or without an actress to play Scarlett O'Hara.

Selznick planned to build Tara on the studio's back lot, which was littered with sets from *The Last of the Mohicans, King Kong, The Garden of Allah,* and *Little Lord Fauntleroy.* Rather than having them carted away, Selznick decided to reconstruct and repaint the sets to represent Atlanta. He could then torch the old sets to clear the way for the construction of Tara and at the same time film the scene of the burning of the munitions warehouses at the Atlanta depot.

Everything was ready for the night of December 10, 1938. Seven Technicolor cameras were positioned to capture the scene at different angles. Three pairs of Rhett and Scarlett doubles were in horse-drawn wagons anticipating their race through the flames. Oil sprinkler pipes were threaded among the sets. Standing by were fire companies from Los Angeles, two hundred studio workers, and various pieces of firefighting equipment just in case the fire got out of control.

Selznick checked his watch as he nervously paced on the platform that rose high above the scene. His mother and a group of friends and colleagues were there to watch the spectacle, and his brother Myron was expected to arrive at any moment. Myron, a Hollywood agent, was dining with clients and had told Selznick that he might be late.

An hour later, Myron had still not arrived, and Selznick was told that the firefighters could wait no longer. Reluctantly, he gave the signal, and suddenly Atlanta was ablaze.

As the flames licked the sky, "Action" was called, the cameras began rolling, and the doubles dashed through the inferno. Sparks flew, smoke billowed, and buildings rumbled. A towering brick wall used in *King Kong* groaned then collapsed in a shower of flames. Selznick reveled in the sensational scene.

As the flames died away, a slightly drunk Myron climbed the platform with his guests, actor Laurence Olivier and a beautiful woman wearing a black picture hat and a mink coat. David Selznick was furious with his brother, but his fury melted when he was introduced to Olivier's companion, Vivien Leigh. "I want you to meet Scarlett O'Hara," Myron said.

"The flames were lighting up her face," David Selznick recalled. "I took one look and knew that she was right, at least as far as her appearance went, at least right as far as my conception of how Scarlett O'Hara looked. I'll never recover from that first look."

That first look told Selznick his two-year search was over. Out of the ashes of Atlanta he had finally discovered his Scarlett, according to the official story.

The Real Story

After reading *GWTW* for the first time, Vivien Leigh hungered for the role of Scarlett O'Hara. Her theater colleagues scoffed at the idea of an unknown English actress stepping into a role coveted by most Hollywood actresses. But Leigh would not be dissuaded. She *would* play Scarlett.

She persuaded her agent to submit her name to Selznick International before the American premiere of her film *Fire Over England*, which was produced by Alexander Korda. Kay Brown gave Leigh's name to Selznick in February 1937, who responded, "I have no enthusiasm for Vivien Leigh. Maybe I will have, but as yet have never even seen photograph of her. Will be seeing *Fire Over England* shortly, at which time will of course see Leigh."

Perhaps *Fire Over England* first kindled in Selznick the desire to have Leigh as his Scarlett. His desire blazed with her coquettish performance in 1938's *A Yank at Oxford*. Between February and August 1938, Selznick viewed all of Leigh's British films and studied photographs of her.

Selznick decided to keep Leigh a closely guarded secret. The American public might reject an English woman playing a Southern belle. Plus, the actresses who believed they had a chance to play Scarlett might go for Selznick's jugular were they to find out he was considering someone else all along. Less backlash would result if Leigh's announcement as Scarlett were to come as close as possible to the start of filming.

In secret correspondence, he urged Leigh and Olivier not to end their respective marriages until after the filming of *GWTW* began. Then Selznick began hush-hush negotiations with Alexander Korda, who had Leigh under exclusive contract. But Korda, who had groomed Leigh's acting talents for the prior three years, was initially unwilling to release his special find to Selznick.

By late 1938, though, Korda was beset with financial difficulties and was ready to make a deal. In November, he and Leigh met Selznick in New York, where the producer was staying after his cruise to Bermuda. There they worked out the terms of the deal (contingent, of course, upon Leigh's screen test for the role) and concocted the story they would feed to the press.

According to the official story, Leigh was in the United States hoping to replace Merle Oberon in *Wuthering Heights* and to star opposite Olivier. This was most unlikely since Oberon was under contract to the film's producer, Samuel Goldwyn.

Leigh flew to Hollywood, where Olivier met her at the airport and drove her to the Beverly Hills Hotel. There she kept a low profile until Selznick could stage a proper entrance for her. It was decided that Leigh would "meet" Selznick on December 10, the night Atlanta's depot would go up in flames.

The plan proceeded almost like clockwork. Leigh and Olivier arrived at the back lot on time, but Myron Selznick was late. This hiccup meant that Leigh and Olivier had to stand around, trying to look inconspicuous.

Among those spotting them was Marcella Rabwin, Selznick's executive assistant, and Wilbur Kurtz, the film's Civil War historian. In his December 10 journal entry, Kurtz recorded that "a charming young lady appeared just before the fire sequences began, squired by a handsome chap. . . . I accosted Marcella as to whom she might be. Marcella cupped a hand to her lips and whispered, 'Vivien Leigh. Mr. Selznick is seriously considering her.'"

Unable to wait any longer for his brother, David O. Selznick signaled for the conflagration to begin. As the last flames lapped at the Atlanta buildings, Myron finally arrived to make his "introduction." And David O. Selznick's "first look" told him that he had "met" his Scarlett.

VIVIEN LEIGH: THE DARK-HORSE SCARLETT

About 1 a.m., after the flames were no more than dying embers, the group returned to Selznick's office for a drink. Selznick showed Leigh the scenes from the script to be used for the screen test and asked her to read Scarlett's lines for him and George Cukor.

Leigh felt an immediate rapport with Cukor. He was equally impressed with her. As she ran through the scenes, both Selznick and Cukor were sure she would be the perfect Scarlett. Despite her clipped British tones, Cukor assured Selznick, "I don't think she'll find the Southern accent any trouble."

Two days after Leigh's reading, Selznick sent a letter to his wife: "Saturday I was greatly exhilarated by the Fire Sequence. . . . Myron rolled in just exactly too late, arriving about a minute and a half after the last building had fallen and burned and after the shots were completed. With him were Larry Olivier and Vivien Leigh. Shhhhh: She's the Scarlett dark horse, and looks damned good. (Not for anybody's ears but your own: It's narrowed down to Paulette [Goddard], Jean Arthur, Joan Bennett, and Vivien Leigh."

TESTING, TESTING, TESTING

Selznick set up the testing schedule for the principal Scarlett candidates and told his staff, "Scarlett will definitely be decided upon as the result of this next group of tests."

Cukor worked with Jean Arthur, Joan Bennett, and Paulette Goddard; and on Wednesday, December 21, it was Vivien Leigh's turn. She had been rehearsing the three screen-test scenes and practicing her Southern accent every night for the past week with Olivier, but she was still nervous.

Before the camera, she displayed a fiery temperament in the lacing scene with Mammy before the barbecue. For the second test, the library scene with Ashley, she was a demanding, passionate Scarlett. In the third test, she fiercely tried to convince Ashley to run away with her to Mexico. Cukor was thrilled with the passion of her performances. Compared with the other candidates, he recalled, "There was an indescribable wildness about her."

Selznick spliced the tests together so that he could see all four actresses consecutively playing each scene. He viewed the scenes over and over again and then sent the film to Jock Whitney in New York for his reaction. Whitney deferred to his producer, and Selznick's decision was definite: Vivien Leigh would play Scarlett.

THE LONG-AWAITED ANNOUNCEMENT

Friday the thirteenth in January 1939 was a lucky day for Vivien Leigh. It was the day that Selznick announced her selection as Scarlett O'Hara. He softened the blow for the unlucky Scarlett contenders by sending each actress orchids and a personal note before the news was announced.

Selznick released the news first to Margaret Mitchell in three long Western Union telegrams that arrived in segments at fifteen-minute intervals. The first wire announced Vivien Leigh's casting as Scarlett, the second detailed the casting of Olivia de Havilland and Leslie Howard, and the third was a lengthy biographical sketch of Vivien Leigh. The bio skirted around Leigh's British nationality by mentioning her birth in India, her education in Europe, and "her recent screen work in England." The release made no mention of Leigh's love, Laurence Olivier, nor their respective impending divorces.

Margaret Mitchell wanted her former colleagues at the *Constitution* to get this scoop of the year, so she ran back and forth between the telegraph office and the newspaper office carrying the pages of the wires as they arrived.

The newspaper, a morning edition, was about to go to press, so the editor tore out a portion of the front page. File clerks scurried around to find a photograph of Leigh, which was placed on the front page alongside the text of the wires as they were received and typeset.

But the clerks had a more difficult time locating a suitable photograph of Olivia de Havilland. According to Margaret Mitchell: "For a bad five minutes it looked as if a picture of Miss de Havilland in a scanty bathing suit was going to appear in the morning paper, bearing the caption 'Here is Melanie, a True Daughter of the Old South.' That picture was the only view of her the file clerk could find at first. I made loud lamentations at this, especially when the editor said, 'We can explain that Sherman's men had gotten away with the rest of her clothes.'" A more suitable photograph was finally found, and Atlanta was the first to learn that *GWTW* had finally been cast.

TELEGRAMS TO MARGARET MITCHELL

After Selznick announced his cast on January 13, 1939, Vivien Leigh, Olivia de Havilland, and Leslie Howard sent telegrams to Margaret Mitchell. The telegrams were published in the *Atlanta Constitution* the following day.

From Vivien Leigh: "Dear Mrs. Marsh: If I can but feel that you are with me on this, the most important and trying task of my life, I pledge with all my heart I shall try to make Scarlett O'Hara live as you described her in your brilliant book. Warmest regards."

From Olivia de Havilland: "Dear Mrs. Marsh: The news that I am to play Melanie means a long-cherished dream realized. Now I hope for one thing more important, that is to play the role to your satisfaction."

From Leslie Howard: "Dear Mrs. Marsh: I am not at all envious of Rhett because thanks to you, it was Melanie, Ma'am, that I wanted. But seriously,

I feel it a great honor to have been selected to enact one of the roles of your book, the title of which escapes me at the moment."

AMERICA'S REACTION

After the long-awaited announcement was officially released, the news was carried by almost every newspaper and radio station from coast to coast. A Gallup poll conducted afterward showed that 35% favored the selection of Vivien Leigh, 16% disapproved, 20% were undecided, and 29% hadn't heard the news.

One group who did hear the news was the Florida Daughters of the Confederacy, and they were not happy. They denounced Leigh's selection and threatened to boycott the film. Southern gentlemen sent outraged letters to newspapers stating their impassioned thoughts on the matter: "The selection of Vivien Leigh is a direct affront to the men who wore the Gray and an outrage to the memory of the heroes of 1776 who fought to free this land of British domination." Others wrote that an Englishwoman's portrayal of Scarlett was an "insult to Southern womanhood."

But the president-general of the United Daughters of the Confederacy saw the selection of Leigh in a different light: "I think Miss Leigh is an excellent solution of the problem, in which all the country has been keenly interested. . . . I have not been able to visualize any known American actress for portrayal of the part assigned to Miss Leigh. The character of Scarlett is interesting and thoroughly objectionable throughout. I do not consider her in any way typical of Southern girls of the [18]60s."

FIVE

Lights! Camera! Chaos!

GEORGE CUKOR: DIRECTOR #1

In Hollywood, George Cukor was considered "a woman's director." He had earned that reputation with his sensitive, insightful handling of women stars such as Katharine Hepburn, Greta Garbo, and Constance Bennett in such films as *A Bill of Divorcement*, *Camille*, and *What Price Hollywood?*

Selznick selected Cukor to direct *GWTW* shortly after buying the film rights. The producer had long admired Cukor's work and felt that relating the story of Scarlett O'Hara needed Cukor's special touch.

From the beginning, Cukor was involved with every aspect of *GWTW*. He advised Selznick on the script; he traveled south to scout filming locations and to seek potential Scarlett candidates. Cukor coached and tested actors and actresses during the casting of the film; he worked with production designer William Cameron Menzies to prepare "a complete script in sketch form, showing actual camera setups, lighting, etc."

Cukor devoted two intense years to the preproduction work on *GWTW*. But only a brief two weeks after he had called "Action!" George Cukor found himself replaced as director of the film.

THE CONTINUING SAGA OF TRANSFORMING
GWTW INTO A SCRIPT, PART TWO

The next writer that Selznick selected to work on Howard's *GWTW* script was well-known script fixer Jo Swerling. Swerling went with Selznick on a two-month working vacation to Bermuda and threw himself into the project. After countless scene rewrites, however, Selznick was still not satisfied with the script.

When Selznick returned from Bermuda, he approached another writer, playwright Oliver H. P. Garrett. An accommodating fellow, Garrett agreed to accompany Selznick on his transcontinental train trip from New York to Los Angeles. As the *Super Chief* train thundered along to the West Coast, Garrett was in his stateroom hard at work revising the *GWTW* script.

What frustrated the writers who worked with Selznick was his insistence that the script contain Margaret Mitchell's dialogue. Selznick was convinced that no more than one hundred lines of new dialogue would be needed. For the writer, that meant endless hunting through the novel, searching for lines of dialogue to use in constructing a scene.

Garrett's tenure on the script was not long. He was soon replaced by yet another writer who was replaced by a succession of still other writers. Those tapped by Selznick included John Van Druten, Charles MacArthur, Winston Miller, John Balderstron, Michael Foster, and Edwin Justus Mayer. Even F. Scott Fitzgerald had a crack at the script.

Fitzgerald's career was on the downslide when he undertook rewriting the *GWTW* script in January 1939. His contract to write for MGM was not being renewed, so during the remaining weeks, the studio lent him to Selznick to rewrite dialogue. He edited the script mercilessly, cutting paragraphs of flowery dialogue that he described as "trite and stagy." But about halfway through his blue-penciling of the script, a snag developed. Selznick was concerned that the character of Aunt Pittypat was not funny enough. Through an all-night conference with Selznick and director Cukor, Fitzgerald struggled to find more amusing lines for the character. But his suggestions bombed, and he was sent home. Selznick fired him the next day.

As a result, on the day before the start of principal shooting, Selznick still didn't have a complete script. Undaunted, he assured Jock Whitney, "Don't get panicky at the seemingly small amount of final revised script. . . . It is so clearly in my mind that I can tell you the picture from beginning to end, almost shot for shot."

What Selznick did have was the novel, the Sidney Howard script, and the Howard-Garrett script. He believed that the Garrett script was superior in its continuity and basic storytelling but not as good as the Howard script in the crafting of individual scenes. "The job that remains to be done is to telescope the three into the shortest possible form," Selznick told Whitney. And Selznick believed he could do that himself. (*To be continued . . .*)

MELANIE'S LABOR PAINS

"Melanie's pains were harder now. Her long hair was drenched in sweat and her gown stuck in wet spots to her body." Olivia de Havilland wanted to portray the scene of Melanie's giving birth as realistically as Margaret Mitchell had written it.

Since childbirth was a foreign experience for her, she prepared for the scene by visiting the Los Angeles County Hospital. There, dressed as a nurse, she observed births in the delivery room. After watching and listening, she noticed that labor pains were not continuous; they came in waves.

She reported this to Cukor as they rehearsed Melanie's labor scene. When filming began, Cukor became inspired. He grabbed and sharply twisted de Havilland's ankle under the blankets whenever he wanted her to simulate a new cycle of pain.

FIRED!

The filming of *GWTW* was progressing as slowly as molasses in January 1939. Because of difficulties with the script, Cukor had to shoot out of sequence. In the two weeks that followed the beginning of principal filming, Cukor had directed the opening scene of Scarlett and the Tarletons on Tara's porch, Ellen O'Hara's return home, the evening prayers sequence, Gerald's walk with Scarlett, Mammy dressing Scarlett for the barbecue, Mammy catching the Widow Hamilton trying on a hat, Rhett's presenting the Paris hat to Scarlett, the birth of Melanie's baby, Rhett's Atlanta rescue, Melanie after the Christmas dinner, and Scarlett giving the sash to Ashley. Cukor was working on the scenes from the Atlanta Bazaar when Selznick fired him.

Things went sour quickly for a number of reasons. The script was the main problem. Changes in scenes and dialogue arrived almost daily on the set. Out of necessity, Cukor substituted dialogue from the novel for the often-unplayable lines of the still-unfinished script. He even rewrote scenes before he shot them to make them more realistic. This not only caused delays in the shooting schedule but incurred Selznick's wrath as well.

After Selznick viewed the rushes, he and Cukor met head-on in heated confrontations. Selznick resented anyone tampering with his masterpiece. He told Cukor he expected to see each scene rehearsed before it was filmed to "avoid projection-room surprises for me." Selznick was concerned that Cukor, in his zeal for capturing the nuances of characters and scenes, was forsaking the panoramic sweep of the film. Selznick then began visiting the set, offering his unasked-for opinions, and driving the director to distraction with his interference.

Clark Gable, too, was becoming dissatisfied with Cukor. He was convinced that the "woman's director" was ignoring him and throwing the film toward its female stars. Gable and Cukor clashed over Rhett's Southern accent. Cukor argued for a more distinctive accent, but Gable resisted and convinced Selznick to back him. Gable also hated the slow pace at which filming was taking place. His view was echoed by Leslie Howard, who wrote to his daughter: "After seven days' shooting they are five days behind schedule."

On February 13, Selznick and Cukor issued a joint statement: "As a result of a series of disagreements between us over many of the individual scenes of *Gone With the Wind*, we have mutually decided that the only solution is for a new director to be selected at as early a date as is practicable." Cukor was out, and production shut down for two weeks.

When Vivien Leigh and Olivia de Havilland heard that Cukor had been fired, they were rehearsing a scene from the Atlanta Bazaar sequence. In their black mourning costumes, they stormed into Selznick's office and pleaded that Cukor be reinstated. Cukor had been the craftsman who had shaped their roles, they implored. Without his guidance, they would be lost. But Selznick would not reconsider. Leigh even threatened to walk off the film until she was warned about the legal ramifications of breaking a contract.

The stars returned to work, but they were distraught. Leigh later wrote to her husband Leigh Holman that Cukor "was my last hope of ever enjoying the film."

Cukor's influence did not end with his firing, though. When Vivien Leigh felt she needed help in understanding an upcoming scene, she secretly met Cukor for direction after regular studio hours. Olivia de Havilland also saw Cukor on the q.t. She met him on Sundays or dined with him when she needed help with development of her character. But neither actress let on to the other what she was doing.

De Havilland, perhaps feeling guilty, questioned Cukor about the propriety of working with him behind Leigh's back. Cukor replied that he didn't see anything wrong with it since Leigh was doing the same thing. Cukor essentially ghost-directed their performances in this way until the end of filming.

VICTOR FLEMING: DIRECTOR #2

To replace Cukor, Selznick approached MGM contract director Victor Fleming. Fleming was not interested in taking over the directorial reins of the troubled *GWTW*. At the time, he was manic with Munchkins on the set of *The Wizard of Oz* and didn't want to take on another exhausting project.

Gable was all for Fleming. Fleming had a reputation of being a "man's director" and had directed Gable in *Red Dust*, *The White Sister*, and *Test Pilot*. The two were also old friends and enjoyed motorcycling, carousing, and drinking together. Gable appealed to Fleming to accept the job on the basis of their friendship. MGM was applying pressure as well, and Fleming reluctantly agreed to take on the project.

Fleming met with Selznick to view the film footage of *GWTW* that had been shot so far. Fleming was never a man to pull any punches. As soon as the lights came up in the projection room, he turned to Selznick and said, "David, your f—ing script is no f—ing good."

THE CONTINUING SAGA OF TRANSFORMING
GWTW INTO A SCRIPT, PART THREE

Once production was underway, Selznick assumed the enormous task of writing the script for *GWTW*. He stayed awake night after night writing and rewriting the scenes that would be shot the following day. Cukor's complaints about the script escalated. Something had to give, and that something proved to be George Cukor.

Since Sidney Howard's original effort, the script had been changed by numerous pens. Selznick had resorted to printing revised pages on different shades of colored paper in an effort to keep track of each writer's contributions. By the time Victor Fleming took over directorial duties, the script resembled a veritable rainbow. Fleming's graphic estimation of the script's quality shocked Selznick into admitting that the script was, indeed, in serious trouble.

Selznick had no time to lose in reviving his script. Each day of suspended filming was costing the studio over $65,000. So Selznick turned to a famous script doctor who had a reputation for working miracles, Ben Hecht.

Hecht, brilliant but cynical, had begun his career as a playwright with his partner Charles MacArthur. Together they penned *The Front Page* and *Twentieth Century*. Lured by more lucrative work in Hollywood, Hecht then turned to writing scripts. He wrote *Design for Living* for Ernst Lubitsch and *Notorious* for Alfred Hitchcock. He always worked for the best price because he was a shrewd bargainer and a fast writer. He had written *Nothing Sacred* for Selznick in two weeks and rewrote *Hurricane* for Samuel Goldwyn in two days.

Selznick and Fleming arrived at Hecht's house early on Sunday morning. They spirited Hecht away in Selznick's car, and on the way to the studio they came to terms: Selznick would pay Hecht $15,000 for one week's work.

At the studio, Selznick was horrified to learn that Hecht had never read *Gone with the Wind*. Fleming admitted that he had not either, so Selznick launched into an oral synopsis that took over an hour. "I had seldom heard a more involved plot," Hecht remembered. "My verdict was that nobody could make a sensible movie out of it."

Hecht read the existing script, a real "humpty-dumpty job." He then asked Selznick if any one of the previous writers had produced a better version. Selznick suddenly remembered Sidney Howard's two-year-old draft and sent secretaries scurrying to find it. Hecht called it a "superb treatment" that needed only substantial editing and agreed to base his rewrite on Howard's script.

In Selznick's office for the next five days and nights, Hecht attacked the script mercilessly in eighteen- to twenty-four-hour stretches. Since he was not familiar with the characters, Selznick and Fleming acted out each scene as Hecht edited.

The pace was arduous and took its toll. Selznick ruled that food interfered with creativity so he banned all sustenance except for bananas and salted peanuts. Selznick took Benzedrine to keep awake and recommended the wonder drug to his cohorts. On day four, Fleming suffered a burst blood vessel in his eye, and the following day, Selznick collapsed while eating a banana. Nevertheless, at the end of the week, Hecht had succeeded in revising the entire first half of the script. (*To be continued . . .*)

THE CONTINUING SAGA OF TRANSFORMING *GWTW* INTO A SCRIPT, PART FOUR

Selznick tried to convince Ben Hecht to stay and finish the second part of the script. Hecht felt "there wasn't enough money in the world for this kind of suicidal work—eighteen to twenty hours a day—and I got out in a hurry."

With Hecht gone, Selznick decided to undertake the rewriting of part two on his own. By April, though, he was hopelessly behind in the rewriting, and the filming was floundering under the awful dialogue. In desperation, he sent out an SOS to the original architect of the script, Sidney Howard.

Howard agreed to work on the script for two weeks and during that time rewrote several major scenes in the second part. He fought with Selznick over the producer's desire to have a large church wedding for Scarlett's marriage to Frank Kennedy and over other issues. Howard tackled the final scene in which Rhett leaves Scarlett and felt his work was done. He was sure, however, that Selznick would rewrite the rewrite, then call him back again to salvage the script. Selznick did attack the script again, but Howard never worked again on it.

TRAGEDY STRIKES SIDNEY HOWARD

Sidney Howard owned a seven-hundred-acre cattle farm in Tyringham, Massachusetts. On August 23, 1939, he was attempting to start a tractor in his shed. What he didn't know was that the tractor had been left in gear. He cranked the handle in front of the tractor, the engine engaged, and the tractor leaped forward. Howard was crushed to death against a wall.

COACHES ON THE SET

Selznick recruited special advisors to work on *GWTW*. The following were among them:

Will Price: A Southern dialogue director, Will Price was charged with coaching the actors in Southern dialects. He worked with acting candidates to prepare them for their auditions, and during filming he coached the stars and the bit players.

Susan Myrick: She was a newspaperwoman with the *Macon Telegraph* and a friend of Margaret Mitchell's. Margaret recommended her to Kay Brown as an expert on Southern speech, manners, and customs. For example, Myrick pointed out to Selznick, but was overruled, that it would be inappropriate for Scarlett to wear a long-veiled street bonnet at the evening Bazaar. She was more successful in convincing him that it would be an insult for Rhett to use Belle Watling's carriage when calling on Scarlett. Myrick's work on the film earned her the title "The Emily Post of the South."

Wilbur Kurtz: This noted Civil War historian, artist, and architect was another recommendation from Margaret Mitchell. She had sought his expertise when checking the accuracy of two chapters of her novel. He worked closely with William Cameron Menzies and provided sketches of the city of Atlanta, common household items, and farm implements. He was the authority on endless historical details: the cropping of horses' tails, the use of oral thermometers, the construction of a well, the design of tombstones. His thirty-two-page description of a typical pre–Civil War Southern barbecue was invaluable during the planning and execution of the set for the Wilkes's barbecue.

LOVE AMONG THE STARS

- Although he was still married to Ria Langham Gable, Clark Gable's romance with Carole Lombard sizzled during the filming of *GWTW*. The pair married on March 29, 1939, when Gable had a break from shooting.
- The love affair between Vivien Leigh and Laurence Olivier was hotter than the flames that swept through the streets of Atlanta. Leigh was married to London barrister Leigh Holman, and Olivier was

married to actress Jill Esmond. Each marriage was blessed with a young child. The lovers were planning to marry as soon as their divorces could be arranged but until then were living together in a Beverly Hills house. Selznick, ever afraid of scandal, appealed to his brother Myron to get Olivier out of town. As a result, after the filming of *Wuthering Heights* ended in April 1939, Olivier departed for a role in the Broadway play *No Time for Comedy*.

- Like Olivier, Leslie Howard was a married man with a family. And Howard was also madly in love and living with a woman who was not his wife. Attractive, red-haired Violette Cunningham was Howard's production assistant, but most people guessed that theirs was a deeper relationship. Unlike Olivier, who was barred from the *GWTW* set, Cunningham accompanied Howard to the set every day.

- Olivia de Havilland was single and dating millionaire aviator Howard Hughes. When he proposed marriage during the filming of *GWTW*, Hughes made it clear he wanted to wait until he turned fifty—in seventeen years—to tie the knot. But Hughes wanted de Havilland to give up her career then and there and devote her life to him. She refused his offer, but they continued to see each other. Their relationship finally ended in June 1939 when, at a party, Hughes spontaneously proposed to de Havilland's sister, Joan Fontaine.

A WHO'S WHO OF SELZNICK'S PRODUCTION TEAM

Edward G. Boyle—Interior Decoration
Ridgeway Callow—Second Assistant Director
Wilfrid M. Cline—Technicolor Associate
Jack Cosgrove—Special Photographic Effects
Lillian K. Deighton—Research
Connie Earle—Production Continuity
Reeves Eason—Second Unit Director
Frank Floyd—Dance Director
Lou Forbes—Associate Music Director
James Forney—Drapes
John Frederics—Scarlett's Hats
Ernest Haller—Photography

Natalie Kalmus—Technicolor Company Supervision
Barbara Keon—Scenario Assistant
Hal C. Kern—Supervising Film Editor
Raymond Klune—Production Manager
Edward P. Lambert—Wardrobe
Frank Maher—Sound Recorder
William Cameron Menzies—Production Designer
James E. Newcom—Associate Film Editor
Ben Nye—Makeup Associate
Fred Parrish—Still Photographer
Joseph B. Platt—Interiors
Walter Plunkett—Costumes
Eddie Prinz—Dance Director
Ray Rennahan—Technicolor Associate
Hazel Rogers—Hairstyling Associate
Lydia Schiller—Production Continuity
Eddie Schmidt—Rhett's Wardrobe
Eric G. Stacey—Assistant Director
Max Steiner—Music
Monty Westmore—Makeup and Hairstyling
Lyle Wheeler—Art Direction
Florence Yoch—Tara's Landscaper
Lee Zavitz—Associate: Fire Effects

COSTUMES

The Man Who Had Designs on Scarlett

Scarlett's exquisite costumes were designed by Walter Plunkett, a contract designer borrowed from Metro-Goldwyn-Mayer.

He had started out at RKO in 1926 and first worked with Selznick in 1937's *Nothing Sacred*. In 1946, Plunkett began a twenty-year association with MGM, where his work earned him kudos as a designer of historical costumes.

After Selznick selected him to design the costumes for *GWTW*, Plunkett traveled to Atlanta to research the styles of clothing worn during the Civil War and Reconstruction periods. He also collected fabric swatches from dresses displayed in Southern museums. These swatches were sent to a Pennsylvania textile mill, which made all the cotton cloth used for the costumes.

When he returned to Selznick's studio, Plunkett was faced with designing gowns and petticoats for an unknown actress, since the role of Scarlett had not yet been cast. Additionally, Plunkett supervised the Civil War fashions industry that had sprung up on the studio lot. Seamstresses, weavers, hatmakers, and shoemakers created hundreds of dresses, uniforms, and accessories. A retired corset maker provided expertise on antebellum foundation garments, and ironworkers forged hoops for skirts.

Plunkett's matchless *GWTW* designs would be unrecognized by an Academy Award since the category of Best Costume Design did not exist at the time. But in 1951, he and two other designers shared the Academy Award for their work on *An American in Paris*. Plunkett's costumes earned him Oscar nominations for *The Magnificent Yankee*, *That Forsyte Woman*, *Kind Lady*, *The Actress*, *Young Bess*, *Raintree County*, *Some Came Running*, *Pocketful of Miracles*, and *How the West Was Won*. In 2000, Plunkett was inducted posthumously into the Costume Designers Guild Hall of Fame.

Gable's Wardrobe Didn't Suit Him

Gable not only had problems with *GWTW*'s script and director Cukor, he was also unhappy with the wardrobe made for him by Selznick's costume department. The shirt collars choked him, and the suits and cravats were ill fitting.

He complained to Selznick, who fired off a memo to the wardrobe department: "I think it is very disappointing indeed to have the elegant Rhett Butler wandering around with clothes that look as though he had bought them at the Hart, Schaffner, and Marx of that period and walked right out of the store with them." Selznick urged his wardrobe staff to observe Gable's personal wardrobe: "Look at how well he looks in his own clothes generally, and compare the fit and the tailoring and the general attractiveness with what I regard as the awful costuming job we are doing with him."

To keep his star happy, Selznick ordered a complete new wardrobe made for Rhett Butler by Gable's Beverly Hills tailor, Eddie Schmidt.

Other Design Notes

- Plunkett fashioned 5,500 wardrobe items for *GWTW* at a cost of $153,818. The women's costumes alone totaled $98,154. The cost for laundering the costumes during production was $10,000.

- Selznick insisted on complete authenticity in the costumes. For instance, he directed Plunkett to use expensive lace to make petticoats for the ladies. Ann Rutherford, playing Scarlett's sister Carreen, voiced her opinion that the cost was extravagant, especially since the audience would not know the lace was there. "But you'll know it's there," was Selznick's reply.

- Scarlett wears a calico dress in various stages of disintegration longer than any other costume in the film. The calico first appears in the shadow sequence in the Atlanta hospital and is seen for the last time when Scarlett tears down her mother's portieres to make the green velvet drapery dress. The calico was accessorized with bonnets, shawls, and aprons in various scenes.

  Actually, twenty-seven copies of the dress were made for Leigh and her stand-ins. Some were used in their original condition for the earlier scenes; other had to be aged for subsequent ones. In the aging process, the calicoes were subjected to rubbings with sandpaper and washings in a solution of water, bleach, and sand. A special dye was added to the wash water when a dingy look was needed. For the later scenes, the calico dress was constructed using the reverse side of the material.

- Probably the most famous costume in movie history is the drapery dress that Scarlett wears to Atlanta. She has to go "looking like a queen" to convince Rhett to give her the tax money for Tara, and the gown symbolizes her firm determination to survive.

- Director Fleming demanded a good deal of cleavage for Leigh's appearance in the décolleté burgundy velvet gown Scarlett wears to Ashley's birthday party. "For Christ's sake, let's get a good look at the girl's boobs," he told Walter Plunkett. Because Leigh's breasts spread sideways naturally, Plunkett had to tape them tightly together. The taping forced her breasts forward and upward, which resulted in the desired deep cleavage.

TURMOIL ON THE SET

Filming resumed on March 2 with Victor Fleming at the directorial helm. At his first meeting with assistant directors Eric Stacey and Ridgeway Callow, Fleming left no doubt about how he would run things. "They tell me that you're supposed to be the best team in the picture business," Fleming snarled. "But I'm going to put both of you in the hospital before this picture is over." Fleming browbeat and drove his cast and crew mercilessly. In just a few days, he was thoroughly disliked by almost everyone.

Gable was happy to have Fleming on board. At last he could feel comfortable in the hands of a director who understood him. Gable relaxed on the set, had lunch with the crew, and joined in their jokes.

Vivien Leigh, on the other hand, was bitter about Cukor's replacement, especially after Fleming declared, "I'm going to make this picture a melodrama." In an attempt to win her over, Fleming nicknamed Leigh "Fiddle-dee-dee," but this just increased her resentment toward him. Adding to her misery was the fact that Olivier had gone to New York. In great despair, Leigh wrote to her husband Leigh Holman, "It is really very miserable and going terribly slowly." A few days later she wrote, "I was a *fool* to have done it." Now the only goal for Leigh was to complete the picture as soon as possible and be reunited with Olivier. To that end she pushed herself by working sixteen-hour days, six days a week.

Leigh's exhaustion and frayed nerves were not helped by Selznick's rewritten script pages, which appeared on the set daily. Since shooting was done out of sequence, Leigh was frequently called upon to switch from a flirtatious Scarlett in one scene to a grieving Scarlett in the very next.

Leigh constantly complained about Selznick's unplayable dialogue and kept a copy of Margaret Mitchell's novel with her to bolster her arguments. Selznick frequently yelled at her to "please put that damn book away."

One dialogue battle that Leigh went head-to-head with Selznick on concerned Scarlett's line when Rhett visits after Frank Kennedy's funeral. A tipsy Scarlett tearfully admits to Rhett that she is glad her mother is dead and can't see her. "I always wanted to be like her—calm and kind—and I certainly have turned out disappointing." Selznick kept cutting the line, but Leigh fought for it. She believed it defined Scarlett's character. Leigh won, and the line stayed in.

Fleming also was no help to Leigh when it came to development of her character since he was more used to working with men in action films. When she would ask how a particular scene should be played, Fleming would reply, "Ham it up."

Leigh also resented Fleming's attempt to portray Scarlett as a horrible woman with no motivating factors. The veneer of professionalism that had characterized their working relationship quickly deteriorated. Quarrels erupted and frequently ended with Leigh in tears and Fleming enraged.

Things finally came to a head on April 29 when Leigh and Fleming were rehearsing the scene in which Scarlett and Melanie encounter Belle Watling outside the Atlanta military hospital. Leigh objected to Fleming's insistence that she convey Scarlett's snootiness and scorn toward Rhett's mistress. "I can't do it, I simply can't do it," Leigh wailed. "This woman is nothing but a terrible bitch." Fleming, apparently at the end of his rope, rolled up his script and with fury in his eyes screamed, "Miss Leigh, you can stick this script up your royal British ass." Then he threw the script at her feet and walked off the set.

While driving home, Fleming had thoughts of steering his car off a cliff and feared he was having a nervous breakdown. His doctor ordered complete bed rest until further notice.

SIX

Endless Trouble for GWTW

Fleming was off the set. Leigh was exhausted from overwork. Gable felt railroaded into playing Rhett Butler. Leslie Howard saw the promise of directorial duties on *Intermezzo* fading in front of his eyes. Olivia de Havilland felt depressed without Cukor's guidance on the set. And the main cause of everyone's misery was David O. Selznick.

Selznick had an overwhelming feeling that *GWTW* was destined to be more than an epic: it would be a masterpiece. His masterpiece. To ensure this, he pushed himself beyond his own perfectionism by trying to control everything.

He personally approved every facet of production from the sets to the hairstyles and sometimes pushed Fleming aside to take over the direction of the film. At night when he should have been sleeping, he was writing the script, viewing the rushes of the day's filming, or gambling for hours at the Clover Club. To stay awake, he took Benzedrine; to fall asleep, he resorted to sleeping pills. His drive took its toll not only on himself but also on his staff, cast, and crew, who viewed him as even more argumentative and tyrannical than ever.

The relentless pace resulted in endless delays. Production costs skyrocketed, and Selznick was forced to seek further financing from his backers. Then he began to doubt the results of his work. He complained that the costumes looked too new, that Tara's fields looked like "the back yard of a suburban home," and that the Southern accents of the actors were not convincing. The filming of *GWTW* was in serious trouble.

DIRECTOR #3

Fleming's breakdown had not been a surprise to David O. Selznick. On April 14, he had confided in a memo to one of his executives that Fleming "is so near the breaking point both physically and mentally from sheer exhaustion that it would be a miracle . . . if he is able to shoot for another seven or eight weeks." Selznick recommended "selecting an understudy . . . so that he could step in on brief notice." That understudy turned out to be MGM contract director Sam Wood, who had just finished filming *Goodbye, Mr. Chips*.

Wood had worked as an assistant director with Cecil B. DeMille, the master of the movie spectacular. While at Paramount Pictures, Wood directed films starring Wallace Reid, Gloria Swanson, and Rudolph Valentino. He transitioned to directing sound films at MGM in 1927, and his recent work for the studio included the Marx Brothers' movies *A Night at the Opera* and *A Day at the Races*.

Only hours after Fleming had stormed off, Wood was on the set. He picked up where Fleming had left off, directing the scene of Belle Watling approaching Melanie. Scenes on his schedule for the first week of May were Scarlett tearing down the green velvet draperies, Scarlett and Ashley embracing at the lumber mill, and Melanie and Belle conversing in the carriage.

While he was a steady, efficient director, Wood was not one with a great deal of imagination. Inventiveness and compelling visual storytelling were hallmarks of Fleming's directing, and Selznick was determined to convince Fleming to return to work.

AN APPEAL TO FLEMING

Selznick, Gable, and Leigh drove to Fleming's house during his recuperation bearing a cage of lovebirds as a peace offering. With harmony established, Selznick asked Fleming to return to the set, even offering him a share of the profits.

"What do you think I am, a chump?" Fleming replied. "This picture is going to be the biggest white elephant in history." Reluctantly, Fleming agreed to return to work.

FLEMING RETURNS!

To the surprise of cast and crew who were just getting used to Sam Wood's style, a recuperated Victor Fleming returned to the set in mid-May. Selznick decided to retain Wood to maintain the filming pace and to take some of the pressure off Fleming.

Wood directed sequences such as Rhett and Bonnie in London and the naming of Bonnie, while Fleming directed Rhett pouring Mammy a drink and Scarlett searching for Dr. Meade. The stars frequently found themselves working with Fleming in the morning and Wood in the afternoon. Others contributing to the directorial duties were William Cameron Menzies, who directed a second camera unit, and Eric Stacey and Reeves Eason, who filmed incidental shots.

GWTW'S JINXED SCENES

Scarlett and the Tarletons on Tara's Porch

On Thursday, January 26, 1939, George Cukor called "Action," and principal photography began. Vivien Leigh in her green sprig silk muslin dress warned the Tarleton boys that one more mention of war would send her right into the house. But when the rushes of that scene were shown, Selznick was aghast that the Tarletons' curly hairstyles had photographed bright orange. He ordered the scene reshot.

Four days later, the trio once more appeared on Tara's porch. This time the Tarletons' hairstyles were straightened and darkened. Selznick was pleased with the results of their coiffures, but their acting abilities left much to be desired.

When Victor Fleming took over directing duties on March 2, the porch scene was shot again. This third time the camera caught Scarlett's flirtations from a different angle, but this was no better than the previous two tries.

On June 14, Vivien Leigh reported for the scene of Gerald's walk with Scarlett in which he declares that "land's the only thing that lasts." While preparing for that scene, she learned that Selznick had decided she would wear the white, high-necked, ruffled dress from the Evening Prayers sequence. White, Selznick believed, would make Scarlett look more virginal. That meant, of course, that all the previously filmed porch scenes had to be scrapped. Not even close-ups could be saved.

The fourth version of the porch scene was filmed on June 26. Vivien Leigh, dressed in white, listened as the Tarletons told her that Ashley was engaged to marry his cousin Melanie. But Leigh's face reflected more than distress at this news. She looked pale, haggard, and worn from five months of grueling work.

On October 13, Victor Fleming directed the fifth version of the porch scene. Leigh, fresh from a vacation, was well rested and once again the beautiful image of sixteen-year-old Scarlett as she complained to the Tarletons that talk of war was spoiling all the fun at every party.

Belle Watling Waiting for Melanie outside the Hospital

Sam Wood directed the scene of Belle Watling waiting for Melanie outside the hospital. Ona Munson's costume was heavily padded to make the slightly built actress look well endowed. But the costume department outdid themselves, and Wood decided that the prominence of Belle's bosom would not be approved by the censors in the Hays Office. He reshot the scene the following week, but this was equally unsatisfactory.

Victor Fleming took a crack at directing this scene on June 2. During the shooting, Munson's bosom was rendered more discreetly, and the scene was successful.

The Arrival of Ellen

On January 28, George Cukor directed Ellen O'Hara's return to Tara. Barbara O'Neil as Ellen informed Robert Gleckler, who was playing Jonas Wilkerson, that she had just come from Emmy Slattery's bedside. Cukor and Selznick were both pleased with that scene as well as others Gleckler had done.

But tragedy struck during a break in production. Gleckler died of uremic poisoning on February 25. Victor Jory was hired to replace Gleckler, and all of the previously filmed scenes were reshot under Victor Fleming's direction.

SELZNICK'S FOLLY

Delays, friction, and dismissals during *GWTW*'s filming caused consternation among Selznick's backers. Production overhead was soaring, and they were beginning to think they would never see a return on their investment. Even those in the movie industry began having second thoughts about Selznick's "folly." Soon the shoptalk around Hollywood buzzed that *GWTW* was going to be a disaster.

Film insiders gossiped about Selznick, made him the butt of their jokes, and predicted his financial ruin. Cecil B. DeMille tweaked Selznick's nose by announcing a nationwide search to find a cigar-store Indian for a scene in his film *Union Pacific*. Even Sid Grauman, who owned the Chinese Movie Theater, added his two cents. At a large dinner party, he unveiled a life-size wax statue of a very old David O. Selznick leaning on a cane. A placard at the base of the statue proclaimed: "Selznick after the final shot of *Gone With the Wind*."

Outsiders hurled epithets such as "bust," "white elephant," and "turkey" in *GWTW*'s direction. But this abuse had the very opposite reaction. It only intensified Selznick's determination that *GWTW* would be the greatest picture ever made.

FUN ON THE SET

To break the tension of the long workdays, stagehands and actors occasionally played jokes on one another, such as:

- Stagehands placed percussive caps beneath the boards of sets under construction. When a workman nailing the boards struck them with a hammer, the caps exploded. The crew in on the gag then burst into screams of "The Yankees is coming!"

- As a prank on Clark Gable, Olivia de Havilland had some stagehands move a large cement block topped with an iron ring under her bed. She tied a rope through the ring, secured the rope around her waist, and hid the rope beneath a bed quilt. For the scene of Rhett's rescue, Gable had to lift a weakened Melanie from her bed and carry her down the stairs to the wagon that would whisk them out of Atlanta. Gable, staggering under the added weight, good-naturedly asked if the crew had nailed de Havilland to the floor.
- Gable turned the tables on Hattie McDaniel during the filming of "Rhett Pours Mammy a Drink." After the birth of his daughter Bonnie, Rhett celebrates by offering Mammy a glass of sherry. Cold tea is the traditional liquor substitute used on movie sets. Gable poured from the decanter while McDaniel delivered her line then downed her drink. An instant later, she froze. Tears came to her reddened eyes, and the cast and crew roared with laughter. In place of the cold tea, Gable had put real scotch in the decanter.
- The joke was on the crew during the filming of "Scarlett Killing the Yankee Deserter." After Scarlett shoots the deserter, she tells Melanie to take off her nightgown so she can wrap it around the soldier's head. Word had spread like wildfire throughout the studio that de Havilland wore nothing underneath the nightgown. On the day of the filming, a large crowd of studio workers gathered behind the lights to watch the scene. As de Havilland slipped off the nightgown, the hopes of the crowd were dashed. There she was without her nightgown, but she wore a camisole and had on a pair of pants that were rolled up to her knees.
- To while away the time between takes, Gable and Leigh retreated to a corner of the set to play games. He taught her the fundamentals of backgammon, and she taught him Battleship, a naval war game of skill and strategy. Time after time, Leigh soundly trounced Gable at both games.

THE FAMOUS CRANE SHOT

Scarlett searching for Dr. Meade at the train depot is one of *GWTW*'s most memorable scenes. Known as the crane shot, the scene begins with Scarlett's arrival at the depot. She walks gingerly among the "hundreds of wounded men . . . stretched out in endless rows." When she finds Dr. Meade, she tells him that Melanie is having her baby, and Meade is incredulous. "Are you crazy? I can't leave these men for a baby! They're dying—hundreds of them." To underscore his words, the camera slowly pulls back and up to show a field of "stinking, bleeding bodies broiling under the glaring sun" and comes to rest on the tattered Confederate flag flapping in the wind.

The planning of this scene started four months before it was filmed. The major problem was getting the camera up to the required height. The camera crew estimated that by the end of the scene, the camera needed to be ninety feet off the ground. But the tallest camera crane available in Hollywood reached only a height of twenty-five feet.

Selznick's production manager, Ray Klune, contacted a Southern California construction company that owned a crane with an extension range of 125 feet. He rented the truck-mounted crane for ten days. During tests, he found that vibrations from the truck's engine shook the camera at the beginning and end of the scene. To solve the problem, Klune ordered the building of a 150-foot-long concrete ramp. The truck slid smoothly down the ramp while the arm of the crane lifted the camera easily into the air to capture the breathtaking panorama.

In addition to the technical problems of the crane shot, Klune was faced with populating the scene, so he turned to Central Casting and ordered two thousand extras. "We prepared far enough in advance, we thought," Klune said. "But Central Casting told us the most they could promise us . . . was about eight hundred people. So we decided to use the eight hundred and intersperse dummies among them." The extras were instructed to rock the dummies to simulate animation.

Later, the Screen Extras Guild tried to extract union dues from Selznick for the dummies as well as for the live extras. Selznick balked and challenged the guild to come up with two thousand extras. They couldn't do it, and they dropped their claim.

WHAT DID YOU DO ON YOUR DAY OFF, CLARK?

On March 8, Ria Gable's divorce came through. Clark Gable was now free to marry Carole Lombard. On the day the news of the divorce broke, Hearst newspaper columnist Louella Parsons asked Lombard about the pair's wedding plans. Lombard told her, "When Clark gets a few days off, perhaps we'll sneak away and have the ceremony performed."

On March 25, Gable learned that because of changes in the shooting schedule, he would have six days off from his work on *GWTW*. Overjoyed, the pair quickly and quietly made elopement plans.

They did not want to alert the press, especially the reporters who had been haunting Lombard's Bel Air house, hoping to scoop the wedding of the year. But luck was with the lovers. Most of the Hollywood press corps was being sent on a junket to San Francisco to cover the world premiere of *The Story of Alexander Graham Bell*, giving Gable and Lombard a perfect opportunity to slip away and be married.

Hollywood's golden couple had a nickel-plated elopement. They packed their wedding clothes in a suitcase and dressed in ragtag shirts and scruffy dungarees. For further camouflage, Lombard wore no makeup and tied her blonde hair in pigtails. The pair, accompanied by MGM's publicity man Otto Winkler, took off at 4:30 in the morning on March 29 in Winkler's blue DeSoto coupe and headed for Kingman, Arizona, 357 miles away.

Along the way, the trio munched on sandwiches and drank Thermos bottles of coffee. Gable and Winkler shared the driving, and during stops for gas, Gable hid in the rumble seat to avoid recognition. One of the last stops before reaching Kingman was to buy wedding flowers: a corsage of pink roses and lilies of the valley for the bride and carnation boutonnieres for the groom and best man Winkler. Total cost: fifty cents.

At four o'clock that afternoon in Kingman's town hall, Gable and Lombard completed the necessary marriage forms, then hurried to the rectory of the First Methodist-Episcopal Church. There they changed into their wedding clothes and met the minister and his wife. The quiet ceremony then began.

Gable, wearing a blue serge suit, a white shirt, and a patterned tie, nervously placed a platinum band on his bride's finger. Dressed in a tailored, light gray flannel suit, Lombard shed tears of joy.

After the ceremony, the newlyweds, with Winkler driving, headed back to Los Angeles. Along the way they phoned the news of their marriage to MGM and wired Louella Parsons and her boss, William Randolph Hearst.

The new Mr. and Mrs. Clark Gable arrived at Lombard's house nearly twenty-four hours after they had left. They had only a few hours to rest up before facing reporters during a press conference scheduled for later that morning. And the most popular tongue-in-cheek question surely was, "What did you do on your day off, Clark?"

LESLIE HOWARD: FOILED AGAIN

"I hate the damn part," Leslie Howard complained in a letter to his daughter. "I'm not nearly beautiful or young enough for Ashley, and it makes me sick being fixed up to look attractive."

Howard's initial uninterest in playing Ashley eventually grew to resentment. He frequently arrived late on the set despite lectures from Selznick. He was unprepared and ruined takes when he flubbed his lines. His feelings about the film were summed up as "a terrible lot of nonsense—heaven help me if I ever read the book."

He never did. Right before filming the paddock scene, Selznick sent a pointed memo to Howard: "I send you herewith a copy of that book you ought to get around to reading some time, called *Gone with the Wind*. I think the book has a good future and might make a very good picture." Selznick reminded Howard of his promise to read that part of the book that contained the paddock scene to get a better understanding of Ashley. If at all, Howard probably read those ten pages and no more.

Howard's mind was on the plum that Selznick had used to snare him into the role of Ashley: *Intermezzo*. In that film, Howard's acting role was the married violinist who falls in love with his accompanist, played by the new Swedish star Ingrid Bergman. He was also supposed to be behind the camera as associate producer.

Unfortunately, delays in filming *GWTW* caused its shooting schedule to overlap with the production start of *Intermezzo*. Howard soon found himself racing from the set of one film to that of the other. Playing two roles simultaneously left Howard precious little time to undertake the production duties promised by Selznick. And tragically, *Intermezzo* would be Leslie Howard's last film.

CARE FOR ANOTHER RADISH, MISS LEIGH?

At the stirring conclusion of part one, an exhausted Scarlett trudges into Tara's backyard and views the Yankee devastation. Seized by hunger, she falls to her knees, and her hand plucks a radish from the garden. She eats the pungent vegetable, but her stomach quickly rejects it.

Slowly, Scarlett rises and, with her fist clenched toward heaven, vows: "As God is my witness . . . As God is my witness . . . they're not going to lick me. I'm going to live through this and when it's all over I'll never be hungry again. No, nor any of my folks! If I have to lie, steal, cheat or kill, as God is my witness, I'll never be hungry again."

Cut and print it. Sounds easy enough, but it wasn't.

Selznick envisioned the scene ending with Scarlett silhouetted against a clear dawn sky. To achieve this, the crew planned to film at the Lasky Mesa in the San Fernando Valley. There the crew laid down a track on which the camera could pull back to capture the long shot of Scarlett, that is, if Mother Nature cooperated. The scene needed to be filmed on a mistless morning in an area of the valley famous for mists rolling in from the Pacific.

Vivien Leigh, Victor Fleming, and the crew had to leave the studio at 2 a.m. to make their way to the mesa. Then, with all eyes on the horizon, everyone waited for the shot to appear. When fog settled in or the sky was overcast, the trip was wasted. Cast and crew trekked to the filming location five different times between late May and early June before the shot Selznick wanted finally materialized.

Leigh didn't mind getting up early in the morning. What she did object to was her response to the radish: retching. She argued with Selznick about eliminating this "unladylike" action from the scene; he wanted to keep it in. Finally, they compromised. The action would stay in, but Leigh could dub in the sound at the studio.

At the studio, Leigh's rendition of retching for the sound editor was unconvincing. Olivia de Havilland thought she could do a better job and proceeded to demonstrate. Hal Kern, the editor, was so impressed he substituted de Havilland's sound effects for Leigh's in the soundtrack.

THE DAY CLARK GABLE CRIED

According to the script, Scarlett has fallen down the staircase and has suffered a miscarriage. A distraught, unshaven Rhett, alone in his room, blames himself for what has happened. But Melanie soon brings news that Scarlett is better. Rhett, filled with relief and remorse, covers his face with his hands and weeps.

"I can't do this!" Clark Gable complained to Olivia de Havilland during rehearsals for the scene. "I won't do it! I'm going to leave acting. . . . I'll quit pictures, starting with this one!"

De Havilland tried her best to encourage him, but Gable was resolute. Leading men in the 1930s just did not cry on screen, and Gable would rather abandon his career than risk the humiliation of audiences laughing at him.

Gable appealed to Fleming. Have the scene rewritten, he begged. Or, better still, eliminate the scene entirely from the picture. Fleming privately assured Gable that crying would create more audience sympathy for Rhett, but Gable was not convinced.

On the day of the filming, an edgy and agitated Gable arrived on the set. He again threatened to walk off the picture, but Fleming proposed a compromise. The scene would be shot two ways: one with tears and the other simply showing a bereft Rhett's back. Whichever one Gable thought was the stronger scene would be the one used. Gable was only partly relieved.

Fleming cleared the set of visitors and extraneous crew members and filmed the two versions in only two takes: the eloquent back first and then the tears. After Gable saw the rushes, he was amazed at his performance. He agreed that the weeping scene was more effective and okayed its use in the film.

GWTW'S FILMING: AN
ENDURANCE TEST FOR ITS STARS

The official shooting of *GWTW* began on January 26, 1939, and ended five months and one day later on June 27, 1939. The stars endured grueling six-day workweeks filled with sixteen-hour days. Here's how long *GWTW*'s stars were at it: Vivien Leigh, 125 days; Clark Gable, 71 days; Olivia de Havilland, 59 days; and Leslie Howard, 32 days.

Filming Ends, Sort Of

Selznick was under pressure from Louis B. Mayer to give *GWTW* a happy ending. Mayer was in favor of a concluding scene showing Scarlett rushing after Rhett, calling his name, and a fade-out shot of them in a loving embrace. Selznick, though, wanted to leave audiences with only the same glimmer of hope that Margaret Mitchell had left with her readers: that Scarlett would, somehow, get him back.

Selznick rewrote the final scene several times. Finally, on the night before the scene was shot, he achieved the version he wanted. As it appears on the screen, Scarlett watches Rhett walk down the front path, put on his hat, and disappear into the mist.

"I can't let him go. I can't. There must be some way to bring him back," she cries. "Oh, I can't think about this now. I'll go crazy if I do. I'll think about it tomorrow." She closes the heavy front door and walks toward the staircase. "But I must think about it, I must think about it. What is there to do? What is there that matters?"

With heart-wrenching sobs, she sinks to the staircase in a flood of tears. Then she hears the voices of her father, Ashley, and Rhett reminding her that she still has Tara.

She slowly rises from the staircase as well as from her despair, and as the camera pulls in for the close-up, she says: "Tara . . . home. I'll go home, and I'll think of some way to get him back. After all, tomorrow is another day." Then, as the film ends, a pull-back shot catches a silhouetted Scarlett with bonnet in hand, looking at Tara.

With that last scene, the official filming schedule ended on June 27, 1939. Selznick sent a telegram to Jock Whitney stating, "Sound the siren. Scarlett O'Hara completed her performance at noon today." That evening, the cast and crew attended the traditional "wrap party," but additional work needed to be done. Selznick ordered the reshooting of certain scenes. The special effects unit was still hard at work, and other fill-in sequences had to be filmed. The filming of *GWTW* had ended, sort of.

Postproduction of *GWTW*

While scenes were being reshot and special effects orchestrated, Selznick busied himself with screening the existing footage and selecting takes of scenes. The selected scenes were assembled, and by early July, with the assistance of film editor Hal Kern, Selznick had a rough cut of the film. But the running time was almost six hours. Then came the process of eliminating this scene and cutting that entrance to shorten the film to a manageable length.

The work was intense. Selznick and Kern spent interminable hours in the cutting room (one session lasted almost forty-eight hours!) until late July, when Selznick had a five-hour version that he showed to cast and crew. At this showing, Selznick presented to each of his stars a leather-bound copy of the script. But this script was not the multicolored mess that had been used for shooting. Selznick had Lydia Schiller, the continuity coordinator, compile the "official" script from the edited version of the film.

Selznick went back to the cutting room and eliminated more time from the film. He showed a four-hour-and-twenty-five-minute version to Louis B. Mayer and other MGM executives. Although Mayer had to excuse himself several times for visits to the men's room, he was enthusiastic about the film.

The film needed narrative titles to bridge one part of the film with another, so Selznick turned to Ben Hecht for this job. Hecht succeeded in writing in the flowery style (e.g., "There was a land of cavaliers and cotton fields called the Old South") that Selznick favored.

For the film's title, Selznick wanted "the biggest main title that has ever been made." To achieve this, each word of the title was hand painted on a sheet of plate glass. The camera was mounted on a dolly, and it pulled the camera along as it photographed the four plate-glass sheets.

Selznick continued to add new footage and to trim existing footage of the film. So from day to day the running time of *GWTW* went up and down like the proverbial yo-yo. Finally, Selznick managed to reduce the film to 20,300 feet, which gave a running time of three hours and forty minutes—the length of the final version.

SNEAK PEEKS

By September, Selznick was ready to preview *GWTW*. Because the film was not completely finished, he didn't want to attract the attention of the press, so plans for the preview were super hush-hush.

The first preview took place in Riverside, California. Selznick, an entourage, twenty-four reels of film, and twenty-four reels of sound track arrived at the Riverside Theater on Saturday, September 9. The audience was told that instead of the expected feature, *Beau Geste*, they were about to see a very long movie. People were given the chance to leave if they wished, but they were warned that once the film started no one would be allowed to exit or to enter the theater.

Murmurs of anticipation rose among the audience. As the title swept across the screen, moviegoers were on their feet with shouts of joy. They jumped to their feet again four hours later when the film ended and gave Selznick a thunderous ovation. Selznick, his wife, and Jock Whitney wiped away tears. Later, Selznick called the evening a "sensational success. The reaction was everything that we hoped for and expected."

A second preview was held on October 18 at the Arlington Theatre in Santa Barbara. That audience was just as wild with excitement as the Riverside audience had been.

Selznick was thrilled when he read the review cards filled out by the audiences. "The greatest picture ever made," said one. "The greatest picture since *Birth of a Nation*," said another. "The screen's greatest achievement of all times," a third noted. But audiences also made critical comments, especially about missing Rhett Butler's "damn" exit line. Selznick paid attention to the audience's negative comments and took the film back into the cutting room for more editing.

MUSIC BY MAX STEINER

In October 1939, Selznick selected Warner Bros. composer Max Steiner to compose the score for *GWTW*. Vienna-born Steiner, who was the godson of composer Richard Strauss, was well known for his work on *Jezebel*, *A Star Is Born*, *Garden of Allah*, and *King Kong*. Selznick told Steiner he wanted "instead of two or three hours of original music, little original music and a score based on the great music of the world, and of the south in particular."

Steiner ignored Selznick's request. The score he composed contained mostly original music, but he did use some Southern favorites such as "Dixie" and "The Bonnie Blue Flag," as well as military and patriotic tunes. Steiner wrote separate themes for Tara and for the leading characters. He also included love themes for the relationships between Melanie and Ashley, Scarlett and Ashley, and Scarlett and Rhett.

Since Selznick feared that Steiner would not be able to meet the short deadline he had been given, Selznick hired composer and conductor Franz Waxman to write an "insurance score." Selznick wasn't pleased with Waxman's work. The producer discreetly talked to Herbert Stothart, MGM's musical director and composer, about taking over the score. Unfortunately, Stothart blabbed that he was taking over for Steiner. This got back to Steiner, and all hell broke loose.

But as a result, Steiner increased his output, and this in turn pleased Selznick, who advised the composer to "just go mad with schmaltz in the last three reels." Steiner ignored this piece of advice, too, and as a result the lushly orchestrated, richly textured score that Steiner produced for *GWTW* was a movie masterpiece.

Musical Notes

- "Mammy's Theme" is the first heard in the film. The theme plays when the credit appears for MGM and Technicolor.
- The most famous theme that Steiner composed was "Tara's Theme." The music was later adapted for the popular song "My Own True Love."
- Steiner did not write a separate theme for Ashley. Instead, the "elegant Mr. Wilkes" was surrounded musically by the two women who loved him in the "Melanie and Ashley Theme" and the "Scarlett and Ashley Theme."
- Steiner borrowed the melody for "Melanie's Theme" from his score of the 1934 RKO film *The Fountain.*
- Steiner used touches of Stephen Foster tunes in *GWTW*'s score. In one humorous instance, Steiner used the Foster melody "Massa's in de Cold, Cold Ground" for the scene in which Scarlett, as the newly widowed Mrs. Hamilton, tries on a stylish purple bonnet.
- Selznick insisted that segments of MGM stock music remain in the film after the previews. These were used in the scenes "Approach of the Yankee Deserter," "Shantytown," and "Rhett Carries Scarlett Upstairs."
- Steiner, under intense pressure from Selznick to complete the score, turned to his colleagues for some help. Franz Waxman, Adolph Deutsch, and Hugo Friedhofer contributed, and Heinz Roemheld composed the music that accompanied the escape from Atlanta and the burning of the depot.
- Selznick suggested to record companies the idea of recording an album of *GWTW*'s music from Steiner's soundtracks. Unbelievably,

the record companies turned down the idea. Although symphonic re-recordings were produced later, they lacked the beauty of the Steiner originals.

THAT DAMN WORD "DAMN"

In the novel, a tearful Scarlett wails, "If you go, where shall I go, what shall I do?" And Rhett exits with the memorable words: "My dear, I don't give a damn." At the outset, Selznick knew he would have problems with that damn word "damn."

The Motion Picture Production Code developed in 1930 by the Motion Picture Producers and Distributors Association of America (known as the "Association") barred from the screen, among other things, the use of profanity. Specifically, it forbade the use of the word "damn."

Sidney Howard, aware of the industry's censorship code, changed the line to "My dear, I don't care." But Selznick knew how much the American public would expect the line to be left intact, so he ordered the scene shot with each version of the line. At the last moment, Selznick added the word "frankly" to the beginning of Rhett's line because he felt the word added an offhanded quality to the delivery. Then Selznick prepared to do battle with the Association and its Production Code.

The code was administered by Joseph Breen, who reviewed shooting scripts and completed films for violations. Breen had the power to grant or to deny the certificate of approval that a film needed in order to be shown in theaters. Under the terms of Selznick's contract with MGM, a studio that supported the code, *GWTW* required a Production Code seal.

After Breen had reviewed *GWTW*'s script, he sent a message to Selznick in June 1939 directing him to eliminate the word "damn" from the dialogue. He concluded the letter with his standard warning: "Our final judgments will be based on the finished picture."

Since Breen refused to permit Gable's stronger version, the September preview audience heard the "I don't care" line. They expressed their disappointment on the preview cards they handed back to Selznick.

Breen, too, saw the "I don't care" version of the film later that month, after which, on September 28, 1939, he granted Certificate No. 5729 to

GWTW. With the seal of approval in hand, Selznick set into motion the next phase of his plan to challenge the Association on his use of "damn."

He shared his strategy in an October 12, 1939, letter to Jock Whitney: "If I can't persuade the Breen office here to see reason on it . . . then I think the best way of getting it through would be for you to . . . insist upon a special Board of Directors meeting being called immediately for the purpose of ruling on it."

When Selznick approached him about the issue, Breen stated that the code was explicit in forbidding "damn." And that was that. Or so it seemed.

Selznick subsequently learned through his story editor Val Lewton, who was the liaison with the Production Code office, that Breen's official position was not the same as his personal position on Selznick's "damn" matter. According to Lewton, Breen encouraged Selznick to go over his head and appeal to Will H. Hays, the Association's president. Doing so, Breen had suggested, might establish a precedent that would be helpful not only to Selznick but also to Breen. But Breen was clear: he could not openly support Selznick's efforts.

In an October 20, 1939, letter to Hays, Selznick laid out his arguments. He stated that the *Oxford English Dictionary* described "damn" not as an oath or curse but as a vulgarism. Selznick also pointed to the public's general acceptance of the word by citing magazines such as *Woman's Home Companion*, *Saturday Evening Post*, and *Collier's* that used the word frequently. Last, he noted the disappointment of preview audiences. "On our very fadeout it gives an impression of unfaithfulness after three hours and forty-five minutes of extreme fidelity to Miss Mitchell's work." (The final cut was five minutes shorter.)

Unmoved by Selznick's arguments, the Hays office ordered Breen to send an overnight letter to the producer outlining the strongest reasons for refusing his request. Receiving that letter left only one avenue open to Selznick: appealing to the Association's Board of Directors and lining up support from the directors who were studio heads and independent producers.

Had the October 27, 1939, board meeting been a Western, the script would have characterized the atmosphere as "rip roaring." Hays opposed Selznick's use of "damn." Aligned with him were the heads of Universal, Paramount, and Twentieth Century Fox. Supporting Selznick was the formidable Nicholas Schenck, president of MGM, the soon-to-be distributor of *GWTW*, whose investment was on the line depending upon the meeting's outcome.

When the dust settled finally, directors representing the major studios and independent producers voted to reverse Breen's ruling and allow Selznick to use "damn." Waiving the profanity rule, Hays warned, might violate federal law and could draw unwanted attention from the Justice Department. So the board took an additional action.

On November 1, 1939, the Association's Board of Directors amended the Production Code. The words "hell" and "damn" continued to be banned except if they "shall be essential and required for portrayal, in proper historical context, of any scene or dialogue based upon historical fact or folklore . . . or a quotation from a literary work, provided that no such use shall be permitted which is intrinsically objectionable or offends good taste."

With the blessing of the Motion Picture Producers and Distributors Association of America, Selznick was permitted to use the word "damn" in a line that has become as famous as Scarlett's "I'll think about that tomorrow." Selznick had cracked the code, and for him the moment was priceless.

FACTS AND FIGURES

Production

- 250,000 staff hours spent in preproduction
- 750,000 staff hours spent during production

Footage

- 449,512 feet of film shot
- 160,000 feet of film printed
- 20,300 feet of film in the final version
- 220 minutes of running time (234–238 minutes with overture, intermission, entr'acte, and exit music)

Actors

- 59 leading and supporting cast members
- 2,400 extras

Animals

- 1,100 horses
- 375 pigs, mules, oxen, cows, dogs, and other animals

Vehicles

- 450 vehicles, including wagons, ambulances, and gun caissons

Sets

- 3,000 sketches drawn of all major scenes
- 200 sets designed
- 90 sets built, using 1,000,000 feet of lumber

Costs

- $3,700,000 actual production cost
- $4,250,000 total cost, including overheads for prints, publicity, advertising, and the like

SEVEN

Test Your GWTW *Knowledge*

THE GREATEST MOVIE OF ALL TIME

1. With whom was Scarlett chatting on the front porch of Tara as the film opens?
2. What secret did they share with Scarlett?
3. During evening prayers, what did Scarlett decide to do?
4. What did Mammy and Scarlett argue about on the morning of the barbecue?
5. At the barbecue, who told Scarlett about Rhett Butler's reputation?
6. From what school had Rhett been expelled?
7. What did a spurned Scarlett break in the Twelve Oaks library? Whom did this rouse from the sofa?
8. Who was Scarlett's first husband?
9. What caused his death?
10. At the Atlanta Bazaar, how much did Rhett bid for the honor of leading the opening reel with Scarlett?
11. Who fainted after Scarlett accepted Rhett's bid to dance?
12. What present did Rhett bring to Scarlett from Paris?
13. How long was Ashley's Christmas leave?
14. What was Ashley's rank?

15. What promise did Ashley extract from Scarlett before he returned to the war?
16. What did Belle Watling give to Melanie outside the Atlanta hospital?
17. Where was Belle's establishment located?
18. For whom did Scarlett search among the wounded soldiers? Why did she need him?
19. Who lied about having childbirthing skills?
20. What did Melanie want to bring on the escape to Tara?
21. Why did Rhett abandon Scarlett on the road to Tara?
22. By the time Scarlett arrived at Tara, who had died from typhoid?
23. What did Scarlett vow in Tara's vegetable garden?
24. Whom did Scarlett shoot on Tara's staircase?
25. How much money did Scarlett need for the taxes on Tara?
26. Who threatened to buy Tara when the plantation was sold at the sheriff's sale?
27. Whom had he married?
28. Where did Scarlett obtain the material for her Atlanta gown?
29. From whom did Scarlett plan to get the needed tax money?
30. What gave away Scarlett's destitution in the Atlanta jail?
31. To save Tara, whom did Scarlett marry? Whom was he supposed to marry?
32. Where did this sign appear: "The war is over. Don't ask for credit."?
33. In what other business enterprise did Scarlett engage?
34. Where was Scarlett attacked? Who rescued her?
35. Who were the members of the evening sewing circle?
36. What book did Melanie read to the sewing circle?
37. Who was wounded during the raid to avenge Scarlett's attack?
38. What did Rhett do when he called on Scarlett after Frank Kennedy's funeral?
39. What gift did Rhett bring back from New Orleans for Mammy?
40. What was Scarlett's waist measurement after giving birth to Bonnie?
41. Who found Scarlett in Ashley's arms?
42. What social function did Rhett force Scarlett to attend alone that evening?
43. The following day, where did Rhett announce he was taking Bonnie?

Author Margaret Mitchell. Photofest

David O. Selznick on the set. Academy of Motion Picture Arts and Sciences.

Scarlett runs to meet her father. Turner Entertainment/New Line Cinema

Gerald O'Hara to Scarlett: "It will come to you, this love of the land." Turner Entertainment/New Line Cinema

Scarlett and Mammy argue about the barbecue dress. Turner Entertainment/New Line Cinema

The O'Hara sisters—Carreen, Scarlett, and Suellen—at Twelve Oaks. Turner Entertainment/New Line Cinema

Melanie declares her love to Ashley at Twelve Oaks. Turner Entertainment/New Line Cinema

Scarlett surrounded by admirers at the barbecue. Turner Entertainment/New Line Cinema

Ashley and Melanie congratulate Mrs. Charles Hamilton. Turner Entertainment/ New Line Cinema

Rhett and Scarlett lead the opening reel at the Atlanta Bazaar. Turner Entertainment/New Line Cinema

Rhett and Scarlett waltz at the Atlanta Bazaar. Turner Entertainment/New Line Cinema

Scarlett and Prissy face a crisis. Turner Entertainment/New Line Cinema

Rhett's farewell to Scarlett on the McDonough Road. Turner Entertainment/New Line Cinema

Rhett comforts the "grieving" Widow Kennedy. Turner Entertainment/New Line Cinema

44. Why was their trip cut short?
45. What caused Scarlett's miscarriage?
46. Why did Rhett warn Bonnie not to jump?
47. Who convinced Rhett to schedule Bonnie's funeral?
48. What was Ashley holding when Scarlett left the dying Melanie's room?
49. Where did Rhett say he was going when he left Scarlett?
50. What did Scarlett decide to do after Rhett walked out?

THE CURIOUS NUMBER OF SCENES TAKING PLACE ON STAIRCASES

On the Staircase at Tara

- From the window on the landing, Mammy spots Ellen O'Hara returning home and grumbles about her ministering to the white-trash Slattery family.
- Scarlett learns from Mammy about Tara's devastation at the hands of the Yankee invaders.
- Scarlett orders the ailing Melanie back to bed when she offers to help with the plantation work.
- Scarlett confronts and shoots the Yankee deserter.

On the Staircase at Twelve Oaks

- Ashley greets Scarlett as she arrives for the barbecue.
- Scarlett flirts with Frank Kennedy and flatters him about his "new set of whiskers."
- Scarlett encounters the Tarleton twins and convinces them to "eat barbecue" with her.
- Scarlett sees Rhett Butler for the first time.
- Scarlett eavesdrops on the men talking about the war over brandy and cigars.
- Scarlett overhears Melanie defending Scarlett's flirting with all the men at the barbecue.
- Charles Hamilton proposes marriage to Scarlett.

- Scarlett views the destruction of Twelve Oaks on her way home to Tara with Melanie, the baby, and Prissy.

On the Staircase at Aunt Pittypat's House

- Melanie explains how she obtained the material for Ashley's Christmas tunic and asks him to make sure it doesn't get torn.
- Scarlett asks to accompany Ashley to the train station at the end of his Christmas leave.
- When she discovers Melanie in labor, Scarlett sends Prissy to fetch Dr. Meade.
- Scarlett threatens to sell Prissy South for not finding Dr. Meade.
- Scarlett slaps Prissy when she reveals her lack of childbirthing skills.
- Scarlett holds a lantern for Rhett as he carries Melanie out to the carriage to escape Atlanta.
- Rhett greets Scarlett after Frank Kennedy's funeral and notices she has been drinking.

On Staircases Here and There

- Lists of Gettysburg casualties are handed to the crowd from the staircase at the newspaper office.
- Belle Watling approaches Melanie and Scarlett with a contribution on the staircase outside the Atlanta church-turned-hospital.
- Melanie chats with a ragged Confederate soldier on the back steps of Tara and learns that Ashley was taken prisoner.

On the Staircase at Scarlett's Atlanta House

- Scarlett hears a drunken Rhett invite her to come into the dining room.
- Rhett sweeps Scarlett into his arms for a night of passion.
- Scarlett admits to Rhett that she is pregnant and, in attempting to strike him, misses and tumbles down the stairs.
- Mammy asks Melanie to speak to Rhett about funeral services for Bonnie.
- Rhett bids farewell to Scarlett as he leaves for Charleston.
- A tearful Scarlett decides that "tomorrow is another day."

THE PLAYERS WHO'S WHO

Match the character in the first column with the actor or actress in the second column who immortalized the role.

1. Mammy	a.	Vivien Leigh
2. Aunt Pittypat Hamilton	b.	Alicia Rhett
3. Rhett Butler	c.	Eddie Anderson
4. Jonas Wilkerson	d.	Rand Brooks
5. Prissy	e.	Laura Hope Crews
6. Scarlett O'Hara	f.	Olivia de Havilland
7. Stuart Tarleton	g.	Harry Davenport
8. Ellen O'Hara	h.	Hattie McDaniel
9. Ashley Wilkes	i.	Victor Jory
10. Uncle Peter	j.	Carroll Nye
11. Belle Watling	k.	Ann Rutherford
12. Melanie Hamilton	l.	Everett Brown
13. Gerald O'Hara	m.	George Reeves
14. Big Sam	n.	Butterfly McQueen
15. India Wilkes	o.	Ona Munson
16. Frank Kennedy	p.	Clark Gable
17. Dr. Meade	q.	Barbara O'Neil
18. Mrs. Merriwether	r.	Leslie Howard
19. Bonnie Butler	s.	Thomas Mitchell
20. Carreen O'Hara	t.	Jane Darwell
21. Charles Hamilton	u.	Ward Bond
22. Tom, the Yankee captain	v.	Cammie King

WHO SAID IT? (#1)

From the following list of characters, decide who spoke the line of movie dialogue.

Scarlett O'Hara   Rhett Butler
Melanie Hamilton Wilkes   Ashley Wilkes

1. "Has the war started?"
2. "Fine thing when a horse can get shoes and humans can't."
3. "She's the only dream I ever had that didn't die in the face of reality."
4. "Here, take my handkerchief. Never at any crisis of your life have I known you to have a handkerchief."
5. "Do you think it would be dishonest if we went through his haversack?"
6. "Panic's a pretty sight, isn't it?"
7. "You must be brave. You must. How else can I bear going?"
8. "I've always thought a good lashing with a buggy whip would benefit you immensely."
9. "You will take good care of it, won't you? You won't let it get— torn. Promise me!"
10. "It's cold, and I left my muff at home. Would you mind if I put my hand in your pocket?"
11. "Oh, can't we go away and forget we ever said these things?"
12. "You go into the arena alone. The lions are hungry for you."
13. "Isn't it enough that you've gathered every other man's heart today? You've always had mine. You cut your teeth on it."
14. "You've lived in dirt so long you can't understand anything else, and you're jealous of something you can't understand."
15. "This war stopped being a joke when a girl like you doesn't know how to wear the latest fashion."
16. "Don't cry. She mustn't see you've been crying."
17. "Nobody cares about me. You all act as though it were nothing at all."
18. "Most of the miseries of the world were caused by wars. And when the wars were over no one ever knew what they were about."
19. "Boys aren't any use to anybody. Don't you think I'm proof of that?"
20. "Take a good look, my dear. It's a historic moment. You can tell your grandchildren how you watched the Old South disappear one night."
21. "I'm too young to be a widow."
22. "You have so much life. I've always admired you so. I wish I could be more like you."
23. "With enough courage you can do without a reputation."

24. "You seem to belong here. As if it had all been imagined for you."
25. "Frankly, my dear, I don't give a damn."
26. "Don't worry about me. I can shoot straight, if I don't have to shoot too far."
27. "It's a pity we couldn't have fought the war out in a poker game. You'd have done better than General Grant with far less effort."
28. "Don't look back. It drags at your heart till you can't do anything but look back."
29. "The happiest days are when babies come."
30. "How could I help loving you? You, who have all the passion for life that I lack!"
31. "I'll go home, and I'll think of some way to get him back."
32. "I shall be proud to speak to you. Proud to be under obligation to you."
33. "Selfish to the end, aren't you? Thinking only of your own precious hide with never a thought for the noble Cause."
34. "War, war, war. This war talk's spoiling all the fun at every party this spring. I get so bored I could scream."
35. "Any of you beauties know where I can steal a horse for a good cause?"
36. "I'll hate you till I die! I can't think of anything bad enough to call you."
37. "Tonight I wouldn't mind dancing with Abe Lincoln himself."
38. "I seem to be spoiling everybody's brandy and cigars and dreams of victory."
39. "Oh, I could never hate you! And—and I know you must care about me. Oh, you *do* care, don't you?"
40. "I'll think about that tomorrow."
41. "All we've got is cotton, and slaves, and arrogance."
42. "My life is over—Nothing will ever happen to me anymore."

THE MASTER'S *GWTW* GAME:
MINOR CHARACTERS MATCH

This game is designed to separate the true Windie from the mere fan. Match the actor or actress in the first column with the minor role undertaken in *GWTW* in the second column.

1. Mary Anderson	a. Bonnie's London nurse
2. Irving Bacon	b. Shantytown attacker
3. Yakima Canutt	c. Mrs. Meade
4. Cliff Edwards	d. Phil Meade
5. Robert Elliott	e. Maybelle Merriwether
6. Olin Howland	f. Reminiscent soldier in Atlanta hospital
7. Paul Hurst	g. The Yankee deserter
8. Lillian Kemble-Cooper	h. The Yankee major
9. J. M. Kerrigan	i. The Yankee corporal
10. Mickey Kuhn	j. Johnnie Gallegher
11. Jackie Moran	k. A Yankee businessman
12. Leona Roberts	l. Beau Wilkes

WHO SAID IT? (#2)

From the following list of characters, decide who spoke the line of movie dialogue.

Gerald O'Hara	India Wilkes
Ellen O'Hara	Cathleen Calvert
Suellen O'Hara	Charles Hamilton
Carreen O'Hara	Frank Kennedy

1. "Why, land is the only thing in the world worth working for, worth fighting for, worth dying for—because it's the only thing that lasts."
2. "How's Ashley today, Scarlett? He didn't seem to be paying much attention to you."
3. "Are you hinting, Mr. Butler, that the Yankees can lick us?"
4. "But what difference does it make who you marry, so long as he's a Southerner and thinks like you?"
5. "She's had three husbands, and I'll be an old maid."
6. "It's only natural to want to look young and be young when you are young."
7. "I've been waiting here two whole days and I've got to tell her—that I was wrong about something."

8. "My dear, don't you know? That's Rhett Butler. He's from Charleston. He has the most terrible reputation."
9. "She can get mad quicker than any woman I ever saw."
10. "I do hate you. You've done all you could to lower the prestige of decent people."
11. "Bonds—they're all we've saved—all we have left—bonds."
12. "What happened this afternoon is just what you deserved! And if there was any justice, you'd have gotten worse!"
13. "I guess things like hands and ladies don't matter so much any more."
14. "If true love carries any weight with you, you can be sure your sister will be rich in that."
15. "Don't cry, darling. The war will be over in a few weeks, and I'll be coming back to you."
16. "You act on me just like a tonic."
17. "Darling, you mustn't think unkindly of her. She's made it possible for us to keep Tara—always!"

I'LL THINK ABOUT THAT TOMORROW

GWTW is peppered with Scarlett's favorite expressions such as "Fiddle-dee-dee" and "Great balls of fire." But she uttered her most famous screen oath only three times.

1. At the opening, when the Tarletons ask if she is planning to eat barbecue with them the next day: "Oh, I haven't really thought about *that* yet. I'll think about that tomorrow."
2. After shooting the Yankee deserter: "Well, I guess I've done murder. Oh, I won't think about that now. I'll think about that tomorrow."
3. After Rhett walks out: "I can't let him go! I can't! There must be some way to bring him back. Oh, I can't think about that now. I'll go crazy if I do. I'll think about that tomorrow."

And, of course, the final lines of the movie contain an unforgettable variation of Scarlett's purposeful procrastination theme. After she hears the disembodied voices of her father, Ashley, and Rhett on the staircase, she says: "Tara! Home! . . . I'll go home—and I'll think of some way to get him back. After all, tomorrow is another day!"

WHO SAID IT? (#3)

From the following list of characters, decide who spoke the line of movie dialogue.

Aunt Pittypat Hamilton   Mrs. Merriwether
Uncle Peter   Bonnie Butler
Dr. Meade   Beau Wilkes
Mrs. Meade

1. "Go on, you trash. Don't you be pesterin' these ladies."
2. "Why do I have to go back to bed? It's morning."
3. "Good Heavens, woman, this is war—not a garden party."
4. "I will so jump! I can jump better than ever 'cause I've grown. And I've moved the bar higher."
5. "Don't go gettin' so uppity even if you is the las' chicken in Atlanta."
6. "For a widow to appear in public at a social gathering! Every time I think of it I feel faint!"
7. "London Bridge! Will it be falling down?"
8. "Were you really there? What did it look like? Does she have cut-glass chandeliers, plush curtains, and dozens of mirrors?"
9. "Where is my mother going away to? And why can't I go along, please?"
10. "There must be a great deal of good in a man who would love a child so much."
11. "I may be a coward but—but—oh, dear, Yankees in Georgia! How did they ever get in?"

GWTW GOOFS

Here and there in *GWTW* are minor mistakes that resulted either from errors in continuity or from slips in the editing process. Did you catch or miss any of these *GWTW* goofs?

1. "I wore this old dress just because I thought you liked it."

   Scarlett delivers this line to the Tarleton twins on the Twelve Oaks staircase on the morning of the barbecue. Audiences might have wondered when the Tarletons had previously seen her in the green sprig silk muslin dress.

   When the film's original opening scene was shot in January 1939, Scarlett was flirting with the Tarletons in this very same gown. However, by June, Selznick decided to reshoot this sequence and have Scarlett wear the white gown she wore during Evening Prayers. So since the dress she wore to the barbecue was not the one they had seen her wearing the afternoon before, her line to the Tarletons lost all its meaning.

2. Shadows out of sync.

   The shadow scene in which Scarlett and Melanie care for the wounded in the Atlanta hospital was filmed with two doubles. Since Leigh and de Havilland were standing at the wrong angle to cast the shadows, two stand-ins were positioned in front of a high-intensity light. The shadows of the doubles were reflected on the wall in back of the actresses, and the result was a stunning visual effect. Yet upon closer look, the gestures of the stand-ins are not totally synchronized with the movements of the stars.

3. Gerald's reprimand.

   In Tara's cotton patch scene, Scarlett speaks sharply to and slaps her sister Suellen. Immediately afterward, Gerald reprimands Scarlett for her ill treatment of the servants. Is this a non sequitur? No, it's another glitch in continuity. Scenes showing an acid-tongued Scarlett speaking to Mammy, Pork, and Prissy were edited out, yet Gerald's admonition remained.

4. Scarlett's breakfast tray.

   After her night of passion with Rhett, Scarlett awakens and delights in the memory of the ravishment. Mammy enters, comes to the bedside, and takes away a tray containing a silver service. An earlier part of this scene showed Bonnie bringing the breakfast tray to her mother, but this was deleted during editing. Without this segment, audiences were left to wonder whether part of Rhett's romantic overtures included a midnight supper.

GWTW GLITCHES

Continuity errors or editing mistakes are easy to miss when you're caught up in *GWTW*'s riveting action. Take a closer look at scenes throughout the film. How many of these *GWTW* glitches did you originally overlook in these four categories?

Fashions and Accessories

- Dressing for the barbecue, Scarlett forgets to tie a small bustle around her waist and clasp a coral necklace around her neck. Yet she is wearing both when Mammy helps her undress for her nap at Twelve Oaks.
- Rhett is bareheaded when he lifts Melanie from her bed during the escape from Atlanta. Yet, when he carries her out of the room, he is wearing a hat.
- Scarlett, too, is hatless as she leaves Aunt Pittypat's house. Yet a black mourning bonnet appears as she and Rhett ride through the depot area, encounter the looters, and follow the retreating Confederate troops. When Rhett stops the carriage on McDonough Road at the turn to Tara, the bonnet has vanished.
- During the exodus to Tara, Rhett borrows Scarlett's shawl to cover the head of the horse frightened by the flames. Yet, after shaking off the garment, the equine dashes bravely into the fiery boxcar area.
- When saying goodbye to Scarlett on McDonough Road at the turn to Tara, Rhett puts his coat on the fence and tosses his hat on the ground. Yet, after Scarlett slaps him, he grabs both his hat and his coat from the fence and disappears into the night.
- When Scarlett encounters and shoots the Yankee intruder, her hair is secured in a white snood that is pinned in the middle of the back of her head. Yet, when she and Melanie discuss what to do with the body, Scarlett's snood is pinned at the top of her head.
- In Tara's paddock, when Scarlett begs Ashley to run away with her to Mexico, her shawl covers one shoulder. Yet, after he speaks of honor and she turns away, her shawl suddenly covers both shoulders.
- Fighting off the Shantytown attackers causes Scarlett to lose her hat. Yet, when Big Sam runs after her, she is wearing the hat until he catches up to her and then the hat is gone once again.

- When Rhett visits after Frank's funeral, Scarlett tearfully admits she's afraid of going to hell and then weeps into her handkerchief. Yet, when Rhett asks what she has done to deserve such a fate, she has no handkerchief. She wipes her nose with her hands until Rhett gives his handkerchief to her.

Furnishings and Fixtures

- After Scarlett flees the Atlanta hospital, the camera captures the panic in the street. The camera pans past a streetlamp that contains a light-bulb, as Scarlett recognizes Big Sam in the Confederate work gang.
- When Rhett and Scarlett argue about going to Tara, the foyer and staircase of Aunt Pittypat's house are bright with light. Yet when they come downstairs with Melanie and Prissy, the staircase and foyer are dark, requiring Scarlett to carry a lamp.
- Rhett and Dr. Meade return from the Shantytown raid with the wounded Ashley. To light the way for Rhett as he carries Ashley into the bedroom, Melanie grabs a lamp that has an electrical cord at its base.
- Following Frank's funeral, Scarlett is alone in her bedroom. The first time she looks at Frank's photograph, the frame rests on the dresser's bare surface. When she turns the photograph face down, the frame rests on the dresser's lace scarf. Then, when she brushes her hair before leaving the room, the framed photograph has vanished.
- On the Butler terrace, Scarlett sits and sips from a teacup while talk-ing with Rhett and watching Bonnie on her pony. Scarlett asks Rhett to stop Bonnie from jumping and places the teacup on the table. Yet, in the next shot, the teacup is missing. Then, when Scarlett stands, the teacup is on the table again.
- After Melanie dies, Scarlett hurries from the Wilkeses' house looking for Rhett. She touches the porch post and it wobbles.

Scamps and Scoundrels

- On McDonough Road at the turn to Tara, Rhett stops the wagon and pulls the brake. Yet, after the scamp abandons her, Scarlett doesn't release the brake before she grabs the reins and leads the horse onto the road.

- After Scarlett kills the Yankee scoundrel, Melanie covers for her by going to the window on the landing. The opaque window bears the silhouette of a tall tree. Yet, when Melanie opens the window to reassure the O'Haras, no tree in the yard is tall enough or close enough to have cast the shadow.
- Gerald mounts his horse and chases the scoundrel Wilkerson from Tara. Hearing the commotion, Suellen and Carreen rush onto the porch, leaving the front door open. Yet, when Scarlett runs down the lawn yelling for her father to come back, her sisters have disappeared from the porch and the door is closed.
- Following Gerald's death, Mammy comforts Scarlett in Tara's parlor. Preoccupied with figuring out ways to get the $300 needed to pay the taxes on Tara, Scarlett thinks of a scamp who can help her: Rhett. Mammy asks: "Who dat? A Yankee?" yet her lips don't move.
- The two Shantytown scoundrels see Scarlett's buggy approaching from their positions below the bridge near a babbling brook. Yet, when Big Sam throws the second attacker off the bridge, the brook has become a river.
- When the two scoundrels attack Scarlett in Shantytown, her buggy rolls backward and teeters on the edge of the bridge. Yet, after Scarlett faints and Big Sam tussles with the second attacker, the camera shows the buggy secure in the center of the bridge.
- After Big Sam has dispatched the Shantytown scoundrels, he climbs into the buggy, takes the reins from Scarlett, and drives away. Yet, when the camera shows the vehicle hurtling through the woods, Big Sam is gone and Scarlett is driving the buggy.

People and Places

- In the barnyard at Aunt Pittypat's house, the last rooster in Atlanta struts by the same woodpile twice while trying to escape from Uncle Peter and his hatchet.
- After Uncle Peter places the tray with the Madeira on the dining table, he stands to Aunt Pittypat's right. Yet, after she warns that the wine is the last, he is suddenly on her left.
- As Scarlett and Rhett's wagon joins the line of retreating troops, a bearded, pipe-smoking soldier passes by carrying a young soldier. Yet, as Rhett looks back, he sees the young soldier collapsing and

being picked up by the bearded soldier who was previously shown carrying him.

- Carrying two water buckets, Scarlett overhears Suellen complaining to Carreen as they work in Tara's cotton field. Scarlett slaps Suellen, yet the camera didn't show her putting the buckets down. Then Scarlett bends down, picks up the buckets, and walks off.
- As Gerald bursts into Tara to announce the end of the war, Melanie stands alone on the staircase. Yet, a moment later in her close-up, she has Beau in her arms.
- In Rhett's bedroom, when he pours sherry to celebrate Bonnie's birth, his cigar is in his mouth. Yet, when he offers the tumbler to Mammy, his cigar is in the hand holding the glass.

WHO SAID IT? (#4)

From the following list of characters, decide who spoke the line of movie dialogue.

Pork	Yankee deserter at Tara
Prissy	Tom, a Yankee captain
Mammy	Belle Watling
Big Sam	Shantytown attacker
Jonas Wilkerson	A Yankee major
Johnnie Gallegher	

1. "We finished plowing the creek bottom today. What do you want me to start on tomorrow?"
2. "I told him you was prostrate with grief."
3. "She's a mighty cold woman. Prancing about Atlanta by herself. She killed her husband same as if she shot him."
4. "He's her husband, ain't he?"
5. "You might as well take my money, Miz Wilkes. It's good money even if it is mine."
6. "Does you know a dyed-hair woman?"
7. "It's hard to be strict with a man who loses money so pleasantly."

8. "What gentlemens says and what they thinks is two different things. And I ain't noticed Mist' Ashley asking for to marry you."

9. "I don't know nothin' 'bout birthin' babies."

10. "Regular little spitfire, ain't you?"

11. "Savannah would be better for you. You'll just get in trouble in Atlanta."

12. "The whole Confederate Army's got the same troubles—crawlin' clothes and dysentery."

13. "There ain't never been a lady in this town nice to me like you was."

14. "Ma says that if you puts a knife under the bed it cuts the pain in two."

15. "There ain't no barn no more, Miz Scarlett. The Yankees done burned it for firewood."

16. "We came out here to pay a call, a friendly call, and talk a little business with old friends."

17. "Here's your new mill hands, Mrs. Kennedy. The pick of all the best jails in Georgia."

18. "Can you give me a quarter?"

19. "Horse, make tracks."

20. "It's about time you Rebels learned you can't take the law into your own hands!"

A UNIQUE MOVIE

What is unique about *GWTW*? It's a Civil War movie that never shows any battle scenes. The audience sees only the effects of war:

- The anxious crowds awaiting the Gettysburg casualty lists
- Trains of incoming wounded as Ashley arrives for Christmas leave
- Ashley's discouraged end-of-the-war speech to Scarlett
- Scarlett and Melanie caring for the wounded and dying in the Atlanta hospital
- The shelling of Atlanta and panic in the streets
- The multitude of wounded at the depot
- The burning of the Atlanta depot

- The Confederate army in retreat from Atlanta
- Scarlett hiding under the bridge with soldiers passing above
- Scarlett and Prissy on their way to Tara crossing a battlefield filled with dead soldiers
- Scarlett viewing the ruins of Twelve Oaks and returning to the ravaged Tara
- The montage of soldiers and cannons that opens part two
- The trespassing Yankee deserter at Tara
- The delousing of Frank Kennedy and feeding the returning "starving scarecrows"
- News that Ashley has been taken prisoner
- Gerald's announcing that the war is over

EIGHT

The Wind *Sweeps America*

PLANS FOR THE PREMIERE

As Selznick worked around the clock to complete *GWTW*, MGM, which would release the film, made plans for the movie's premiere. Selznick wanted to make sure everything went perfectly, so he bombarded MGM's publicity director, Howard Dietz, with endless memos and telegrams concerning all phases of the premiere.

In one cable, Selznick noted: "I want you to be very careful of the paper you select for the program—stop—Sometimes their crackling noise makes it difficult to hear the dialogue—stop—promise you will attend to this." In a return telegram, an exasperated Dietz declared that program noise would not be a problem, then added: "Have made tie up with *Gone With the Wind* peanut brittle company assuring each patron of the picture a box of peanut brittle as he enters the theater."

The world premiere was scheduled for Friday, December 15, 1939, in Margaret Mitchell's hometown. In honor of the film's debut, Georgia Governor Eurith D. Rivers proclaimed the day of the premiere an official state holiday. Not wanting to be a slouch, the mayor of Atlanta, William B. Hartsfield, proclaimed a municipal half-day holiday and ordered three days of celebrations including parades, citizens dressing up in period costumes, and a Junior League ball.

The site of the premiere was the Loew's Grand Theatre on Peachtree Street. The façade of the two-thousand-seat theater was false-fronted with giant white columns to make it resemble Twelve Oaks. High above street level was a two-story-high portrait of Vivien Leigh and Clark Gable.

Tickets for the gala event, which were selling for ten dollars apiece, quickly sold out, and scalpers got as much as two hundred dollars for a single ticket as the day of the premiere drew closer. Nearly one million visitors filled the city and battled for rooms in Atlanta's hotels and guest cottages. Citizens of Atlanta agreed that the hometown premiere of *GWTW* was the biggest thing to hit the city since William Tecumseh Sherman.

On December 11, just four days before the Atlanta premiere, Selznick sent this wire to Jock Whitney: "Have just finished *Gone With the Wind*. God bless us one and all."

THE ATLANTA FESTIVITIES

On Wednesday, December 13, the governor of Georgia and the mayor of Atlanta headed the airport contingent that welcomed the Selznick entourage. Selznick was accompanied by his wife Irene, his brother Myron, Vivien Leigh, Laurence Olivier, Olivia de Havilland, Evelyn Keyes, and Ona Munson. Conspicuously absent were Leslie Howard, Clark Gable, and Victor Fleming.

Howard had returned to England in August after war was declared in Europe. Fleming had decided to boycott the premiere after reading a newspaper publicity story. In the story, Selznick was quoted as saying he had supervised all the film's directors. This was the last straw for an enraged Fleming, who broke off all further relations with Selznick.

Gable had decided to support Fleming and boycott the film as well until MGM convinced both men to attend. Sadly, Fleming's longtime friend and mentor, Douglas Fairbanks Sr., died on December 12, giving the devastated director a legitimate excuse for opting out of the Atlanta festivities.

Without Fleming, Gable couldn't stand the thought of spending the long flight in Selznick's company, so he, his wife Carole Lombard, and a group of MGM executives flew to Atlanta on December 13 in a DC-3. On the side of Gable's plane were the words "MGM's *Gone With the Wind*" painted in large letters.

That afternoon, at the bunting- and Confederate-flag draped airport, a forty-piece band struck up "Dixie" as Gable's plane landed and he joined the earlier Hollywood arrivals for the procession into Atlanta. As Vivien Leigh walked down the red carpet amid the crush of reporters and popping flashbulbs, she recognized the tune being played by the band. "Oh, they're playing the song from the picture," she said. A quick-thinking Howard Dietz, who didn't want the comment attributed to Scarlett O'Hara, told a reporter who had overheard the remark that Olivia de Havilland had said it.

The luminaries were ushered into thirty open-topped cars for the motorcade trip to the Georgian Terrace Hotel. Along the Peachtree Street route, throngs of people (some dressed in contemporary clothing but many in hoopskirts and Confederate uniforms) cheered, shouted the rebel yell, and waved flags at the celebrities.

When the motorcade arrived at the hotel, the mayor officially welcomed the stars and introduced them to the crowd, which broke into renewed pandemonium. Confetti flew, and giant spotlights lit up the mayor as he presented his guests with Wedgwood coffee-and-tea sets.

Later that evening, the Hollywood stars were the guests of honor at a Junior League charity ball held at the Atlanta Municipal Auditorium, designed to resemble *GWTW*'s Monster Bazaar and decorated for the occasion in Confederate red and blue. After a procession of debutantes and their escorts, the master of ceremonies introduced the celebrities. The Kay Kyser Orchestra then began a lilting waltz, and Gable shared a dance with Mayor Hartsfield's daughter.

All of the stars were eager to meet *GWTW*'s author. But Margaret Mitchell had decided to settle an old score with the Junior League, which had denied her membership so many years before. She had sent regrets that, because her father was ill, she would not be able to attend the ball.

The next day, December 15, the mayor took the stars on a tour of the city, including a stop at the Cyclorama. Luncheons were held at Rich's department store for the Macmillan contingent and at the Governor's Mansion for the stars and for the governors of Tennessee, Alabama, Florida, and South Carolina, who were to attend the premiere. Georgia Governor Rivers made Selznick, Gable, and Wilbur Kurtz honorary colonels in the Georgia National Guard.

That afternoon, the Atlanta Women's Press Club hosted a tea in Margaret Mitchell's honor at the Piedmont Driving Club. Attending were friends and colleagues of the author, the mayor and governor, representatives from Macmillan, the Hollywood stars, and studio executives. Selznick finally met Margaret. But when the producer began to discuss a sequel to the movie, she politely excused herself. Afterward, she was presented to Clark Gable.

The pressure of the crowd around her was so great that she took Gable by the arm and hustled him into a quiet room. Behind locked doors, the petite author and the actor who played her hero chatted in private. Later, Gable mentioned that Margaret Mitchell was "the most fascinating woman I've ever met." The Atlanta festivities culminated that evening with the long-awaited event, the four-hour premiere of *GWTW*.

THE PREMIERE OF *GWTW*

Crowds gathered early in front of the Loew's Grand Theatre, which was illuminated by nine searchlights. People didn't have a chance of getting in to see the film; they were there to watch the stars. Four hundred Georgia National Guardsmen formed a human cordon to hold back the enthusiastic crowd of almost 18,000 that surged forward as each star arrived.

Gable's arrival caused some women to scream with joy and others to faint dead away. The premiere was covered by radio stations, and Gable made a gentlemanly request of the audience when it was his turn at the microphone: "Tonight I am here just as a spectator. I want to see *Gone With the Wind* the same as you do. This is Margaret Mitchell's night and the people of Atlanta's night. Allow me to see *Gone With the Wind* as a spectator."

In addition to the Hollywood stars, Jock Whitney was attending the premiere with his silver-spooned friends, including the Vanderbilts, Herbert Bayard Swope, Nelson Rockefeller, J. P. Morgan, and John Jacob Astor. Also attending were Atlanta's favorite citizens, Margaret Mitchell and her husband, John Marsh.

As the title swept across the screen and Max Steiner's music swelled through the theater, many in the audience gasped at the beauty of the Technicolor production. They followed Scarlett from her innocent days as a flirtatious belle through her beleaguered days in war-torn Atlanta. They cheered when Scarlett shot the Yankee deserter and held their breaths as she fended off the Shantytown attacker. By the end of the movie, as Melanie lay dying, many openly sobbed into handkerchiefs.

When the heavy curtains swept across the stage, the audience stood and broke into wild applause for Selznick, his stars, and Margaret Mitchell. In the speeches that followed the premiere, Margaret Mitchell, for the first time, shared her feelings about the film. She thanked Selznick "on behalf of me and my poor Scarlett" for "the grand things these actors have done." Although emotionally drained, the audience renewed their ovations with new spirit and echoed the author's sentiments. David O. Selznick, with tears in his eyes, basked in the unrestrained praise. The endless trouble and months of hard work were finally worth it.

OTHER "PREMIERES"

Following the Atlanta premiere, *GWTW* blew to New York City and hit the Big Apple with hurricane force. Simultaneous "premieres" were held on Tuesday, December 19, at the Astor Theatre and at the Loew's Capitol Theatre. The opening night at the Capitol was covered by a new medium—television—that broadcast the arrival of the stars and special guests to several hundred television sets in the area.

Most city newspapers sent reviewers to cover one or the other premiere, but the *New York Daily News* dispatched a reviewer to each theater. The next morning, the *Daily News* printed both four-star reviews on the same page under the headline "*Gone With the Wind* in Two Gala Openings." Kate Cameron, who saw the film at the Capitol, wrote: "There are a dozen or more scenes and passages in the film that have never been equaled on the screen." Wanda Hale, who attended the premiere at the Astor, wrote: "After three years of impatient waiting . . . we are finally rewarded, ten-fold, by this stunning production."

The critic for the *New York Times*, Frank Nugent, wrote: "The greatest motion picture mural we have seen and the most ambitious film-making venture in Hollywood's spectacular history." The *Post*'s Archer Winsten noted: "Just as *Birth of a Nation* was a milestone of movie history, *Gone With the Wind* represents a supreme effort."

The next major premiere for *GWTW* took place in Los Angeles on Thursday, December 28, at the Fox Carthay Circle Theatre. This most glamorous premiere of all was held three days before the deadline set by the Academy of Motion Picture Arts and Sciences for films to qualify for 1939's Academy Awards. And all of Hollywood's glitterati attended, including *GWTW*'s cast, the unsuccessful contenders, Selznick's detractors, and his well-wishers, too. Selznick was enjoying the pinnacle of his success.

SELZNICK'S SEQUEL IDEAS

Almost as soon as the previews were over, Selznick started seriously thinking about a *GWTW* sequel. He asked Kay Brown to approach Margaret Mitchell about writing the further adventures of Scarlett and Rhett or selling the rights to the characters. Margaret, though, refused to consider either possibility.

But Selznick was undaunted and wrote to Brown: "If we can't get a sequel I would still be delighted to have a story to be called *The Daughter of Scarlett O'Hara*, with Vivien playing the daughter. Don't you think we might persuade Mitchell to write such a story as a novel, or a novelette, or even as a short story?

"I realize that we killed off Bonnie Blue, and it is not clear to me as to how Scarlett would get herself pregnant again, but then Scarlett, after all, was Scarlett, and there must have been other men in her life after Rhett walked out the door. Maybe we could talk about a marriage beyond Rhett, or perhaps even have an opening sequence in the story and in the picture dealing with her fourth husband."

Margaret Mitchell turned down that idea as well, and Selznick gave up hope of reprising the story of Scarlett O'Hara.

HOW *GWTW* CHANGED THE OSCAR PRESENTATIONS FOREVER

February 29, 1940, 8:30 p.m. The place: the Cocoanut Grove of the Ambassador Hotel in Los Angeles. The event: the twelfth annual awards presentation of the Academy of Motion Picture Arts and Sciences.

Hollywood was abuzz and aglitter with Oscar fever that Thursday afternoon. As was the custom, the names of the Oscar winners were revealed in advance to the press, with newspapers making a solemn promise not to break the news before the ceremonies. But one newspaper couldn't contain the excitement.

The *Los Angeles Times* printed the names of the winners and splashed *Gone With the Wind* in banner headlines across the front page. The results greeted Academy Award–goers as they arrived for the banquet and prompted the academy to initiate a protocol for future award presentations.

Since then, the names of the winners have been sealed in envelopes by PricewaterhouseCoopers, a multinational professional services firm. This ensures that the results are, indeed, kept secret until the presenter says, "And the winner is . . ."

THE 1939 ACADEMY AWARDS: "THE WINNERS ARE . . ."

Gone With the Wind, Best Picture

GWTW took top honors—and was the first color film to do so—in a resplendent field that included *Dark Victory*; *Goodbye, Mr. Chips*; *Love Affair*; *Mr. Smith Goes to Washington*; *Ninotchka*; *Of Mice and Men*; *Stagecoach*; *The Wizard of Oz*; and *Wuthering Heights*.

Vivien Leigh, Best Actress, *Gone With the Wind*

Spencer Tracy presented the Oscar for Best Actress to Vivien Leigh for her portrayal of Scarlett O'Hara. The other nominees included Bette Davis (*Dark Victory*), Irene Dunne (*Love Affair*), Greta Garbo (*Ninotchka*), and Greer Garson (*Goodbye, Mr. Chips*).

Robert Donat, Best Actor, *Goodbye, Mr. Chips*

Clark Gable as Rhett Butler lost the Best Actor Award to Robert Donat for his touching portrayal of schoolteacher and headmaster Charles Edward Chipping, fondly known as "Mr. Chips." The other contenders were Laurence Olivier (*Wuthering Heights*), Mickey Rooney (*Babes in Arms*), and James Stewart (*Mr. Smith Goes to Washington*).

Hattie McDaniel, Best Supporting Actress, *Gone With the Wind*

Her performance as Mammy earned the Best Supporting Actress Award for Hattie McDaniel, the first African American performer to win an Oscar. In presenting the award, Fay Bainter remarked: "To me it seems more than just a plaque of gold. It opens the doors of this room, moves back the walls, and enables us to embrace the whole of America. An America that almost alone in the world today recognizes and pays tribute to those who give of their best regardless of creed, race, or color." McDaniel was up against Olivia de Havilland (*Gone With the Wind*), Geraldine Fitzgerald (*Wuthering Heights*), Edna May Oliver (*Drums Along the Mohawk*), and Maria Ouspenskaya (*Love Affair*).

Thomas Mitchell, Best Supporting Actor, *Stagecoach*

Thomas Mitchell was nominated in this category for his role in *Stagecoach*, not for his portrayal of *GWTW*'s Gerald O'Hara, nor for his work in *Mr. Smith Goes to Washington*. Yet this trifecta of noteworthy roles made him a predicted winner. His competition included Brian Aherne (*Juarez*), Brian Donlevy (*Beau Geste*), and double nominations from *Mr. Smith Goes to Washington*—Harry Carey and Claude Rains. Leslie Howard's portrayal of Ashley Wilkes was bypassed as a nomination for Best Supporting Actor.

Victor Fleming, Best Director, *Gone With the Wind*

Although Victor Fleming was one of three directors to work on *GWTW*, he received sole on-screen credit and garnered the Academy Award for Best Director. Among his competition were Frank Capra (*Mr. Smith Goes to Washington*), John Ford (*Stagecoach*), Sam Wood (*Goodbye, Mr. Chips*), and William Wyler (*Wuthering Heights*).

Other competitive Academy Awards for *GWTW* were:

- Sidney Howard, Best Screenplay
- Ernest Haller and Ray Rennahan, Best Cinematography, Color
- Lyle Wheeler, Best Art Direction
- Hal C. Kern and James E. Newcom, Best Film Editing

David O. Selznick received the honorary Irving G. Thalberg Memorial Award "for the most consistent high quality of production during 1939." An honorary plaque went to William Cameron Menzies "for outstanding achievement in the use of color for the enhancement of dramatic mood in the production *Gone With the Wind*."

With an unprecedented thirteen nominations in twelve categories (double nomination for Best Supporting Actress), *GWTW* might have swept the Academy Awards. But the film did not win in every nomination category. In addition to Gable's loss of the Best Actor Award, Jack Cosgrove lost the Best Special Effects Award to *The Rains Came*, Max Steiner lost the Best Musical Score Award to *The Wizard of Oz*, and Thomas Moulton lost the Best Sound Recording Award to *When Tomorrow Comes*. However, by the end of the Oscar presentations, *GWTW* had won a record-breaking eight competitive Academy Awards.

TIDBITS FROM OSCAR NIGHT

- Star of a popular radio program, comedian Bob Hope made his first appearance as the Oscars' master of ceremonies. Walter Wanger, the academy's new president, introduced Hope as the "Rhett Butler of the airwaves." Hope commented to the audience, "What a wonderful thing, this benefit for David Selznick."
- Sidney Howard's win for Best Screenplay made him the first posthumous Academy Award winner.
- When Hattie McDaniel's name was announced as the Best Supporting Actress winner, she whooped a "Hallelujah" and hurried to the podium. Being selected for the award, she said, "has made me feel very, very humble, and I shall always hold it as a beacon for anything I may be able to do in the future. . . . My heart is too full to tell you just how I feel." She sobbed a quiet "thank you and God bless you" and hurried back to her table. There she buried her face in her hands and cried. Olivia de Havilland, who had lost to McDaniel, went to offer her congratulations. Then, feeling overcome by her own disappointment, de Havilland left the room and burst into tears herself.

- Spencer Tracy, the presenter of the Oscars for Best Actor and Best Actress, had left a hospital bed where he was suffering from strep throat to attend the awards ceremony.
- After the ceremony, David Selznick sat silent and sullen as he rode to a post-Oscar party with his publicity director, Russell Birdwell. Suddenly Selznick turned to Birdwell. "I don't know why we didn't get the best-actor award for Gable. Somewhere you failed. You didn't put on the proper campaign; otherwise, Clark would have been sure to get it." Birdwell was stunned, especially because of all the Oscars *GWTW* did get. When Birdwell didn't show up at work for two days, Selznick phoned him and apologized. "I was a pig. I worked so hard and waited so long. I got piggish and wanted everything."
- Gable, too, was disappointed with not having won an Oscar for Rhett Butler. On the way home from the Academy Award ceremony, his actress-wife Carole Lombard tried to snap her husband out of his bad mood. "Aw, don't be blue, Pappy. I just know we'll bring one home next year." "No, we won't," Gable said dejectedly. "This was it. This was my last chance." Lombard was furious: "Not you, you self-centered bastard! I mean me!"

GWTW CAPTURES OTHER HONORS

- In December 1939, the New York Film Critics voted Vivien Leigh their Best Actress. Victor Fleming ranked third in the critics' Best Director category.
- The *Photoplay* magazine Gold Medal Award was the only one granted on the basis of balloting by the moviegoing public. In 1939, this oldest industry award was bestowed upon David O. Selznick for *GWTW* as "the best photoplay of the year."
- The National Board of Review Awards published an annual listing of the ten best movies. Voting was done by a Committee on Exceptional Films, and in 1940, the National Board ranked *GWTW* ninth on its top ten list. Number one was *The Grapes of Wrath*, and number ten was *Rebecca*.
- The *Film Daily* annually polled movie critics across the country and compiled a list of the ten best films. *GWTW* was included in the 1941

poll because the film was then in general release. Of the 548 ballots cast, 452 were enough to declare *GWTW* the first-place winner.

EVERYONE WANTS TO SEE *GWTW*

During the film's first run, theaters showed *GWTW* either three times a day with unreserved seating or twice a day with reserved seating. Selznick was in favor of reserved seats because this eliminated long lines of patrons waiting outside the theater for the next showing. Generally, patrons paid seventy-five cents for a matinee ticket, while evening showings cost one dollar. Evening loge seating was $1.50. Regular movie tickets at this time were usually around twenty-five cents and rarely cost more than fifty cents.

Despite the high admission prices, everyone wanted to see *GWTW*. Within a week of its opening, the movie grossed an astounding $945,000. In its first year of release, *GWTW* earned $14 million. And more than twenty-five million people in the United States had been overcome by Scarlett fever.

THE PHENOMENON OF *GWTW* BEGINS

Although most films had a short first-run life of several weeks, Selznick believed he could hold the public's interest in *GWTW* for at least two years with careful planning.

When *GWTW*'s first run ended in June 1940, MGM and Selznick International took the film out of circulation. To whet the appetites of those who hadn't been able to afford the premium prices of the film's initial run, print ads promised that *GWTW* would return the following year at reduced admissions.

To kick off the popular-priced engagements, MGM planned a First Anniversary Premiere bash in Atlanta for December 12, 1940. Another talent search was arranged, not for a new Scarlett, but for a Georgian miss to preside over the celebration. Louella Stone of Atlanta was chosen Miss Anniversary.

The top of the Loew's Grand Theatre was decorated with a replica of a three-tiered birthday cake complete with one sparkling candle. Guests paid

$2.50 a ticket (which benefited the British War Relief Society) to see the film and to greet Vivien Leigh, Laurence Olivier, and Alfred Hitchcock, who were to make special appearances. Unfortunately, bad weather delayed the arrival of the celebrities until the following day.

Moviegoers were ecstatic when *GWTW*'s general release began. Print ads shouted, "Nothing cut but the price!" Twenty-four million people flocked to large cinemas in major cities as well as to small neighborhood theaters to see Scarlett battle hunger and despair. Matinee tickets sold for forty cents, while evening tickets cost fifty-five cents. *GWTW*'s second release not only earned $5 million but made the film the #1 box-office draw for 1941.

At the end of the 1941 general release, MGM decided to withdraw *GWTW* again. The prints were battered, but the studio believed one final fling for *GWTW* was possible. The film returned to movie theaters for the third time in the spring of 1942 and stayed in release until late 1943.

When MGM finally pulled the film from exhibition, all worn-out prints were destroyed, and *GWTW* was at last declared out of circulation. MGM, which by then had sole ownership of the film, announced that *GWTW* had grossed over $32 million. But the phenomenon was only beginning.

GWTW IS A HIT OVERSEAS

GWTW was not just an American phenomenon. *The Wind* swept overseas as well:

- In 1940, *GWTW* opened at the Ritz Theatre in war-torn London where the film played for 232 consecutive weeks, nearly four and a half years.
- Adolf Hitler apparently was smitten with *GWTW*'s saucy heroine and her damn-Yankee attitude. But when der Führer learned that *GWTW* was a source of encouragement to the underground resistance, he banned both the novel and the film from all German-occupied countries.
- In the postwar years, *GWTW*'s message of survival spoke to thousands of newly liberated people who crammed European theaters to see Scarlett O'Hara triumph over her oppressors.

- *GWTW* debuted in West Berlin in 1954 and played for two and a half years. By the time four prints of the film had bit the dust, over 600,000 had viewed the movie.

NOT EVERYONE LOVED *GWTW*

The Catholic Church's Legion of Decency gave *GWTW* a "B" rating, which meant the film was "morally objectionable in part for all." The legion did not approve of "the low moral character, principles, and behavior of the main figures as depicted in the film; suggestive implications; the attractive portrayal of the immoral character of a supporting role in the story." (Belle Watling, perhaps?)

Usually such forceful censure of a film was enough to keep crowds away from the movie house, but not so with *GWTW*. Many saw the film despite the objections of their church.

GWTW MERCHANDISING MANIA

Not only were millions of people seeing *GWTW*, they were also buying hundreds of products with *GWTW* tie-ins:

- La Cross promoted three shades of nail polish—Scarlett O'Hara Morning, Noon, and Night—with this warning: "Scarlett O'Hara Danger! . . . Wear it for romance . . . A nail polish so glamorous you'll want to live up to it . . . Sirenizing deep red to add Scarlett glamour like a jewel."
- The Rhett Butler bow by Slim Jim Bows was inspired by the cravats worn by Clark Gable in the film.
- A series of Scarlett O'Hara dolls was popular. The dolls wore costumes reminiscent of various scenes in the movie.
- A Chinese checkers–type game called Bet Chu Can't was sold as "The Scarlett O'Hara game."
- A simulated cameo brooch, designed to resemble the one worn by Vivien Leigh, was offered for fifteen cents and three wrappers from Lux toilet soap.

- Nunnally's, "The Candy of the South," packaged a box of Scarlett chocolates. The box looked like a book, had a photograph of Vivien Leigh on the cover, and contained candy pieces named after the film's characters: Scarlett Fantasies, Rhett Caramels, Melanie Molasses Strings, Tara Pecans, Ashley Brazils, Tarleton Strawberries, Prissy Peppermints, and Gerald O'Hara Almonds.
- The "Scarlett O'Hara Morning Glory" was awarded a gold medal from the All-America Seed Selections Society.
- Hundreds of other merchandising tie-ins were authorized by Loew's Inc. Among them were Scarlett and Rhett wristwatches and statuettes; Scarlett O'Hara perfume, perfume decanters, and dress patterns; *GWTW* fashions including costumes, handkerchiefs, scarves, snoods, turbans, hats, and veils. Fashions for the home included living room furniture, *GWTW* quilts, slipcovers, and drapery valences. Adults enjoyed *GWTW* leather products; kids had fun with *GWTW* paper dolls and paint boxes.

In honor of the film, the Southern Comfort Corporation debuted two new potent potables:

Scarlett O'Hara Cocktail

Juice of ¼ fresh lime
1 jigger cranberry juice
1 jigger Southern Comfort

Combine the ingredients in a cocktail shaker filled with cracked ice. Shake well, and strain into a cocktail glass.

Rhett Butler Cocktail

Juice of ½ lime
Juice of ⅓ lemon
½ teaspoon sugar
1 barspoon Curacao
1 jigger Southern Comfort

Combine ingredients in a cocktail shaker filled with cracked ice. Shake well, and strain into a cocktail glass.

The slogan for the new cocktails was "no more than two lest you be *Gone With the Wind*." The American public immediately took to the cocktail named after its favorite heroine, and the drink remains a classic today. But what about the Rhett Butler Cocktail? The drink never achieved popularity, and it disappeared from the scene as quickly as its namesake left for Charleston at the end of the film.

COOKING UP A STORM
WITH THE *GWTW* COOKBOOK

Purchasers of Pebeco toothpaste received an unparalleled premium: *The Gone With the Wind Cookbook*. The forty-eight-page cookbook presented suggestions for *GWTW* parties as well as 128 "famous Southern cooking recipes," from soup to nuts. Included were:

Southland Vegetable Soup
Gerald O'Hara Ham Steak
Tara Supper Deviled Crabs
Tarleton Twins' Broiled Oysters on the Half Shell
Mammy's Creole Rice
Plantation Corn Omelet
Atlanta Waffles
Twelve Oaks Plum Pudding
Aunt Pittypat's Coconut Pudding
Georgia Peach Trifle
Melanie's Sweet Potato Pie

The cookbook contains no recipes for Ashley Artichokes or Rhett Butler Rutabagas. You're on your own with those.

GWTW IS AN INSPIRATION

- *Kiss the Boys Goodbye* by Clare Boothe opened on Broadway in September 1938 and told the story of an Alabama beauty who longs for

Hollywood and the chance to play Velvet O'Toole. The play became a film in 1941.

- In *Strike Up the Band*, Mickey Rooney and Judy Garland sang the praises of Scarlett and Rhett in "Our Love Affair."
- The 1940 Broadway musical revue *Keep Off the Grass* featured a hilarious *GWTW* takeoff with Ilka Chase playing Scarlett, Ray Bolger as Ashley, and Jimmy Durante in the role of Rhett Butler.
- Cecil B. DeMille's 1941 film *Reap the Wild Wind* teamed Paulette Goddard (with a Southern accent), Louise Beavers as Mammy, Hedda Hopper as a swooning aunt, and Oscar Polk (*GWTW*'s Pork) as house servant "Salt Meat" in a merry Technicolor romp that included various and sundry disasters.

GWTW IS SOLD

Huge profits from *GWTW* were pouring into Selznick International. Because his lawyers feared that most of the profits would go toward taxes, Selznick was advised to dissolve Selznick International Pictures and to sell his interest in *GWTW*.

Selznick was reluctant to let go of his share of the film. But the tax attorneys advised that unless he did so, the capital-gains strategy they had worked out with the government might be challenged. Besides, they argued, the public would soon grow tired of *GWTW*, and there couldn't be more than another million dollars in profits to be made. So in August 1942, Selznick sold his interest in the film to Jock Whitney for $400,000 in cash plus the interest in the studio's accounts receivables and dissolved the company. (Selznick subsequently formed another film company.) In September 1943, Whitney sold his interest in *GWTW* for $2.2 million to MGM, the ultimate triumph for Louis B. Mayer.

With their respective windfalls from the sales, Selznick and Whitney sent a check for $50,000 to Margaret Mitchell to show their gratitude to the Atlanta author. This brought the total amount she received for the movie rights to $100,000.

Postscript: When *GWTW* was re-released in mid-1947 and played through 1948, the film brought in $9 million. When Selznick learned about the profits he missed out on, he became enraged: "I could strangle [the tax lawyers] with my bare hands in cold blood."

WITH A GUST, *THE WIND* RETURNS

Americans had not seen *GWTW* since November 1943 when MGM put the film into mothballs after its successful third reissue. However, fans wanted to know when it would reappear.

They wrote letters to Selznick asking when the film would be shown again. Selznick received a petition signed by every student of Western State High School in Kalamazoo, Michigan, requesting to see the "supreme film" one more time. Even Margaret Mitchell took pen in hand: "So many children who were not old enough to see it when it was last here have requested that I ask you when it will be back. So I am asking for them, and because I'd like to see it myself." Selznick passed all the mail on to MGM, which decided to bring *GWTW* back to theaters in June 1947.

MGM splurged on the 1947 revival of *GWTW*. New Technicolor prints and a spanking new ad campaign debuted. Posters for the film for the first time showed Rhett holding Scarlett in his arms and boasted that "Everybody Wants to See *Gone With the Wind*."

And everybody did. Crowds this time around rivaled those that had waited on line for tickets in 1939. Many who saw the film during its first release returned to see if the film was as good as they remembered it. They brought their children, too, to introduce a new generation to the story of Scarlett and Rhett.

In Atlanta alone, records for popular-price admission were shattered. Thousands stood in double lines at the Loew's Grand Theatre on the first day of *GWTW*'s return. Some fans, eager for tickets, stood in line at the box office as early as 8 a.m. to make sure they saw the film. When *GWTW*'s fourth reissue run ended in late 1948, the film had earned $9 million.

NINE

The Stars Shine On

THE AFTER-THE-MOVIE LIVES OF *GWTW*'S STARS

Leslie Howard

After completing work on *Intermezzo*, Leslie Howard sailed to England. There he started his own filmmaking company so he would finally be able to realize his dream of directing. He immersed himself in directing *Pimpernel Smith* and *The First of the Few*.

England was at war. Howard undertook a lecture tour on behalf of the British Council and traveled to Spain and Portugal, where he spoke in various cities about the theater. Spain was still neutral, and it was whispered even then that Howard was really on a secret mission for the British government.

On June 1, 1943, Howard, at the end of his tour, boarded a commercial airplane in Lisbon, Portugal, bound for England. In a tragic coincidence, Prime Minister Winston Churchill was at the same time flying back to England on another plane after attending a military meeting.

At 12:45 p.m., as Howard's plane crossed the Bay of Biscay, the pilot sighted the approach of eight German fighter planes. Whether the Germans believed that Churchill was on the plane or whether they mistook the craft for Churchill's remains open to speculation. But in the next few seconds, the fighters opened fire on the unarmed civilian aircraft. The plane exploded into flames and crashed into the sea. All aboard, including fifty-year-old Leslie Howard, were killed.

In September 2011, the ninety-minute documentary *Leslie Howard: The Man Who Gave a Damn*, produced by Tom Hamilton of Repo Films, debuted during an event held at Howard's former home, Stowe Maries, in Dorking, Surrey, England. The film explored Howard's life, loves, and career; shared the memories of his daughter, Ruth; showed never-seen-before Howard family home movies; and examined Howard's role in the British war effort and the events that led up to his 1943 disappearance.

British film and television actor Derek Partridge narrated the film and added a chilling, personal footnote to Howard's story. In 1943, seven-year-old Partridge and his nanny were bumped from the Lisbon-to-Bristol flight so their seats could be given to agent Alfred T. Chenhalls and his client Leslie Howard.

Clark Gable

Relieved that *GWTW* was finished, Gable returned to work at MGM and life with Carole Lombard. But their idyllic happiness was shattered when the Japanese bombs found their targets at Pearl Harbor.

Lombard, a dyed-in-the-wool patriot, agreed to help in the war effort by traveling to her home state of Indiana on a bond-selling tour. The tour was wildly successful. In Indianapolis alone, Lombard sold over $2 million in defense bonds. She was on her way home to Gable on January 16, 1942, when, a few minutes after taking off from Las Vegas, her plane smashed into Mount Potosi. Everyone on board, including Lombard, her mother, and MGM's staff publicist Otto Winkler, was killed.

Lombard's death devastated Clark Gable. Despite the objections of his studio, he enlisted in the Army Air Force. He flew in bombing missions over Germany during his two-year tour of duty and was discharged with the rank of major.

When Gable returned home from the war, he returned to the only life he knew: making movies. MGM teamed him with young actresses such as Greer Garson, Ava Gardner, and Grace Kelly, and Gable recaptured his success in films such as *Adventure, Lone Star,* and *Mogambo.*

In 1954, at the height of his popularity, Gable left MGM over a contract dispute and began a freelance acting career. Gable had a lingering resentment toward MGM that he had never been offered a percentage of *GWTW*'s enormous profits. He was determined that future contracts would include percentage clauses.

In the area of love, Gable was less successful. He continually searched for a replacement for Carole Lombard and thought he had found her in an Englishwoman, Lady Sylvia Ashley. Their 1949 marriage, though, ended in divorce two years later. Gable had better luck in his fifth trip to the altar. In 1955, he married Kay Williams Spreckels and at last found the happiness that had eluded him since Lombard's death.

His film work now found him playing opposite actresses such as Susan Hayward, Jane Russell, and Eleanor Parker in films for various studios. In 1957, he starred in another story of the Old South, *Band of Angels* with Yvonne DeCarlo. *Variety* called Gable's character, a reformed slave trader, "reminiscent of Rhett Butler."

In 1960, Gable signed to star as an aging cowboy in Arthur Miller's *The Misfits*. He was teamed with Marilyn Monroe, Montgomery Clift, Eli Wallach, and Thelma Ritter in a story filmed on location in the scorching Nevada flats. Tensions on the set resulting from script problems and an unstable Marilyn Monroe drove Gable to distraction, but he always remained professional. He even insisted on doing his own stunt work for scenes, including a horse-roping sequence in which he was dragged four hundred feet through an alkali bed.

Throughout the production, Gable stayed sane by looking ahead to the future. His wife was pregnant with their first child, and he was thrilled at the prospect of becoming a father. He was committed to making one more film after *The Misfits*, and then he planned to retire to raise his child—a son, he hoped.

But *The Misfits* took its toll. Shortly after filming ended, Gable suffered a heart attack. Ten days later, on November 16, 1960, the "King of Hollywood" was dead at age fifty-nine. As a sad postscript, the child he always wanted but never saw—a son, John Clark Gable—was born on March 20, 1961.

In 1994, John Clark Gable had a small role as army officer Terry in the biographical TV film *A Burning Passion: The Margaret Mitchell Story*, starring Shannen Doherty. The Hollywood Foreign Press Association named him Mr. Golden Globe in 1995.

In 2011, John Clark Gable accepted a Golden Boot "Centennial Award" in commemoration of his father's one-hundredth birthday at the nineteenth annual Golden Boot Awards ceremony in Hollywood. Sponsored and presented by the Motion Picture & Television Fund, the awards honor achievement in Western television and movies. Divorced, Gable has two children, Kayley Gable, who was born in 1986, and Clark James Gable, who was born in 1988.

In 2012, model, actor, and grandson of the "King of Hollywood," Clark James Gable became the new host of the nationally syndicated reality show *Cheaters* for its thirteenth season.

Vivien Leigh

After *GWTW*, Vivien Leigh's film career continued with her roles in *Waterloo Bridge* with Robert Taylor and in *That Hamilton Woman* with Laurence Olivier. In her personal life, Leigh was now starring as Mrs. Laurence Olivier, and the couple worked together in various stage and screen projects. She moved comfortably into the role of Lady Olivier when her husband was knighted in 1947.

Leigh was playing Sabine in Thornton Wilder's *The Skin of Our Teeth* when she was first diagnosed as having a tubercular patch in her right lung. Seeming to ignore the seriousness of her condition, she continued to smoke and drink excessively and to work to the point of exhaustion.

What she could not ignore were the periods of manic depression (now called bipolar disorder) she suffered. During the depressive phase, she was miserable, had difficulty thinking and concentrating, and lost her appetite as well as her ability to sleep. In the manic phase, she became wild and lashed out at others for no reason. Her judgment was poor during these times, and she often was sexually indiscriminate. Frequently, only electroshock therapy could restore her mental stability.

In 1949, Leigh starred in the London production of *A Streetcar Named Desire*, directed by Olivier. Leigh's outstanding portrayal of the fading Southern belle Blanche DuBois won her the role in the Warner Bros. film and subsequently her second Academy Award. The role also earned Leigh a British Academy of Film and Television Arts (BAFTA) Award for Best British Actress and a New York Film Critics Circle Award for Best Actress.

No matter where Leigh traveled, she was recognized as Scarlett O'Hara. Fans of *GWTW* packed theaters to see her in plays; shouted to her on the street; and hounded her for autographs at train stations, airports, and hotels. "Did Scarlett get Rhett back?" they always asked, and Leigh replied that she didn't think so. In 1960, the question became poignant on a personal level when Olivier, the love of her own life, asked for a divorce.

Crushed by the end of her marriage, Leigh sought solace in the arms of Jack Merivale, a British actor who had worked with the Oliviers in the 1940 production of *Romeo and Juliet*. The relationship provided love, care, and stability to the fragile Leigh as she plunged herself into work as an antidote to the pain of losing her beloved Larry.

She starred in the 1961 film *The Roman Spring of Mrs. Stone* and accepted a role in the 1963 Broadway musical *Tovarich*. In the musical, Leigh sang and danced her way into the hearts of the critics, and her performance earned her a Tony Award.

After her stage triumph, Leigh was overcome by another cycle of manic depression. Her recuperation was slow, but she eventually felt well enough to undertake the role of a Southern woman in decline in the 1965 film *Ship of Fools*.

In 1967, fifty-four-year-old Leigh began rehearsals for the London production of Edward Albee's *A Delicate Balance*. But she was forced to withdraw from the play at the end of May. The tuberculosis that wracked her body was found to have spread to both lungs.

Leigh refused hospitalization. She chose instead to remain at home for the three months the doctors said it would take to recover from this latest and most serious bout of illness. Those three months were not hers to have.

Newspapers around the world that carried the news of her July 8 death sadly announced: "Scarlett O'Hara Is Dead." The evening after her passing, in recognition of their loss, all the theaters in London's West End extinguished their lights for one hour to honor the memory of Vivien Leigh.

In 1999, the American Film Institute ranked Leigh sixteenth on its list of the top fifty greatest screen legends in American film history.

In 2013, London's Victoria and Albert Museum acquired Leigh's archive from her grandchildren. Among the personal and professional items were Leigh's diaries that she kept from age sixteen until her death; more than two hundred love letters exchanged with Laurence Olivier, including forty that Leigh wrote when she was making *GWTW*; press clippings, annotated theater and movie scripts, and awards; more than 7,500 personal letters from Winston Churchill, Noel Coward, Tennessee Williams, T. S. Eliot; and photographs, including stills from *GWTW*.

Olivia de Havilland

After Olivia de Havilland's appearance in *GWTW*, Warner Bros. lent her to other studios. She played in *Raffles* for Samuel Goldwyn and in *Hold Back the Dawn* for Paramount. Although *Hold Back the Dawn* brought her a second Academy Award nomination, an Oscar remained tantalizingly out of reach.

Just as Jack L. Warner had predicted, de Havilland became dissatisfied with the projects the studio offered her. They tossed her a few bones that she enjoyed such as *Strawberry Blonde*, *The Male Animal*, and *In This Our Life* with Bette Davis. She was hungry, though, for a meaty role that could capture the elusive Oscar. When she refused to accept unsuitable parts, Warner suspended her without salary.

She endured seven such suspensions, and when her contract expired in 1943, de Havilland decided not to renew. But Warner had an ace up his sleeve. He ordered the nine months she had spent on suspension added to the end of her contract. By this time de Havilland had had it with Warner's dictatorial ways. She decided to take him to court.

She fought her case in three successive courtrooms until the Superior Court of California ruled that a seven-year contract ended after the seventh year. Warner was foiled but not for long; he initiated a squeeze play. He brought the case to the appellate court, then warned every Hollywood producer not to hire her since de Havilland was still his contract player.

When the dust of this fight finally settled nearly two years after it began, de Havilland was the winner. The appeals judge ruled that adding suspension time to her contract "would amount to virtual peonage." This precedent-setting decision for contract actors signaled the death knell for the powerful movie studio system.

Fresh from her legal victory, de Havilland accepted the role of an unwed mother fighting to regain custody of her child in Paramount's *To Each His Own* in 1946. Her heart-wrenching performance finally won the long-sought Academy Award as Best Actress. This was followed by her role in *The Snake Pit* in 1948, which earned her a fourth Oscar nomination, and in *The Heiress* in 1949, which captured her second Academy Award. The year proved to be a good one personally as well. Her 1946 union with Marcus Goodrich was blessed in 1949 with a son, Benjamin.

After 1951, de Havilland accepted roles on the stage, in films, and on television. Following the crumbling of her marriage, she found happiness again with Pierre Galante. They married in 1955, and de Havilland moved to France. They had a daughter, Giselle, in 1957. But the second marriage was fated to end as well; they were divorced in 1979.

Her career continued in the 1980s on television. She played Henry Fonda's wife in *Roots: The Next Generation*. In 1986, she crossed to the other side of the Mason-Dixon Line when she played Mrs. Neal, a Northerner and hospital administrator, in the twelve-hour miniseries *North and South, Book II*. That same year she starred with Rex Harrison and Amy Irving in the four-hour miniseries *Anastasia: The Mystery of Anna*. For her role as the Dowager Empress Maria, de Havilland earned a Golden Globe Award for Best Supporting Actress in a Miniseries and was nominated for an Emmy Award for Outstanding Supporting Actress in a Miniseries.

De Havilland finds it ironic that she is the last of *GWTW*'s four stars since she was the only one to die in the film. Her connection to the movie remains strong. For its sixtieth anniversary, she and her daughter were guests of honor at a special screening in Paris.

In 2004, she returned to Hollywood to help promote the new *GWTW* DVD and to accept a lifetime achievement award—the first-ever "Legend" award—at *Premiere* magazine's annual "Women in Hollywood" awards luncheon. That same year, Turner Classic Movies produced *Melanie Remembers*, a retrospective film in which de Havilland reminisced about *GWTW*'s casting and filming, as a sixty-fifth-anniversary tribute to the film.

In 2006, the Academy of Motion Picture Arts and Sciences honored de Havilland with a two-and-a-half-hour, ninetieth-birthday salute hosted by TCM host Robert Osborne. The tribute included clips from fifteen of her films, including *GWTW*, and praise from colleagues. In accepting their acclaim, she recalled being asked by Errol Flynn at their first meeting what she wanted from life. "Respect for difficult work well done," had been her response. "You here tonight . . . have made me feel that, perhaps after all, I have achieved that young dream," de Havilland told the adoring audience.

Two years later, de Havilland received from President George W. Bush the National Medal of Arts, the United States' highest honor given to an individual artist. The medal celebrated "her persuasive and compelling skill as an actress in roles from Shakespeare's Hermia to Margaret Mitchell's Melanie. Her independence, integrity, and grace won creative freedom for herself and her fellow film actors."

Not to be outdone, de Havilland's adopted country awarded her its highest award, the French Legion of Honor, in 2010. French President

Nicolas Sarkozy praised her long, distinguished film career and said, "You honor France for having chosen us."

WHATEVER HAPPENED TO . . .

Thomas Mitchell (Gerald O'Hara)

- Had roles in *other* key 1939 films, including, *Mr. Smith Goes to Washington, Only Angels Have Wings, The Hunchback of Notre Dame*, and *Stagecoach*.
- Notable films following *GWTW*: *Our Town, This Above All, Tales of Manhattan, Immortal Sergeant, The Fighting Sullivans, Wilson, The Keys of the Kingdom, It's a Wonderful Life* (playing Uncle Billy), and *High Noon*.
- Entered the new medium of television in the 1950s and appeared in a range of roles in series such as *The Alcoa Hour, Playhouse 90, Kraft Theatre, Goodyear Theatre*, and *Zane Grey Theater*.
- Became the first person to win the Triple Crown of acting awards: He won the Best Supporting Actor Academy Award for *Stagecoach* in 1939, the Emmy Award for Lead Actor in a Drama for *The Doctor*, and the Tony Award for Best Actor in a Musical for *Hazel Flagg*, both in 1953.
- Continued his work in television with appearances in the thirty-nine-episode television series *Glencannon* and in films, including 1961's *Pocketful of Miracles*.
- Died on December 17, 1962, at the age of seventy.

Barbara O'Neil (Ellen O'Hara)

- Notable films after *GWTW*: *I Remember Mama, Whirlpool, Angel Face*, and *The Nun's Story*.
- For her role as Duchesse de Praslin in 1940's *All This, and Heaven Too*, she was nominated for an Academy Award for Best Supporting Actress.
- Was artist-in-residence at the University of Denver from 1958 to 1960.
- Retired from acting to live in Connecticut.
- Died on September 3, 1980, at the age of seventy.

Evelyn Keyes (Suellen O'Hara)

- Worked under contract with Columbia Pictures for eight years and had roles in *Here Comes Mr. Jordan, Ladies in Retirement, A Thousand and One Nights,* and *The Jolson Story.*
- Left Columbia to pursue film work on her own. Keyes captured roles in *Enchantment, Mrs. Mike, The Prowler, The Seven Year Itch,* and *Around the World in 80 Days.*
- Was married four times, to businessman Barton Bainbridge (1938–1940), director Charles Vidor (1943–1945), director/writer/producer/actor John Huston (1946–1950), and musician Artie Shaw (1957–1985). She was a companion to producer Mike Todd from 1950 to 1956, after which he left her for Elizabeth Taylor.
- Became an author in 1971 with the novel *I Am a Billboard.* The book detailed the efforts of a Southern actress to make it big in Hollywood.
- Starred with Don Ameche in the 1972 nationwide stage tour of *No, No, Nanette.*
- Wrote two autobiographies: *Scarlett O'Hara's Younger Sister* (1977), which detailed her marriages and love affairs, and *I'll Think about That Tomorrow* (1991), about her efforts to succeed as a performer, writer, and lover.
- Had occasional television roles in notable series such as *The Love Boat; Amazing Stories;* and *Murder, She Wrote.*
- Appeared in the 1988 documentary *The Making of a Legend:* Gone With the Wind and returned to Atlanta as an honored guest in 1989 for *GWTW*'s fiftieth anniversary.
- Died on July 4, 2008, at the age of ninety-one.

Ann Rutherford (Carreen O'Hara)

- Notable films after *GWTW: Pride and Prejudice, Orchestra Wives, The Secret Life of Walter Mitty,* and *The Adventures of Don Juan.*
- Played the on-screen girlfriend, Carol Lambert, of radio detective Wally "the Fox" Benton, played by comedian Red Skelton in the early 1940s series of mystery/comedies *Whistling in the Dark, Whistling in Dixie,* and *Whistling in Brooklyn.*
- Married (1942) and divorced (1953) David May II, the grandson of the founder of the May Company department stores. In 1953, she

married William Dozier, who would go on to create the *Batman* television series (1966–1968). He had been formerly married to Joan Fontaine, which made Rutherford stepmother to Olivia de Havilland's niece.

- Honored in 1960 with a star on the Hollywood Walk of Fame at 6834 Hollywood Blvd. for her work in motion pictures.
- Had a small role in 1972's *They Only Kill Their Masters* with June Allyson and Peter Lawford for MGM.
- Made television guest appearances on four episodes of *Perry Mason* and two episodes of *The Bob Newhart Show*. In the latter, she played Aggie Harrison, the mother of Emily Hartley (Suzanne Pleshette).
- Returned to Georgia as an honored guest for *GWTW*-related celebrations, including the film's fiftieth anniversary, the 2004 Margaret Mitchell Birthday commemoration in Jonesboro, and 2007's "The Heart and History of Hollywood" event at the Marietta *Gone With the Wind* Museum in Marietta.
- Died on June 11, 2012, at the age of ninety-four.

George Reeves (Stuart Tarleton)

- Notable films after *GWTW*: *So Proudly We Hail!*; *Winged Victory*; *From Here to Eternity*; and *Westward Ho, the Wagons!*
- Starred for the first time as Superman/Clark Kent in the 1951 film *Superman and the Mole Men*. That appearance led to the *Adventures of Superman* television series (1952–1958) and earned Reeves national celebrity—and typecasting—as the Man of Steel.
- Died of a gunshot wound to the head on June 16, 1959, at the age of forty-five in an incident that was officially ruled a suicide. The controversial circumstances of his death—was it suicide, an accident, or murder?—were explored in the 2006 film *Hollywoodland* starring Ben Affleck.

Fred Crane (Brent Tarleton)

- Notable work after *GWTW*: *The Gay Amigo*, a 1949 Cisco Kid film; TV roles on *Surfside 6*, *Lawman*, *Lost in Space*, *Peyton Place*, *Bonanza*, *77 Sunset Strip*, and *General Hospital*.

- Had a long career as a classical music announcer on the Los Angeles radio station KFAC until being fired, along with other older staff members, in 1987. He filed suit against the radio station for age discrimination and won.
- Worked at radio station KKGO, which featured jazz and classical music programming.
- With his fifth wife, Terry Lynn, bought an antebellum mansion south of Atlanta, Georgia, in 2000 and transformed the property into Tarleton Oaks, a bed and breakfast with an adjacent *GWTW* museum.
- Died on August 21, 2008, at the age of ninety.

Hattie McDaniel (Mammy)

- Notable films after *GWTW*: *In This Our Life* (playing with Olivia de Havilland), *Thank Your Lucky Stars*, *Since You Went Away*, and Walt Disney's *Song of the South*.
- Continued to make radio appearances and entered the world of television with her radio character "Beulah," but her career was stopped by cancer.
- Died on October 26, 1952, at the age of fifty-seven.
- Honored in 1960 with two stars on the Hollywood Walk of Fame: one at 6933 Hollywood Blvd. for her contributions to radio and one at 1719 Vine Street for her contributions to motion pictures.
- Inducted posthumously into the Black Filmmakers Hall of Fame in 1975.
- Profiled in the 2001 television documentary *Beyond Tara: The Extraordinary Life of Hattie McDaniel*, which won the 2001–2002 Daytime Emmy Award for Outstanding Special Class Special.
- Featured for the first time by Turner Classic Movies in its 2013 "Summer Under the Stars" showcase. McDaniel's films, including *GWTW*, were spotlighted for twenty-four hours on August 20.

Butterfly McQueen (Prissy)

- Notable films after *GWTW*: *Cabin in the Sky* (playing with Eddie Anderson), *Mildred Pierce*, and *Duel in the Sun*.

- Costarred in the early 1950s with Ethel Waters in the television series *Beulah*, playing Oriole, the scatterbrained friend of the title character.
- Had a brief run in 1969 with her own off-Broadway show, *McQueen and Friends*.
- Appeared in the film *Amazing Grace* in 1974.
- Honored by the Black Filmmakers Hall of Fame in 1975.
- Earned a Bachelor of Arts degree in Political Science from City College of New York in 1975 at the age of sixty-four.
- Played Aunt Thelma, a fairy godmother, in the 1978 ABC children's special *The Seven Wishes of Joanna Peabody* and won a Daytime Emmy Award for her performance. She reprised the role the following year in the ABC children's special *Seven Wishes of a Rich Kid*.
- Costarred with Harrison Ford in 1986's *The Mosquito Coast*.
- Divided her time between the Harlem area of New York City and Augusta, Georgia, where she was a community volunteer for civil rights and animal- and social-welfare causes.
- Attended the 1989 celebration of *GWTW*'s fiftieth anniversary in Atlanta as a guest of honor.
- Died on December 22, 1995, at the age of eighty-four from critical burns she received in a fire caused by a kerosene heater that destroyed her one-bedroom Augusta cottage.

Victor Jory (Jonas Wilkerson)

- Notable films after *GWTW*: *The Shadow*, *Tombstone: The Town Too Tough to Die*, *The Miracle Worker*, and *Papillon*.
- Played the lead role of a San Diego police detective, Howard Finucane, in the seventy-eight-episode syndicated television crime drama *Manhunt* (1959–1961).
- Recorded the narration for Atlanta's Cyclorama in 1967.
- Made guest appearances on episodes of television series, including *Kraft Theatre*, *Playhouse 90*, *Dr. Kildare*, *The Untouchables*, *Rawhide*, *Hawaiian Eye*, *Gunsmoke*, *Bonanza*, *F Troop*, *Ironside*, *The Virginian*, *McCloud*, and *The Rockford Files*.
- Died on February 12, 1982, at the age of seventy-nine.
- Honored in 1960 with a star on the Hollywood Walk of Fame at 6605 Hollywood Blvd. for his work in motion pictures.

Alicia Rhett (India Wilkes)

- Returned to South Carolina after *GWTW* and retired from filmmaking.
- Worked as a radio announcer at WTMA, Charleston's second-oldest AM radio station.
- Pursued the life of an artist. Volunteering her talents, she painted portraits of schoolchildren, laborers, and World War II servicemen.
- Became a professional portrait painter. Among her commissioned portrait subjects was nineteen-year-old Charleston native Alexandra Braid in 1953. In 1991, Braid would be known as Alexandra Ripley, the author of *Scarlett*, the sequel to *GWTW*.
- Was one of seven local Charleston artists that launched in 1953 the Charleston Artist Guild, an organization dedicated to the practice, teaching, and recognition of fine arts in Charleston.
- Retired to a quiet life in Charleston.
- Died on January 3, 2014, at the age of ninety-eight.

Rand Brooks (Charles Hamilton)

- Had roles in numerous films throughout the 1940s and 1950s, including *Northwest Passage*, *Cheers for Miss Bishop*, *Joan of Arc*, and *The Cimarron Kid*.
- Was Marilyn Monroe's first leading man in 1948's *Ladies of the Chorus* and gave the future film legend her first on-screen kiss.
- Played Hopalong Cassidy's sidekick, Lucky Jenkins, in the 1940's Western film series. When the films were nationally televised in 1952, he gained another audience of fans.
- Was married to Lois Laurel, the daughter of comedian Stan Laurel.
- Moved to guest roles in television Westerns such as *The Adventures of Wild Bill Hickok*, *The Roy Rogers Show*, *The Lone Ranger*, *Sky King*, *Maverick*, *Bat Masterson*, *Laramie*, *Gunsmoke*, *Bonanza*, and *The Virginian*. He costarred from 1954 to 1959 as Corporal Randy Boone in *The Adventures of Rin Tin Tin*.
- Returned to the screen in the 1960s for roles in the Westerns *Comanche Station*, *Stagecoach to Dancer's Rock*, and *Requiem for a Gunfighter*.

- Started an ambulance service in Glendale, California, in 1966 that he and his wife, Lois, grew into the largest private ambulance company in Los Angeles County. Within a decade, the award-winning firm was considered one of the finest paramedic services in the country.
- Phased out his acting career in the mid-1970s because of the success of his ambulance business.
- Attended the 1989 celebration of *GWTW*'s fiftieth anniversary in Atlanta as a guest of honor. With tears, he read a letter sent by Olivia de Havilland for the occasion in which she sent Brooks "my fond eternal greetings to the sole representative of the Hamilton clan."
- Sold his ambulance company in 1994 and retired to his Santa Barbara County ranch, where he and his second wife, Hermine, bred champion Andalusian horses.
- Died on September 1, 2003, at the age of eighty-four.

Carroll Nye (Frank Kennedy)

- Had roles in only four films after *GWTW*, three of which were uncredited, bringing to an end his sixty-film acting career.
- Became the radio editor at the *Los Angeles Times*.
- Died on March 17, 1974, at the age of seventy-two.

Laura Hope Crews (Aunt Pittypat)

- Notable films after *GWTW*: *The Hunchback of Notre Dame*, *One Foot in Heaven*, and *The Man Who Came to Dinner*.
- Accepted the role of Abby Brewster in Broadway's *Arsenic and Old Lace* in June 1942 but was forced to leave the production after being stricken with a kidney ailment in October 1942.
- Died on November 13, 1942, at the age of sixty-two.
- Honored in 1960 with a star on the Hollywood Walk of Fame at 6251 Hollywood Blvd. for her work in motion pictures.

Eddie Anderson (Uncle Peter)

- Notable films after *GWTW*: *Kiss the Boys Goodbye*; *Cabin in the Sky*; and *It's a Mad, Mad, Mad, Mad World*.

- Took his "Rochester" character from radio to television in the 1950s on *The Jack Benny Show*. His character remained a staple during the decade the show was on the air. He reprised the character for several Jack Benny specials.
- Honored in 1960 for his work in radio with a star on the Hollywood Walk of Fame at 6513 Hollywood Blvd.
- Appeared in episodes of television series such as *Bachelor Father*; *The Dick Powell Show*; *It Takes a Thief*; and *Love, American Style*.
- Voiced cartoon characters in the 1970s television series *Harlem Globe Trotters* and *The New Scooby-Doo Movies*.
- Honored by the Black Filmmakers Hall of Fame in 1975.
- Died on February 28, 1977, at the age of seventy-one.

Harry Davenport (Dr. Meade)

- Notable films after *GWTW*: *The Ox-Bow Incident*; *All This, and Heaven Too*; *Foreign Correspondent*; and *Meet Me in St. Louis*.
- Was active professionally right up to his death on August 9, 1949, at the age of eighty-three. His acting career spanned seventy-eight years.

Jane Darwell (Dolly Merriwether)

- Among her more than 170 film credits were roles in *Huckleberry Finn*, *Jesse James*, *The Devil and Daniel Webster*, *The Ox-Bow Incident*, *My Darling Clementine*, and six Shirley Temple movies.
- Won an Academy Award for Best Supporting Actress for her portrayal of Ma Joad in 1940's *The Grapes of Wrath*, a role that star Henry Fonda had insisted be given to Darwell.
- Guest starred on episodes of 1950s and 1960s television series such as *The Loretta Young Show*, *The Pepsi-Cola Playhouse*, *Studio 57*, *Playhouse 90*, *The Real McCoys*, and *Wagon Train*.
- Honored in 1960 with a star on the Hollywood Walk of Fame at 6735 Hollywood Blvd. for her work in motion pictures.
- Appeared last as the Bird Woman in the "Feed the Birds" sequence in 1964's *Mary Poppins*. Walt Disney personally selected and persuaded Darwell to accept the role.
- Died on August 13, 1967, at the age of eighty-seven.

Ona Munson (Belle Watling)

- Accepted supporting roles in film Westerns and dramas such as *Wagons Westward, Lady from Louisiana, The Cheaters, Dakota*, and *The Red House*.
- Played the Chinese dragon lady "Mother" Gin Sling in Josef von Sternberg's *The Shanghai Gesture*, starring Gene Tierney, Walter Huston, and Victor Mature. But the 1941 film and Munson's performance were panned by the critics.
- Made guest appearances in the television series *Broadway Television Theatre, Martin Kane*, and *Armstrong Circle Theatre* in the early 1950s.
- Ended her life with an overdose of sleeping pills on February 11, 1955, at the age of fifty-one.
- Honored in 1960 with a star on the Hollywood Walk of Fame at 6250 Hollywood Blvd. for her work in motion pictures.

Ward Bond (Tom, a Yankee Captain)

- Had supporting roles in more than two hundred movies, including *It Happened One Night* (with Clark Gable), *Bringing Up Baby, Drums Along the Mohawk, The Grapes of Wrath, The Maltese Falcon, Sergeant York, A Guy Named Joe, It's a Wonderful Life* (with Thomas Mitchell), as well as in twenty-three John Wayne films.
- Moved into television where, from 1957 to 1960, he starred as Major Seth Adams the wagon master on the series *Wagon Train*.
- Died on November 5, 1960, at the age of fifty-seven.

SEE WHAT A SMALL PART CAN DO FOR YOU

Most of **Mary Anderson**'s portrayal of Maybelle Merriwether ended up on the cutting-room floor. She is seen blushing briefly as her escort bids for her at the Atlanta Bazaar. But her screen career was launched with her *GWTW* appearance. She found roles in *All This, and Heaven Too* and *Cheers for Miss Bishop*. Her part in Broadway's *Guest in the House* led to a contract with Twentieth Century Fox and impressive roles in *The Song of Bernadette*,

Lifeboat, and *Wilson*. In 1946, she starred with Olivia de Havilland in *To Each His Own*. The Alabama native made guest appearances on television series in the 1950s and 1960s and was best known for playing Catherine Peyton Harrington in the series *Peyton Place*. She died on April 6, 2014, at the age of ninety-six.

Cliff Edwards played a Reminiscent Soldier in the Shadow Scene in the Atlanta church-turned-hospital. Audiences never saw him; they only heard his sad story. The Missouri native sang and played the ukulele in vaudeville; was a successful recording artist; and performed on radio, in movies, and on television. His film career began at MGM in 1929 after producer Irving Thalberg heard Edwards playing at the Orpheum Theater in Los Angeles and hired him for early sound movies. Edwards is best known for his recording of "Ja Da" and for "Singin' in the Rain," a song he performed in *The Hollywood Revue of 1929*. His other film credits include *So This Is College*, *Saratoga* (in which he sang with Clark Gable and Hattie McDaniel), *Maisie*, and *His Girl Friday*. But his best-remembered role was actually a famous voice: Jiminy Cricket in Walt Disney's *Pinocchio*. During the film, Edwards sang "When You Wish Upon a Star," which won the Academy Award for Best Original Song in 1940. Edwards died on July 17, 1971, at the age of seventy-six.

Olin Howland played the Yankee businessman who greets Scarlett outside the Wilkes and Kennedy store and remarks that "Business is certainly growing, ain't it?" The fifty-year acting career of Colorado-born Howland included appearances on the Broadway stage from 1909 to 1928, in silent and sound films from 1918 to 1958, and on television from 1952 to 1959. His notable films include *Angel and the Badman* (1947), *Them!* (1954), *The Spirit of St. Louis* (1957), and *The Blob* (1958). On the small screen, Howland is remembered as the character Charley Perkins, who appeared in five episodes of the ABC sitcom *The Real McCoys*, starring Walter Brennan, in 1958 and 1959. Howland died on September 20, 1959, at the age of seventy-three.

Isabel Jewell, who played Emmy Slattery, had only one scene in the second part of the film (when she and husband Jonas Wilkerson pay a call at Tara) and only one line of dialogue ("Yes, it's me). The role just seemed larger because of the talk about Emmy's white-trash ways in part one of the movie.

The Wyoming-born actress seemed destined for small roles. Her pre-*GWTW* film work included supporting roles in thirty-nine films. She was the innocent seamstress who accompanies Ronald Colman to the guillotine in *A Tale of Two Cities* in 1935 and played Gloria Stone, a lady of the evening, in 1937's *Lost Horizon*. Post-*GWTW* film work included supporting parts in *Northwest Passage, High Sierra, The Bishop's Wife* (she was the hysterical mother whose runaway baby carriage Cary Grant rescues), and *The Snake Pit*. She accepted sporadic roles on television series in the 1950s and 1960s. Despite being honored in 1960 with a star on the Hollywood Walk of Fame (1560 Vine Street) for her work in motion pictures, Jewell's career declined.

Hard times hit in her personal life as well. Jewell ran afoul of the law in 1959 when she was arrested for passing bad checks in Las Vegas. In 1961, she was arrested for drunk driving and sentenced to a five-day jail term and a year's probation. She died on April 5, 1972, at the age of sixty-four.

Marjorie Reynolds's part as a guest at Twelve Oaks was so small she was seen coming down the staircase with Melanie and India but said her one line of dialogue ("Well, men may flirt with girls like that, but they don't marry them") off camera. Larger roles awaited her, though, such as playing opposite Bing Crosby and Fred Astaire in *Holiday Inn*. Her other films included *Star Spangled Rhythm, Dixie, Ministry of Fear, Duffy's Tavern, The Time of Their Lives* (with Abbott and Costello), *That Midnight Kiss*, and *Home Town Story*. But Idaho-born Reynolds found greater fame in television. In 1953, she began a five-year stint playing unflappable Peg Riley opposite William Bendix in *The Life of Riley*. She was honored for her work in television in 1960 with a star on the Hollywood Walk of Fame at 1525 Vine Street. She died on February 1, 1997, at the age of seventy-nine.

WHAT A CHARACTER!

Oscar Polk, who played Pork, the O'Hara's house servant, debuted on Broadway in the 1927 original melodrama *The Trial of Mary Dugan*. He secured roles in fourteen other Broadway productions from 1929 to 1943, including *Face the Music*, the 1932 Moss Hart–Irving Berlin musical-comedy collaboration; *The Green Pastures*, the 1935 musical play that retold Old Testament stories through African American perspectives; and *Swingin' the Dream*, the 1939 musical comedy that included cast mate Butterfly McQueen. Polk reprised his role of Gabriel in the 1936 film version of *The*

Green Pastures, which featured Eddie "Rochester" Anderson in the part of Noah.

After *GWTW*, Polk's film career continued, most notably with 1942's *Reap the Wild Wind*, in which he played the character Salt Meat, and 1943's *Cabin in the Sky*, in which he played dual characters, Deacon and Fleetwood, in the all–African American musical.

He was scheduled to begin a major role in the play *Leading Lady* when he stepped off a curb in New York City's Times Square and was fatally struck by a taxicab. Polk died on January 4, 1949, at the age of forty-nine.

Everett Brown, who played Tara's foreman and Scarlett's Shantytown rescuer Big Sam, began acting in 1927, playing Nahalo in *South Sea Love*. Most other film roles throughout his twenty-six-year career had him typecast as natives or slaves. Look for him in *The Mask of Fu Manchu* (1932); *I Am a Fugitive from a Chain Gang* (1932); *Jungle Jim* (1936); *Nothing Sacred* (1937), playing a policeman; and *Boys Town* (1938). The last of his forty films was *White Witch Doctor* in 1953. Brown died on October 14, 1953, at the age of fifty-one.

Howard C. Hickman was a veteran stage actor, director, screenwriter, and motion picture character actor by the time he was tapped to play John Wilkes in *GWTW*. He had pre-*GWTW* roles in more than two hundred films, including *Twentieth Century* (1934), *Libeled Lady* (1936), and *May Time* (1937).

After *GWTW*, Hickman appeared in sixty-six films, including *Boom Town* (1940), which reunited him with Clark Gable; *Strike Up the Band* (1940); and *Cheers for Miss Bishop* (1941), which reunited him with Mary Anderson, Rand Brooks, and William Bakewell. Hickman died on December 31, 1949, at the age of sixty-nine.

Leona Roberts brought a wealth of acting experience to the role of Mrs. Meade. In 1926, she debuted both in the original Broadway play *Saturday Night* and in her first feature film, starring in the lead role of *Poor Mrs. Jones*. Settling into supporting roles, Roberts appeared in thirty Broadway productions from 1926 to 1937, and then Hollywood beckoned. She had character roles in twenty-five films, most notably Sister Clarke in *Of Human Hearts* (1938), house servant Mrs. Hannah Gogarty in *Bringing Up Baby* (1938), and Caroline Meade in *GWTW*.

After *GWTW*, Roberts had supporting roles in four Broadway plays and nineteen films, including 1940's *The Blue Bird*, which reunited her with Laura Hope Crews. Roberts's last film was 1949's *Chicago Deadline*. She died on January 29, 1954, at the age of seventy-four.

Paul Hurst played the Yankee deserter and Tara trespasser whom Scarlett shoots in self-defense. Multitalented Hurst was a silent film screenwriter and director and character actor in hundreds of silent and sound films from 1912 to 1953. The California native is best remembered for his *GWTW* role and for the part of Monty Smith, the drunken, sadistic vigilante in 1943's *The Ox-Bow Incident*. After appearing as Frederick Carson, the cantankerous old rancher in *Angel and the Badman* (1947), Hurst was signed by Republic Pictures to play the comic sidekick to singing cowboy Monte Hale in a series of Westerns. Diagnosed with terminal cancer in late 1952, Hurst ended his life on February 27, 1953, at the age of sixty-four.

J. M. Kerrigan was an Irish character actor known for playing menacing types such as the purveyor of Scarlett's mill hands, Johnnie Gallegher, who demanded "no questions and no interference." Dublin-born Kerrigan had a long acting career that included Broadway productions from 1908 to 1947, silent and sound films from 1916 to 1956, and guest appearances on television series from 1954 to 1960. Among his post-*GWTW* films were *The Wolf Man* (1941), *Call Northside 777* (1948), and *20,000 Leagues Under the Sea* (1954). Kerrigan was honored in 1960 for his work in film with a star on the Hollywood Walk of Fame at 6621 Hollywood Blvd. He died on April 29, 1964, at the age of seventy-nine.

Jackie Moran played Phil, the son of Dr. and Mrs. Meade. After learning that his brother Darcy has been killed, Phil tells his mother he's going to enlist, only to be hushed by Melanie, who declares she's "never heard of anything so silly." John E. Moran was discovered by actress Mary Pickford, who persuaded his mother to take the twelve-year-old to Hollywood in 1935 for a screen test. That led to a name change—Jackie Moran—and to his first supporting role in 1936's *And So They Were Married*. He came to the attention of David O. Selznick, who cast him as Huckleberry Finn in *The Adventures of Tom Sawyer* (1938), a costarring role that made Illinois-born Moran a popular teenage star. He also costarred in 1939's *Buck Rogers*, in which he played Buster Crabbe's buddy, George Wade.

Selznick cast Moran as a grocer's son in *Since You Went Away* (1944), a small yet memorable part that marked the end of dramatic roles for the twenty-one-year-old. A string of teenage musical comedies followed from 1945 to 1946, and Moran aged out of film work. He returned to his home state and worked in public relations for the Chicago Roman Catholic Archdiocese. He died on September 20, 1990, at the age of sixty-seven.

Lillian Kemble-Cooper was best known for playing Bonnie's London nurse and brought an impressive theatrical pedigree to the role. The London-born actress was a member of the renowned Kemble family, the thespian dynasty that began in England in the late eighteenth century. She was the daughter of stage actor Frank Kemble-Cooper and the sister of Anthony, Greta, and Violet Kemble-Cooper.

Following her Broadway debut in 1906's *The Man of the Hour*, she earned roles in seventeen other stage productions from 1917 to 1949, including the original *Hitchy-Koo*, Cole Porter's 1919 musical revue. She appeared in twenty films from 1916 to 1964 and made guest appearances in eight television series from 1956 to 1960. In her last film, *My Fair Lady*, she was uncredited in the role of Lady Ambassador. Kemble-Cooper died on May 4, 1977, at the age of eighty-five.

Marcella Martin as Cathleen Calvert warns Scarlett about Rhett's "most terrible reputation" on the morning of the Twelve Oaks barbecue. Max Arnow, one of Selznick's talent scouts, discovered Illinois native Elsie Marcella Clifford Martin during the final search for Southern talent. Arnow reported to Selznick in a November 16, 1938, memo that "The results of the eighteen day trip through the South were quite meager with one exception. In Louisiana, at the Shreveport Little Theatre, ran across a girl by the name of Marcella Martin. This girl is quite good looking, has a nice figure, and is a grand actress. Without doubt she is the best of the hundreds of people that I interviewed during my trip." Although she originally tested for Scarlett, Martin was cast in the supporting role of Cathleen Calvert.

After *GWTW*, Martin appeared as Carol Barnet in *West of Tombstone* (1942), as Daphne Turner in *The Man Who Returned to Life* (1942), and as Steffa Wertbowsky in *Voyage to the End of the Universe* (1964). In 1969, she made one guest appearance, playing Ruth Collier, on the television series *The F.B.I.*, which starred Efrem Zimbalist Jr. Martin died on October 31, 1986, at the age of seventy.

Irving Bacon played the Yankee Corporal who escorts Scarlett to Rhett's Atlanta jail cell. As a character actor, Missouri-born Bacon excelled at portraying a range of service professionals from bartenders, butlers, and chauffeurs to doctors, photographers, and reporters in nearly five hundred silent and sound films from 1915 to 1958 and on more than thirty television programs from 1950 to 1965. Bacon's bits included the gas station attendant in *It Happened One Night* (1934) who trades a fill-up for Peter (Clark Gable) Warne's hat, the long-suffering mailman in the *Blondie* film series from 1938 to 1943, and the frustrated railroad information clerk in the all-star Hollywood spoof *It's a Great Feeling* (1949). His television roles included Mr. Townsend, Roberta's father, on the series *My Little Margie* (1954–1955); Will Potter, Ethel Mertz's father, on one episode of *I Love Lucy* (1955); and Howard Anderson on one episode of *The Real McCoys* (1958). Bacon died on February 5, 1965, at the age of seventy-one.

William Bakewell played the Confederate cavalry officer Scarlett stops on Peachtree Street who confirms that the Yankees are coming and advises her to "Better refugee South—right quick, ma'am." Los Angeles–born Bakewell started his film career at the age of sixteen as an extra in 1924's *Fighting Blood*. That led to larger roles and memorable performances as Louis XIV and his twin brother in *The Iron Mask* (1929); as Wally in *Gold Diggers of Broadway* (1929); as Albert in *All Quiet on the Western Front* (1930); and as Rodney in *Dance, Fools, Dance* (1931).

His post-*GWTW* films included *Hop Harrigan* (1943), *The Farmer's Daughter* (1947), and *The Bachelor and the Bobby-Soxer* (1947). From the 1950s through the 1970s, he made guest appearances on television series such as *The Cisco Kid*, *Sky King*, *Lassie*, *Leave It to Beaver*, *Mr. Ed*, *That Girl*, *Green Acres*, and *Nanny and the Professor*. He was best known for playing Major Tobias Norton on the popular Disney series *Davy Crockett* (1954–1955).

In 1991, Bakewell published a book, *Hollywood Be Thy Name: Random Recollections of a Movie Veteran from Silents to Talkies to TV*, in which he shared details from a career spanning 118 films and seventy television shows. Bakewell died on April 15, 1993, at the age of eighty-four.

Eric Linden played the Confederate soldier in the Atlanta hospital who learns that his gangrenous leg must be amputated. Linden was born in New York City to parents of Swedish descent. His father had been an actor with Stockholm's Theater Royal. With an early aptitude for acting, handsome, fair-haired Linden was accepted for membership in New York's Theatre Guild and appeared in several guild productions before debuting on Broadway in 1928.

His acting chops drew the attention of film director Wesley Ruggles, who signed Linden to an RKO contract and cast him as Eddie Brand, the lead role in the 1931 crime drama *Are These Our Children?* Other roles followed in the 1930s for the twenty-two-year-old actor RKO promoted as "The Boy Sensation of the Theatre Guild," including *The Crowd Roars*; *The Age of Consent*; *The Past of Mary Holmes*; *Sweepings*; *The Silver Cord* with Laura Hope Crews; and *Ah, Wilderness!*

In the late 1930s, Linden had fewer good roles and, after appearing in *GWTW*, made only one other film, 1941's *Criminals Within*. He left motion pictures and returned to the stage, but his theater work was interrupted by military service during World War II. After his return from war, the only battle he couldn't win was restarting his career. He abandoned acting for a municipal job in Orange County, California. Linden died on July 14, 1994, at the age of eighty-four.

Yakima Canutt doubled for Clark Gable during the burning of the Atlanta depot sequence and played the renegade who accosts Scarlett on the Shantytown bridge. Enos Edward "Yakima" Canutt was one of Hollywood's most celebrated pioneer stuntmen.

Colfax-born Canutt learned the arts of riding, roping, and shooting while growing up on his family's eastern Washington ranch. In 1912, at the age of seventeen, he won the title of "World's Best Bronco Buster" at the Whitman County Fair in Colfax and thereafter turned to rodeo riding professionally. While competing in the 1914 Pendleton Round-Up in Pendleton, Oregon, he was misidentified in a newspaper caption as "The Cowboy from Yakima," even though he was from Colfax. The nickname "Yakima" stuck, and friends called him "Yak."

Bronco riding, steer wrestling, and roping were among the specialties that won world championships and fame for Canutt as he traveled the rodeo circuit. While in Los Angeles for a rodeo, Canutt met Tom Mix, who recruited him as a cowboy extra for 1915's silent short *Foreman of Bar Z Ranch*, which began his film career. Canutt balanced playing the rodeo circuit with stunting and acting, usually as the heavy, in silent and sound films.

He adapted rodeo techniques to stunt work and innovated safe, foolproof stunts for Western staples such as horse falls, wagon crashes, cattle stampedes, covered-wagon races, cavalry battles, and drops from stagecoaches. As stunt coordinator, he executed and doubled for John Wayne in the famous stagecoach drop sequence in 1939's *Stagecoach*.

After sustaining serious injuries in *Boom Town* (1940) and *In Old Oklahoma* (1943), he retired from stunt work and became a second-unit director, filming stunts and action sequences not involving principal actors. His most famous achievement in that role was the staging and direction of the spectacular chariot-race sequence in 1959's *Ben-Hur*, for which Canutt won a special citation from the National Board of Review. Other accolades followed.

In 1967, he was given an Honorary Academy Award "for achievements as a stunt man and for developing safety devices to protect stunt men everywhere." He won the Western Heritage Trustees Award in 1971 "for more than 50 years of outstanding contributions to motion pictures," was inducted into the National Cowboy & Western Heritage Museum in 1975, and in 1984 won the Golden Boot Award that honors achievement in Western television and movies. In 1985, he was honored for his work in motion pictures with a star on the Hollywood Walk of Fame at 1500 Vine Street.

Cannutt's legacy includes 246 credits for stunt work from 1915 to 1975, 186 credits for acting from 1919 to 1985, 57 credits for second-unit directing from 1931 to 1975, 15 credits for directing from 1935 to 1966, five credits for producing from 1925 to 1926, four credits for writing from 1925 to 1932, and one credit for production manager for 1965's *Cat Ballou*. Cannutt died on May 24, 1986, at the age of ninety.

Louis Jean Heydt played the hungry Confederate soldier who befriends Beau on Tara's back porch and brings Melanie news that Ashley had been captured. News was Heydt's initial career—he worked as a reporter for the *New York World*—and led to his first theatrical role. He visited a friend during rehearsals for *The Trial of Mary Dugan*, was introduced to the producers, who needed to cast the reporter role in the production, and won the part. (Among the other players was Oscar Polk.)

In subsequent appearances in eleven Broadway productions from 1929 to 1948 and in 166 appearances in movies and television from 1933 to 1960, Heydt mastered the character of the hapless, timid, or down-on-his-luck everyman. His post-*GWTW* films included *The Great McGinty* (1940), *Thirty Seconds Over Tokyo* (1944), and *The Big Sleep* (1946).

On January 29, 1960, Heydt was performing in the play *There Was a Little Girl* opposite Jane Fonda at Boston's Colonial Theatre. After completing the first scene, he left the stage and collapsed, dying instantly of a heart attack at the age of fifty-six.

Robert Elliott portrayed the Yankee Major playing poker with Rhett when his "sister" Scarlett arrives at the Atlanta jail for a visit. Ohio-born Elliott debuted on Broadway in 1900 and appeared in three other productions over the next twenty-four years. He became a silent-screen leading man following his film debut in 1916's *The Kiss of Hate* with Ethel Barrymore. After the transition to talkies, Elliott was consigned to supporting roles in films such as *The Divorcee* (1930), *The Finger Points* (1931) with Clark Gable, *The Maltese Falcon* (1931), and *The Roaring Twenties* (1939). He was often cast as a policeman, detective, or military officer. Elliott died on November 15, 1951, at the age of seventy-two.

Frank "Junior" Coghlan played the young collapsing soldier on the retreat from Atlanta. Connecticut-born Coghlan appeared as an extra in his first film, 1920's *Daredevil Jack*, at the age of three. In the 1920s and 1930s, mop-topped, freckled-faced Coghlan was one of the most sought after child actors for shorts and feature films. He made an easy transition to sound films, with notable appearances in *The Public Enemy* (1931), *Hell's House* (1932), and *The Last of the Mohicans* (1932). His post-*GWTW* work included his best-known role, Billy Batson in the twelve-episode serial *Adventures of Captain Marvel* (1941).

During World War II, Coghlan served as an aviator for the U.S. Navy. After the war, he continued his naval career with assignments in the 1950s and 1960s that included liaison and technical advisor on Hollywood films such as *The Caine Mutiny*, *The Bridges at Toko-Ri*, *Mister Roberts*, *PT 109*, and *In Harm's Way*. Coghlan retired in 1965 with the rank of lieutenant commander.

He resumed his acting career with roles in films such as *The Sand Pebbles* (1966) and *Valley of the Dolls* (1967) and on television series such as *The Beverly Hillbillies* (1965) and *Dragnet* (1966). His last role was a 1974 cameo appearance in one episode of *Shazam!*, the television series based on DC Comics' superhero Captain Marvel. In 1993, Coghlan published his autobiography, *They Still Call Me Junior*. He died on September 7, 2009, at the age of ninety-three.

OH, YOU KID! *GWTW*'S CHILD PLAYERS

Kids Who Played Bonnie Blue Butler

Kelly Griffin, at two weeks of age, played Bonnie as a newborn. Griffin's father was fountain manager in Schwab's Drug Store, located at 8024 Sunset Boulevard, a popular Hollywood haunt for those in the movie industry. Griffin's mother—pregnant with her at the time—was in the right place at the right time. Someone from Selznick International Pictures came into Schwab's, greeted the Griffins, and noted Mrs. Griffin's condition. The SIP rep explained about the need to cast a baby for *GWTW* and inquired delicately about the mother-to-be's due date. After some quick calculations that the baby would be the right age at the time of filming, a deal was made on the spot. Following her brief screen debut, Kelly Griffin returned to private life.

Julia Ann Tuck was seven months old when she played Bonnie at six months of age. Tuck appears in the scene during which a sour Scarlett and a resolute Rhett wheel their daughter in a toy-horse-drawn baby carriage, with Bonnie clutching the reins, on Peachtree Street, greeting members of Atlanta's Old Guard. To make her coo for the camera, director Victor Fleming smiled, walked backward, and waved his handkerchief at the baby, who laughed at his antics. Following her film debut, playing younger than her age, Julia Ann Tuck returned to private life.

Phyllis Callow was cast to play Bonnie at age two for the scene in which Rhett on horseback asks Mrs. Merriwether for advice on how to get Bonnie to stop sucking her thumb. Los Angeles–born Callow was the two-year-old daughter of *GWTW*'s second assistant director, Ridgeway Callow, and his wife, Margaret Watts, a Ziegfeld girl and socialite.

After her *GWTW* debut, Callow appeared in supporting roles in twelve films from 1948 to 1971, including uncredited parts in *Raintree County* (1957) and *Andy Hardy Comes Home* (1958). On television, she appeared in two episodes of *Batman* (1967), both times as Josie. In two episodes of *Star Trek*, she appeared first as Yeoman Mears in "The Galileo Seven" (1967) and then in an uncredited part in "The Way to Eden" (1969).

After leaving the entertainment industry, where she was known professionally as Phyllis Douglas, she worked for more than three decades as a real estate broker in California. She married and divorced Macgregor Douglas, then married Robert B. Boyce. Her family included a son and two daughters. Phyllis (Callow) Boyce died on May 12, 2010, at the age of seventy-three.

Cammie King was the best known of the child players who portrayed Rhett and Scarlett's daughter. Los Angeles–born Eleanore Cammack "Cammie" King first appeared on film in the uncredited role of Millie in *Blondie Meets the Boss*, released in March 1939. After *GWTW*, King was the voice of Young Faline, the female fawn and future mate of *Bambi* (1942). "I peaked in show business at the age of five," she said. "Imagine being in two classics and never doing another thing after that."

Since she was only four when she performed in *GWTW*, the adult King's memories of making the film were like "snapshots," she said. She recalled Clark Gable as "such a warm, friendly man. When he kissed me, his mustache tickled. I'd tell that to my mother's friends and they'd swoon." Between scenes, Gable chatted and played games with her. During scenes, he was protective of her. Too many takes of a scene prompted him to say, "Come on, fellows. Let's wrap it up—the baby is tired."

By contrast, Vivien Leigh's high stress during filming charged the atmosphere on the set for King. In the scene when Bonnie returns from London and runs up the stairs to greet her mother, King was certain that viewers looking closely "can see a little hysteria in my eyes."

King even had an incident with Victor Fleming. Her mother rehearsed dialogue with her so King would be ready for her scenes. But one day during filming King acted the role of brat and flubbed her lines repeatedly. So the director knelt down and looked her in the eye. He explained patiently that he, the actors, and crew members had children like her at home. Working on the film allowed the grown-ups to feed their little boys and girls. If she didn't know her lines, the daddies and mommies would have no work to do. Then they wouldn't be able to take care of their children. Embarrassment etched that memory in her mind. "I never forgot another line," she said.

She remembered liking her pony and her blue riding habit. She also recalled her confusion at seeing on the set a girl her size smoking a cigarette and wearing an identical riding costume. The little girl turned out to be a little person—a thirty-five-year-old stuntman—about to enact Bonnie's fatal pony ride.

For the next scene, King was instructed to lie on the ground and pretend to be dead. But each time Gable picked her up, her eyelids fluttered, ruining the takes. The problem was solved by making a mold of her face—a process that frightened her to tears—and creating a death mask that she wore during the scene.

Because her mother wanted her to have a normal childhood, King retired from film work at the age of eight. She grew up and went to school with Judy Lewis (Clark Gable's biological child with Loretta Young), who became a close friend. King graduated in 1956 from the University of Southern California with a bachelor's degree in communications. She worked as a production assistant on the CBS-TV anthology series *Climax!* She married Walter Ned Pollock in 1957, raised a son and daughter, and was widowed in 1968. She married Michael W. Conlon in 1971, but they divorced in 1976.

After a 1980 move to Mendocino County, King worked as a museum director, as a publicist for an inn, and as a marketing coordinator for a chamber of commerce. She attended the 1989 celebration of *GWTW*'s fiftieth anniversary in Atlanta as a guest of honor.

She used her *GWTW* celebrity to promote good causes and hosted Bonnie Blue Butler tea parties as fund-raisers. In 2009, she published a book *Bonnie Blue Butler: A* Gone With the Wind *Memoir* under the name Cammie King Conlon. She died on September 1, 2010, at the age of seventy-six.

Kids Who Played Beau Wilkes

John Joseph Waterman Jr. was one of several newborns cast to appear as the infant son of Ashley and Melanie Wilkes. Beau makes five newborn appearances in the film: when Scarlett hands the blanket-wrapped baby to Prissy before leaving Aunt Pittypat's house, when Prissy places Beau into Melanie's arms as she lies in the wagon, when Melanie clutches Beau to her as the looters attack the wagon, when Melanie pulls Beau close after the horse refuses to move into the fiery boxcar area, and when Beau cries and Melanie shades his eyes as the wagon rolls through the battlefield on the way to Tara. Following his screen debut in *GWTW*, Waterman returned to private life.

Ricky Holt was cast to play eleven-month-old Beau, who makes friends with the hungry Confederate soldier on Tara's back porch. Rehearsals for the scene did not include one-year-old Holt because director Victor Fleming feared tiring out the tyke. But when the cameras rolled, the toddler cried prematurely. Fleming shot the scene four times with the same result. The director sat down on the porch with Holt to soothe him and even asked for orange juice in case the child was thirsty. Then Fleming had a brainstorm. He gave Holt a wooden spoon to play with during the scene and captured an endearing image of baby Beau helping a soldier eat his meager meal.

Richard "Ric" Arlen Holt was born in Studio City, California, to an acting family that included his older siblings, David and Betty. After high school and then service in the Air Force, Holt appeared in several commercials before leaving the entertainment industry for a career with Gulf Oil. From 1964 to 1975, Holt was married to Peggy Goldwater, daughter of Arizona Senator Barry Goldwater. In the early 1980s, Holt moved to southern Oregon, where he busied himself with ranching and politics. He attended the 1989 celebration of *GWTW*'s fiftieth anniversary in Atlanta as a guest of honor.

The following year, he was elected commissioner in Jackson County and served for twelve years. After leaving public service in 2002, Holt returned to private life.

Patrick Curtis was about nine months old when he appeared as baby Beau in Melanie's arms during the war-is-over sequence. Since his screen debut, Curtis grew up to be a film producer who met and made Raquel Welch an international star. They married in 1967 and divorced in 1972. Curtis attended the 1989 celebration of *GWTW*'s fiftieth anniversary in Atlanta as a guest of honor.

Mickey Kuhn was an experienced child actor when he was selected to portray Ashley and Melanie's son. Early film roles for Illinois-born Theodore Matthew Michael Kuhn Jr. were uncredited in *Change of Heart* (1934), *A Doctor's Diary* (1937), and three films in 1939: *King of the Underworld*, *S.O.S. Tidal Wave*, and *Bad Little Angel*. But Hollywood's Golden Year also brought Kuhn rich roles in films with Hollywood royalty. He played Crown Prince Augustin in *Juarez*, starring Paul Muni and Bette Davis; the boy in *When Tomorrow Comes*, starring Irene Dunne and Charles Boyer; and capped off the year with the role of Beau Wilkes in *GWTW*.

When he and his mother arrived for his interview at the Culver City casting office for Selznick's epic, Kuhn's reputation for always knowing his lines and being easy to direct preceded him. After he gave his name to the receptionist, she announced to the more than sixty other juveniles in the room that the part of Beau had been cast.

Six-year-old Kuhn was known for his ability to complete a scene in one take. One of the few exceptions was the scene with Cammie King and Clark Gable in Bonnie's nursery, during which Kuhn had a single line: "Hello, Uncle Rhett." During the first take, Kuhn greeted Gable with "Hello, Uncle Clark." Kuhn made the same mistake during the second take. "This was unheard of for me, and I was really embarrassed," Kuhn said. "That was when Clark Gable took me to one side and said, 'You're right. I am Uncle Clark, but in the movie I'm Uncle Rhett. Okay?' The third take got it."

Kuhn nailed the scene of Melanie's death thanks to help from Victor Fleming. Before shooting the scene, Fleming spoke privately to the young actor: "You know, it's a very sad day. Your mother is dying. How would you feel if your mother was dying? She's dying, and she's very, very sick." That turned on the waterworks. Fleming handed the sobbing boy to Leslie Howard, and they did the heartbreaking scene in one take. Afterward, Fleming comforted Kuhn before bringing him back to his mother.

Kuhn's post-*GWTW* film work included roles in twenty-three films from 1940 to 1956. Most notably, he portrayed Junior in *Dick Tracy* (1945), Walter as a boy in *The Strange Love of Martha Ivers* (1946), and Matt as a boy in *Red River* (1948). Kuhn had a small role in 1951's *A Streetcar Named Desire*, which reunited him with Vivien Leigh. In the film's beginning, Kuhn was the sailor who helped Leigh's character Blanche DuBois board the correct New Orleans streetcar for her destination.

In real life, Kuhn joined the navy in 1951 and served in naval aviation as an aircraft electrician until his discharge in 1955. He resumed his acting career with uncredited film roles. He also appeared in three 1957 episodes of the television series *Alfred Hitchcock Presents.*

After leaving the entertainment industry, Kuhn was employed by American Airlines from 1965 to 1995 when he retired. He and his second wife, Barbara, were guests of honor for *GWTW*'s fiftieth anniversary celebration in 1989. In 2005, he was honored with the Golden Boot Award as one of the "Kids of the West."

Bonnie *and* Beau: This Child Actor Played Both

After previewing *GWTW*, David O. Selznick didn't think the infant actors looked convincing as newborns. He ordered reshoots of the scenes in which Melanie holds her son Beau in the wagon and in which Melanie helps to name Bonnie.

Reps from Selznick International descended upon Rice Maternity Hospital in Los Angeles and chose from the nursery blue-eyed Gregory Giese, who had been born on September 24. Giese's parents signed a contract on October 4, and their baby was whisked away for three days of work, making Giese at less-than-two-weeks of age *GWTW*'s youngest player.

After his film debut, Giese returned to private life. In 1989, he attended the celebration of *GWTW*'s fiftieth anniversary in Atlanta as a guest of honor.

REMEMBERING VICTOR FLEMING

After rescuing two troubled 1939 productions—*The Wizard of Oz* and *GWTW*—and picking up the Best Director Oscar for the latter, Victor Fleming tackled his next cinematic challenges: *Dr. Jekyll and Mr. Hyde* (1941), *Tortilla Flat* (1942), *A Guy Named Joe* (1943), *Adventure* (1945), and *Joan of Arc* (1948).

Fleming was on a family vacation in Arizona when he died suddenly of heart failure on January 6, 1949, at the age of fifty-nine. His death stunned Hollywood, and those who mourned him remembered that Fleming:

- Was hired as a driver and stuntman in 1912 after fixing the car owned by the top filmmaker at the American Film Manufacturing Company (aka Flying "A" Studios). Repairing a camera that had been ruining film introduced Fleming to moviemaking and led to his becoming an assistant cameraman.
- Joined the Triangle Film Corporation in 1915, where director D. W. Griffith tapped him as one of several cameramen for *Intolerance* (1916).
- Worked as a cameraman for and became friends with Douglas Fairbanks Sr.
- Served in the photographic unit of the Signal Corps during World War I and became chief cameraman for President Woodrow Wilson's European tour.
- Directed his first film, *When the Clouds Roll By*, in 1919.
- Made stars of Clara Bow with *Mantrap* (1926), Gary Cooper with *The Virginian* (1929), and Clark Gable with *Red Dust* (1932).
- Directed now-classic films such as *Bombshell* (1933), *Treasure Island* (1934), and *Captains Courageous* (1937).

In 2007, when the American Film Institute issued its "100 Years . . . 100 Movies" list, Victor Fleming was distinguished as the only director with two films in the top ten: *The Wizard of Oz* and *Gone With the Wind*.

EPILOGUE: MARGARET MITCHELL

"I have been writing since I was five and a half years old, and until I got so busy cleaning up after *Gone with the Wind*, I always had something going." Now that the Atlanta premiere and the Academy Award presentations were over, Margaret again yearned to get "something going." But circumstances intervened.

With the world at war, Margaret spent her days working with Atlanta's Civilian Defense and the Red Cross. She sold war bonds, wrote letters to servicemen, and served as hostess and seamstress at army canteens. In September 1941, Margaret traveled to Kearney, New Jersey, to christen a new cruiser, the USS *Atlanta*.

Margaret kept busy fighting personal battles as well. Her ill and hospitalized father, Eugene Mitchell, depended on Margaret for his care until his death in 1944. Her novel also needed tending to: Margaret had to keep on top of the authorized foreign translations of *GWTW* as well as the pirated editions printed by unscrupulous publishers around the world.

On the home front, Macmillan published a "Victory" edition of *GWTW* on August 25, 1942. This hardcover volume was a sized-down version of the original and was printed on a cheaper grade of paper because of the wartime paper shortage. The dust jacket proudly carried the liberty insignia that urged citizens to buy war bonds and stamps. First-year sales of the book, which retailed for $1.49, climbed to 23,572 copies, and an additional 42,450 copies were sold from 1943 to 1944. During the last year of the war, book buyers scooped up another 56,710 copies of *GWTW*.

Margaret hoped to return to her typewriter after the war ended. But her husband, John Marsh, suffered a heart attack that nearly killed him in December 1945. His subsequent care took most of Margaret's time for the next two years. He retired from his position at the Georgia Power Company in September 1947 and assumed much of the foreign *GWTW* business that Margaret had been handling herself. As she wrote to a friend, "The work seems to get heavier and heavier as time goes on instead of getting lighter, and any hope of ever having an opportunity to do more writing is something I never even think about."

The early months of 1949 finally afforded Margaret some breathing space. Business pressures were easing, and Margaret had time to think about a new writing project. Maybe a continuation of Atlanta's history up to World War I. A play perhaps? Margaret toyed with the idea of a drama concerning a woman who writes a wildly successful book. But Margaret was sure of one thing: she would not write a sequel to *GWTW*. For her, the story of Scarlett and Rhett ended just as she had written it.

With hopes stirring for the beginning of a new work, Margaret and John endured the stifling early days of an Atlanta August. The fiery heat of Thursday, August 11, gave way to a cool evening breeze. Margaret had felt ill all day and thought that a night at the movies would be a welcome treat. She and John decided to see *A Canterbury Tale* at the Peachtree Arts Theatre.

Margaret parked their car on the west side of Peachtree Street and with John at her side began to cross the street. As they were about in the middle of the thoroughfare, a speeding car rounded the curved street and headed straight for the couple. John hurried forward, but Margaret for some reason turned and retraced her steps. Brakes squealed. The car skidded and swerved into Margaret. She never made it back to the curb. The man behind the wheel, an off-duty taxi driver, admitted he had been drinking that afternoon.

Unconscious and terribly injured, Margaret was rushed to Grady Hospital. Doctors determined that her most serious injuries were a fractured skull and pelvis.

Crowds began gathering outside the hospital waiting for news about the forty-eight-year-old author. The hospital's switchboard was deluged with calls from all over the country. Radio news programs supplied hourly bulletins about her deteriorating condition. Margaret lingered for five days, and then her struggles ended. On August 16, radio stations announced the sad news of her death by playing "Tara's Theme."

AMERICA REMEMBERS MARGARET MITCHELL

Personal messages of condolence flooded Atlanta. President Harry S. Truman wired John Marsh on August 17: "The nation to which she brought international fame through a creative work of lasting merit shares the sorrow which has come to you with such sudden and tragic force. Great as an artist who gave the world an eternal book, the author of *Gone with the Wind* will also be remembered as a great soul who exemplified in her all-too-brief span of years the highest ideals of American womanhood."

Tributes appeared in newspapers across the nation and around the world. The *New York Times* wrote: "The South and the Nation have lost one of their most beloved and admired personages. Certainly she will always be one of our most remarkable literary figures." The *Charleston News and Courier* said that Margaret was "a dear, sweet woman who had the charity that vaunteth not itself. Her life and her book were the realization of genius, goodness, and modesty."

Sorrow over Margaret's death was quickly replaced with anger when it was revealed that the man who had run her down, twenty-nine-year-old

Hugh D. Gravitt, had a string of arrests and convictions for traffic violations. When he was brought to trial in November 1949, he was convicted of involuntary manslaughter and handed a sentence of twelve to eighteen months. He served ten months and twenty days.

An outpouring of public sentiment screamed for safer driving. The Boy Scouts and Girl Scouts combined forces to promote a "Margaret Mitchell Minute" for the first anniversary of her death. Americans were urged to spend sixty seconds of silence remembering the author of *GWTW* and how suddenly a careless driver can take a life. The National Safety Council used the tragedy of Margaret's death in their campaigns. The Atlanta traffic safety board renamed itself the Margaret Mitchell Safety Council in honor of the city's most famous citizen. (It has since become part of the National Safety Council.) Margaret was gone, but America wanted to remember her and keep her memory alive.

MARGARET MITCHELL INFLUENCES THE LAW

Margaret Mitchell's influence was felt not only in literary circles but in the international legal world as well. When her novel was published, Margaret believed her United States copyright would protect her book all over the world. She was wrong.

At the time, the United States was not a member of the Universal Copyright Convention, so American authors were not protected in foreign countries. Margaret found that foreign publishers blatantly pirated *GWTW*. They changed the novel any way they wanted, published the book without her permission, and refused to pay her royalties. The most brazen of these foreign pirates was a publisher in Holland, and Margaret fought for her rights in the Dutch court system.

On the home front, Margaret lobbied legislators and wrote to members of the State Department, impressing upon them the need to extend United States copyright protection abroad. Unfortunately, Margaret's death ended her fight for America's authors. But her attorney brother, Stephens Mitchell, took up her battle in 1954 by presenting a summary of Margaret's *GWTW* copyright problems to a U.S. Senate committee. This convinced Congress of the importance of international copyright protection, and the United States became a member of the Universal Copyright Convention the following year.

PROOF POSITIVE

Margaret left all rights to *GWTW* to her husband, John Marsh, who carried on the novel's daily business after her death. Part of that business, he realized, meant securing evidence that Margaret had written *Gone with the Wind*.

He placed into a large envelope several typewritten chapters of *GWTW* with handwritten corrections, drafts of chapters with their changes, proof sheets, chronologies of the book's events compiled by Margaret, notes made by Margaret concerning the book, and several of the manila envelopes that had held Margaret's chapters during the writing of *GWTW*. Marsh sealed this large envelope, wrote his name over the seal, and placed the parcel in a safe-deposit box at Citizens and Southern National Bank in July 1951.

He also added a codicil to his will that established a trust fund to pay for perpetual box rental and directed that envelope be unsealed only if Margaret's authorship were questioned: "I am confident it can be proved not only that my wife, Margaret Mitchell Marsh, wrote *Gone with the Wind*, but that she alone could have written it."

John Marsh died on May 5, 1952. Under the terms of his will, the rights to *GWTW* were bequeathed to Margaret's brother, Stephens Mitchell, who oversaw the daily business of *GWTW* for more than thirty years.

TEN

From the Big Screen to TV

HAPPY FIFTEENTH ANNIVERSARY, *GWTW!*

America couldn't wait for the fifteenth anniversary of *GWTW* in December 1954. So MGM began the celebration early with a May 20 anniversary "premiere" at the Loew's Grand Theatre in Atlanta.

Rich's department store joined the festivities by featuring a display of Margaret Mitchell memorabilia. MGM and Atlanta's Smith College Club teamed up to host a "premiere" party. At the event it was announced that proceeds from premiere ticket sales would benefit the college's newly established Margaret Mitchell Scholarship. (Margaret's education at Smith had been cut short by her mother's death in 1919. But in 1939 the college granted Margaret an honorary Master of Arts degree.) More surprises occurred the night of the premiere: *GWTW* had changed!

GWTW was now in CinemaScope. The film had been reprocessed for showing on the now-popular wide screen. The new process made the spectacular scenes more powerful, but the color was faded and grainy in certain parts of the film. MGM had made other alterations as well. *GWTW* had been transferred from volatile nitrate film to acetate safety film, thus preserving *GWTW* for the future. Another addition was Perspecta stereophonic sound.

From Atlanta, *GWTW* traveled to New York, where it opened at the Loew's State Theatre on May 29 and played for most of the summer. But the highlight of the fifteenth anniversary was the spectacular Hollywood premiere at the Egyptian Theatre on August 10.

Hollywood's top stars attended the glittering fete. On display in the lobby were the Oscars *GWTW* had won, along with David O. Selznick's Thalberg Award. A touching ceremony honored the surviving stars of the film as well as its producer. Then the guests took their seats to view the "new" *GWTW*—still the greatest motion picture ever made.

ATLANTA REMEMBERS

The City of Atlanta chose the fifteenth anniversary of the film to honor the memory of the book's author. The Atlanta City Council named a street Margaret Mitchell Drive. The Atlanta Board of Education christened a new elementary school the Margaret Mitchell School. In the auditorium, a portrait of Vivien Leigh as Scarlett O'Hara was unveiled. The Atlanta Public Library established the Margaret Mitchell Room as a site to exhibit a collection of Mitchell materials bequeathed by John Marsh.

HIGH-FIDELITY *GWTW*

In 1954, fans could not only see *GWTW* in theaters, they could listen to *GWTW*'s music on their home stereos. RCA Victor released a ten-inch, long-playing album of *GWTW* music written and conducted by Max Steiner. But this wasn't a soundtrack. Steiner composed a special arrangement of *GWTW*'s individual themes. The music was interpreted by a thirty-piece orchestra under Steiner's direction.

The best known of *GWTW*'s themes, "Tara's Theme," also acquired a lyric by Mack David in 1954. Titled "My Own True Love," the song was a successful recording for several vocalists.

THE NOVEL GOES PAPERBACK

GWTW enjoyed its sixty-eighth printing in 1954. The book retailed for $4.50, although a $2.95 cheap edition was also available. But in April,

Margaret Mitchell's novel made history again: it was published in paperback.

Doubleday, owner of the subsidiary rights, announced a Permabook edition of *GWTW*. The book, which the company called "the longest modern pocket-sized book ever to be published," had 862 pages and sold for seventy-five cents.

THE NOVEL: TWENTY YEARS AND COUNTING

In June 1956, *GWTW* celebrated its twentieth anniversary of publication. Macmillan proudly announced that worldwide sales hovered at around eight million copies. Readers in thirty-one countries enjoyed editions of *GWTW* in twenty-four different languages.

THE RECORD BREAKER'S RECORDS ARE BROKEN

Until the 1950s, no other film had come close to breaking *GWTW*'s championship records for winning the most Academy Awards and being the top box-office grosser. But inevitably, records fall.

In the Oscar category, 1953's *From Here to Eternity* and 1954's *On the Waterfront* both equaled *GWTW*'s sweep of eight Academy Awards. The 1958 musical *Gigi* was victorious in every category for which it was nominated and captured nine Oscars. However, one of the categories was Best Costume Design—a category that did not exist in *GWTW*'s days—so Windies refused to concede the championship. The record was broken for good, though, with the 1959 appearance of MGM's *Ben-Hur*. This spectacular religious production earned a total of eleven Academy Awards exactly twenty years after *GWTW*'s own record-setting win.

GWTW's championship as top box-office grosser also fell in 1960. In *Variety*'s yearly list of the top ten moneymaking movies, Cecil B. DeMille's *The Ten Commandments* took control of the number-one position with total rentals of $34,200,000. *GWTW* had slipped to second place with a total of $33,500,000.

GWTW CELEBRATES THE CIVIL WAR CENTENNIAL

In honor of the one-hundredth anniversary of the Civil War, MGM planned another Atlanta "premiere" of *GWTW* for March 10, 1961, that promised to duplicate the hoopla of the film's 1939 debut.

The Hollywood contingent, including Vivien Leigh, Olivia de Havilland, and David O. Selznick, arrived at the airport and were greeted by welcoming crowds and brass bands. The celebrities then enjoyed riding in a motorcade along Peachtree Street, lined with waving, enthusiastic fans. That evening, a Centennial Benefit Costume Ball was held at the Biltmore Hotel. Guests at the Ball included the governors from fourteen Southern states.

The following evening, attendees entered the glittering Loew's Grand Theatre and took a step back in time. The theater was decorated exactly as it had been in 1939. But many things had changed since that time, and this premiere was bittersweet for the surviving members of *GWTW*'s family. So many of those connected with the film were gone, including Clark Gable, who had died of a heart attack just four months before. When Gable appeared on the screen at the foot of the Twelve Oaks' staircase, Vivien Leigh gasped, "Oh look at Clark; he looks so young and gorgeous!" However, the film's message of hope for tomorrow sliced through the momentary gloom. The thunderous applause that filled the theater at the end of the film acknowledged once again how much audiences loved *GWTW*.

After the Atlanta premiere, *GWTW* opened at the Hollywood Paramount Theatre in Los Angeles on March 24 and at the Loew's State Theatre on Broadway in New York City on April 26. The film played other first-run engagements in America and Canada, then made the rounds of smaller neighborhood theaters.

Audiences may have noticed that the film's color was darker than they remembered. This was the result of Metrocolor, a modern technique used to process new prints of the film that had replaced the more expensive Technicolor process. Fans didn't care. *GWTW* was back, and they flocked to see it.

At the end of 1961, *GWTW* had earned another $7.7 million, which boosted it back to the top of *Variety*'s list of champions with total rentals of $41,200,000. In second place was *Ben-Hur* ($40,000,000), and in third place was *The Ten Commandments* ($34,200,000).

POSTSCRIPT ON DAVID O. SELZNICK

The Academy Awards for *GWTW* sealed David O. Selznick's reputation as producer extraordinaire. Yet in the years that followed, Selznick was haunted by the ghost of *GWTW*.

The specter loomed before him with every film he considered. If the new project would not be as great as *GWTW*, he turned it down. He bought the rights to *The Keys of the Kingdom* and *Waterloo Bridge*. But when he could not get excited about making the films, he sold the rights to other studios. To keep his studio financially afloat, he loaned his stable of stars to other producers.

"You know what my problem is?" he said during a story conference. "I know that when I die the stories will read, 'David O. Selznick, producer of *Gone With the Wind*, died today.' I'm determined to leave them something else to write about."

Selznick thought he'd found that "something else" in a new actress discovered by Kay Brown and in a best-selling novel written by Margaret Buell Wilder.

Selznick found shy, retiring newcomer Phylis Isley fascinating. He placed her under contract, began grooming her, and changed her name to Jennifer Jones. He initially matched her with Twentieth Century Fox director Henry King, who was looking for an unknown to star in *The Song of Bernadette*. Jones landed the role, and her performance earned the Academy Award for Best Actress. Her star was on the rise.

The novel *Since You Went Away* dealt with another war, World War II, and the changes it brought to the lives of an American family. Selznick thought this would be the perfect vehicle for Jones and bought the rights for $30,000.

Selznick was excited about filmmaking again. He wrote the script, chose the director, and selected the distinguished cast, which included Claudette Colbert, Shirley Temple, and Lionel Barrymore. During the filming, Selznick also fell in love with his leading lady. Selznick crowned the 1944 film with the slogan: "The four most important words since *Gone With the Wind—SINCE YOU WENT AWAY!*" The film was a success, but it wasn't a *GWTW*. Selznick, still feeling the need to better his best, began searching for another project.

The next film was *Duel in the Sun*, starring Jennifer Jones, Gregory Peck, and Joseph Cotten. Almost from the beginning the film was beset with problems, such as script rewrites, fights, firings, and reshootings. It took Selznick over two years and more than $6 million to complete the project. He viewed the 1946 film as a Western version of *GWTW*. The critics hated it.

By this time Selznick was reeling from personal as well as professional crises. His marriage was over, his brother Myron was dead, and Selznick seemed to have lost his moviemaking touch. The cost overruns for two films, *The Paradine Case* and *Portrait of Jennie*, had drained the company's finances. Selznick was $12 million in debt and had no other choice but to liquidate the company in 1949. Most of the studio's assets were sold, including the costumes used in *GWTW*, and Selznick withdrew from filmmaking to pay off his debts and to contemplate his future.

The hope of making another *GWTW* rekindled for Selznick in 1957 when he decided to remake *A Farewell to Arms*. As his stars, he chose his new wife Jennifer Jones and Rock Hudson; for the script, he tapped Ben Hecht. In a memo to Hecht, Selznick implored, "Let's really try to do a job that will be remembered as long as *Gone With the Wind*, something that we can be proud of in the years to come." The movie turned out to be quite the opposite. Critics blasted the film for its poor acting, overproduction, and antiquated style. Selznick was devastated, and *A Farewell to Arms* was his farewell to the movie industry.

In 1961, when MGM honored the Civil War Centenary by re-releasing *GWTW* and restaging the Atlanta premiere, Selznick was reunited with the two surviving stars of his epic: Vivien Leigh and Olivia de Havilland. He seemed lethargic and uninterested during the ceremonies that preceded the showing of the film. When he was introduced and came on stage, though, the wild applause of the crowd seemed to electrify him. The hard years peeled away from his lined face. He brushed back his white hair, stood tall, and basked in the adulation.

GWTW was now a benevolent spirit. If Selznick couldn't beat it, he would join forces with it. So Selznick decided to turn *GWTW* into the greatest musical Broadway had ever seen.

He needed to secure the stage rights and entered into negotiations with the agent who represented Margaret Mitchell's estate—Kay Brown, the former Selznick associate who had urged him to buy the film rights to the novel. Once the stage rights were his, Selznick began looking for the best composers and writers. Richard Rodgers and Oscar Hammerstein II turned him down, as did Harold Rome and Dimitri Tiomkin. They feared that their stage version would compare poorly to the film. Selznick planned to write the libretto himself and even thought about building a grand-scale theater specifically for the magnificent production he envisioned. But he was unable to unite the elements he needed to create the *GWTW* musical, and the idea died.

The man who produced *GWTW* died of a heart attack on June 22, 1965. He was sixty-three. And newspaper obituaries across the country remembered Selznick just as he had always thought they would.

GWTW REACHES THE STAGE

David O. Selznick had dreamed of bringing *GWTW* to Broadway. He was not able to realize this dream in his lifetime, but he probably would have been pleased to know that *GWTW* finally made it to the off-Broadway stage. Way off Broadway. In fact, the play *GWTW* debuted in Japan.

The five-hour production opened on November 3, 1966, at Tokyo's Imperial Theatre. Although it had twenty-one scenes, the play covered only the first half of the novel. Still, the production ran for five months and in its 197 performances drew a total audience attendance of 380,000.

A second play with a running time of four hours opened the following summer and presented the second half of the novel. This play was as successful as the first and enjoyed four months of performances. Then in the fall of 1967 the two plays were combined, and a condensed six-hour version hit the stage.

GWTW IN 70 MM SPLENDOR

Bigger isn't always better, and this axiom was proved true in 1967 when *GWTW* was reissued in a 70-millimeter wide-screen version. In the process, each of *GWTW*'s 35-millimeter frames was stretched to fit the wider 70-millimeter format. To achieve this, however, the tops of heads and the bottoms of legs were sacrificed, ruining the composition. The film's title lost its sweeping grandeur, too. The main title was replaced with four small words, stationary on the screen.

Another new feature was the addition of a stereophonic soundtrack, very different from the enhancement made in 1954. The new soundtrack amplified sounds such as the rustle of hoopskirts or the clop of horses' hooves, but often these extraneous sounds muffled essential dialogue.

Despite its drawbacks, this latest version of *GWTW*—with its new "flaming embrace" movie poster artwork—kept theater seats filled. At the close of 1967, *GWTW*'s total rentals reached $47,400,000. One year later, at the end of the first-run engagements, the total had soared to $70,400,000. Although *GWTW* had been on the top of *Variety*'s list of box-office winners for weeks, the film was supplanted at the end of 1968 by *The Sound of Music*, whose higher-priced tickets brought rental totals to $72,000,000.

GWTW: ALL IS FORGIVEN

In 1968, the National Catholic Office for Motion Pictures had a change of heart about *GWTW*. The former Legion of Decency took another look at the film and reclassified *GWTW* as "morally unobjectionable for adults and adolescents."

Why the turnabout after nearly thirty years? In the words of the National Catholic Office, "the social changes following World War II have made what once appeared as daring scenes seem almost innocent on the screen today."

GWTW: THE MUSICAL

If *GWTW* could be transformed into a play, could a musical be far behind? A musical version of *GWTW* called *Scarlett* opened at Tokyo's Imperial Theatre on January 2, 1970.

Playwright Kazuo Kikuta wrote the script based on his 1966 stage version. Broadway veteran Harold Rome wrote the music and lyrics, and award-winning Broadway stager Joe Layton was director and choreographer. Toho Company Ltd., a Japanese conglomerate, put up $1.7 million for the four-hour musical, which played to standing-room-only audiences.

After its Tokyo run, *Scarlett* was translated into English, renamed *Gone With the Wind*, and headed to the British stage. The musical, under the creative direction of Joe Layton, opened on May 3, 1972, at London's Theatre Royal, Drury Lane. Show business writers called the production, with an estimated budget of $450,000, the most expensive musical ever staged in London.

Although audiences thrilled to the staged spectacle, including the nightly burning of the Atlanta depot, the critics were less impressed. Critic Haskel Frankel, writing for the *National Observer*, noted: "The biggest disappointment is American Harve Presnell as Rhett Butler. He has the looks and voice for the part, but God's gifts are all he brings to the role; Presnell does not even attempt the Southern accent, and he's about as dashing as warm water." Frankel was kinder to the leading lady. "The surprising star is June Ritchie as Scarlett. A British actress, she is as Southern as a julep and, if not as ruthless as she should be, Miss Ritchie at least manages to smoulder in the part."

Gone With the Wind crossed the Atlantic and opened in Los Angeles on August 28, 1973. Lesley Ann Warren and Pernell Roberts took over the principal roles, but the critics gave the production many failing marks. On October 23, 1973, the musical debuted in San Francisco, again, to poor notices.

Sherry Mathis as Scarlett and David Canary as Rhett took a touring version of the musical on the road. The musical played to theater audiences in the South with stopovers in Dallas, Kansas City, Miami Beach, and Atlanta. However, the dream of making it to Broadway faded.

THE NOVEL'S FORTIETH ANNIVERSARY

To commemorate the seventy-fifth anniversary of Margaret Mitchell's birth, Macmillan published a slipcased edition of the novel in 1975. The special edition, which retailed for $14.95, contained an introduction written by James A. Michener.

The following year Macmillan marked the novel's fortieth anniversary by printing *GWTW*'s eighty-fifty standard edition, which retailed for $9.95. Macmillan also published two books with *GWTW* tie-ins. *Scarlett, Rhett and a Cast of Thousands* by Roland Flamini told the story of the making of the movie. *Margaret Mitchell's* Gone with the Wind *Letters, 1936–1949*, edited by Richard Harwell, was a collection of more than three hundred letters showing how the publication of *GWTW* changed Margaret Mitchell's life.

GWTW'S WORLD TELEVISION PREMIERE

The National Broadcasting Company paid $5 million to MGM for the one-time showing of *GWTW*. Everyone was waiting for the classic film to appear for the first time on television. But as it turned out, *GWTW* did not make its world television premiere on NBC.

While NBC was busy selling commercial time at a record $234,000 a minute, MGM struck a deal with Home Box Office. The deal allowed HBO to broadcast *GWTW* commercial-free fourteen times during the month of June 1976. On June 11 at 2:30 p.m., *GWTW* made its actual world television premiere on cable—five months before its network debut.

Dick Cavett was the genial host for *GWTW*'s world premiere. He shared with the cable audience some of the stories connected with the casting and filming of Margaret Mitchell's masterpiece. The film was then shown in its uninterrupted entirety, and the broadcast was repeated that evening at eight o'clock. Twice-a-day broadcasts took place on six other dates in June, and cable viewers loved it. *Variety* later estimated that 382,500 viewers, which was more than 85 percent of HBO's total audience of 450,000 subscribers, had watched the film at least once.

GWTW ON NETWORK TELEVISION

In the midst of a presidential election that saw Georgia-born Jimmy Carter elected to the Oval Office, America's attention turned to another "native" of that fair state: Scarlett O'Hara. NBC would be broadcasting *GWTW* on two successive nights, November 7 and 8, 1976.

TV Guide featured Scarlett and Rhett on its cover that week, and in the "This Week's Movies" section reviewer Judith Crist stated: "This is *Gone with the Wind*'s week, and television, via NBC, will be on trial with its presentation of the 1939 classic." Crist expressed concern about the distribution of seventy-eight minutes of commercials and station breaks during the film. NBC also planned to extend part one beyond the normal intermission break.

Olivia de Havilland had already expressed her displeasure about the manner in which the film would be broadcast. NBC had asked her to introduce the film, but she had refused. "I was appalled to learn that they planned to give so much time to commercials . . . a break in the showing every twenty minutes. I object to that," de Havilland said.

Despite her objections, on Sunday, November 7, at 8:00 p.m., the announcer for *The Big Event* called *GWTW* "the most eagerly awaited event in television history." Then, even before the film began, the network went immediately into commercials.

The film opened as usual with the Selznick International trademark and the running of credits. Then Scarlett was on the porch with the Tarletons and discovers that Ashley is to marry Melanie. The Sunday-night presentation of *GWTW* continued past Scarlett's vow to never be hungry again, and the broadcast ended with Scarlett starting her lumber business with Ashley's help.

The conclusion of *GWTW* took place the next evening, Monday, November 8, ironically the anniversary of Margaret Mitchell's birth. But instead of being *The Big Event*, *GWTW* was billed as *Monday Night at the Movies*. The trademark and credits were run again, then NBC provided a synopsis of what had been shown the night before. Finally, viewers rejoined the story as Scarlett becomes a businesswoman and followed her (with commercials, of course) through to her tearful final scene.

GWTW AND THE NIELSEN RATINGS

How did *GWTW* fare in the ratings war? According to the Nielsen ratings, the Sunday, November 7, broadcast of the film had a 47.6 rating and a 65 percent audience share. The Monday, November 8, broadcast had a 47.4 rating and a 64 percent audience share. When the figures were combined and averaged, *GWTW* scored an overall rating of 47.5 and a 65 percent of total audience. In terms of actual numbers, NBC estimated that 33,890,000 homes had watched *GWTW* on Sunday and 33,750,000 on Monday. NBC proudly proclaimed that *GWTW* was "the highest-rated television program ever presented on a single network."

TELEVISION PARODIES OF *GWTW*

GWTW was in for some high-spirited ribbing after making its television debut. During the ABC broadcast of *The John Denver Special*, Joanne

Woodward, in a Southern-belle organza gown and a straw picture hat, sat in a rowboat munching an apple and clutching a parasol. Courting beau Denver worked the oars as well as his charms. The placid scene was interrupted by the menacing music from *Jaws*, and then suddenly the great white himself rose up from the water. One gigantic gulp later, the ocean denizen had devoured Denver, half the boat, and turned Scarlett O'Woodward into the Lady of the Lake.

Carol Burnett's parody of *GWTW* on the November 13, 1976, episode of *The Carol Burnett Show* was a rollicking sketch called "Went With the Wind." Burnett as "Starlett O'Hara" tormented Dinah Shore's "Melody" until that gentle soul finally pushed "Starlett" down a staircase. Vicki Lawrence fared just as well. She played "Sissy," a white servant, who took great pleasure in returning a slap across the face to her domineering mistress. Harvey Korman was a dashing "Rat Butler" in the funniest portion of the sketch. He greeted "Starlett" as she walked down the staircase of her plantation home, Terra, in her drapery dress with curtain rods still in place.

THE CBS DEAL FOR *GWTW*

In April 1978, CBS and MGM concluded an unprecedented twenty-year deal for *GWTW*. CBS bought exclusive television rights to broadcast the film twenty times during the length of the agreement at a price tag of $35 million, the largest license fee ever paid for a single film in the history of television.

GWTW ON VIDEOCASSETTE

"If you could own just one film on videocassette," the ad read, "which would it be? Of course it would." The *GWTW* video that Windies had hungered for hit the market in March 1985. The double-cassette deluxe edition carried a price tag of $89.95.

The production of the video was as meticulous as Selznick's production of the film itself, and the process was blessed by a stroke of luck: the discovery of an original, virgin negative of *GWTW* stored in a former salt mine in Hutchinson, Kansas. (Film studios used the vault as backup storage for perishable materials.) In executing the transfer from film to tape, technicians remastered the soundtrack digitally. The result was a *GWTW* that looked and sounded better than ever.

As soon as it appeared on store shelves, the *GWTW* video soared toward the top of the sales chart. For a solid three weeks, *GWTW* was the number-two best seller behind *Star Trek III*.

Since then, the *GWTW* video has been released on DVD and Blu-Ray Disc formats.

ELEVEN

At Long Last, the Sequels

THE CONTINUATION OF *GWTW*

After *GWTW* was published, fans inundated Margaret Mitchell with mail asking what happened after Rhett walked out on Scarlett. Margaret was always firm: "I do not have a notion of what happened to them and I left them to their ultimate fate. With two such determined characters, it would be hard to predict what would happen to them." She rejected both Selznick's and MGM's requests to write a sequel, and after her death in 1949, her brother Stephens Mitchell continued refusing sequel offers through the 1950s and 1960s.

But Stephens was aware that the battle could not be waged forever. He was getting on in years and couldn't remain Margaret's champion indefinitely. Also, the expiration of *GWTW*'s copyright in 2011 would no doubt unleash countless continuations of the story. So in the 1970s, Stephens considered authorizing a sequel.

In 1975, Kay Brown, the agent for Margaret's estate, met with Richard Zanuck and David Brown of Universal, who were famous for producing grand-scale movies such as *Jaws* and *The Sting*. Would they be interested in a sequel to *GWTW*? They took less time saying yes than Scarlett did after hearing Charles Hamilton's marriage proposal. However, MGM claimed some rights to a sequel. An option deal was worked out in June 1976 that brought Universal and MGM into partnership for a sequel to *GWTW*.

Zanuck and Brown estimated that their budget for *Gone With the Wind, Part II* would be jointly financed by Universal and MGM to the tune of about $12 million. They also stated that in their casting of the leading roles they would not seek performers who looked like Clark Gable or Vivien Leigh.

The writer selected for the project was Anne Edwards, author of the biographies *Judy Garland* and *Vivien Leigh*. Her sequel would be adapted into a screenplay, and the book's paperback publication would be timed to coincide with the release of the film.

The manuscript that Edwards submitted, *Tara: The Continuation of Gone with the Wind*, supposedly was set in 1872–1882 and showed more intrigue between Scarlett and Rhett, a marriage for Ashley and Beau's governess, Ashley's death in a Klan raid, a reconciliation for Scarlett and Rhett after Mammy's death, a Klan raid that destroys Tara and kills Rhett while he saves Scarlett, and her vow to rebuild the plantation in Rhett's memory. Although producers Zanuck and Brown were satisfied with the story, MGM was not. MGM turned thumbs down on Edwards's book and the screenplay written by James Goldman. The book was shelved in 1980, and the deal collapsed. (Contractually, Edwards can never publish her manuscript.)

STEPHENS MITCHELL GOES TO COURT

In 1981, Stephens Mitchell took MGM to federal court to challenge the studio's assertion that it held certain sequel rights. MGM stated that Stephens had relinquished sequel rights when MGM's option on his sister's novel was renegotiated in 1961.

The court battle raged for four years and ended in September 1985 with the Eleventh District United States Court of Appeals ruling in favor of Margaret Mitchell's estate. But Stephens Mitchell did not live long enough to savor this victory. He died on May 12, 1983.

His two sons, Eugene Muse Mitchell and Joseph Reynolds Mitchell, became Margaret's heirs through two trusts established as the Stephens Mitchell Trusts. In his will, Stephens designated a trust committee of three Atlanta attorneys along with the estate's executor, the Trust Company of

Georgia, to manage the rights to *GWTW*, and this included the responsibility for arranging a sequel to *GWTW*.

AT LAST, THE SEQUEL TO *GWTW*

The path to publication for a *GWTW* sequel had as many twists and turns as did Scarlett's harrowing journey from Atlanta to Tara. The saga began in 1986 when the trustees representing the Mitchell estate engaged the William Morris Agency to find a writer equal to the task. The trustees considered twelve candidates for the project before selecting novelist Alexandra Braid Ripley, a native of Charleston, South Carolina. Ripley's agent, Robert Gottlieb, thought she was the perfect choice as she had "the skill and sensibility to bring the post–Civil War era—and the formidable Scarlett—back to life."

Ripley developed the sequel's plot in consultation with the trustees, since the lawyers wanted to make sure that the integrity of Margaret's novel remained intact. Ripley was firm on two points: She would handle sex more openly in her novel, although she would avoid graphic sexuality. She would also avoid the thick slave dialect favored by Margaret, believing it difficult to read and demeaning to African Americans.

As part of her research, Ripley made several trips to Atlanta and Charleston. She studied train timetables between those two cities from the year 1873, maps of city streets, letters, diaries, and old newspapers. Scenes from the movie helped her imagine the rooms in Scarlett's Atlanta house. Ripley chose Charleston buildings dating from the sequel's period as the respective homes of Scarlett's aunts and Rhett's mother.

The sequel's time frame proved a stumbling block for Ripley in plotting the novel. She found it difficult developing story elements that would dovetail with the post–Civil War historical period. She told the *New York Times*: "I read seven books on Wall Street and the economy. This was the big thing happening. Not only was I reading things I did not understand, it bored me senseless. There were things going on in the Balkans, but can you see Scarlett saying, 'I think I'll grow cotton in the Balkans'?" That's when Ripley's research provided an epiphany. She realized that Ireland's turbulent times mirrored the pre–Civil War days of *GWTW*. "I said, 'Oh thank you, God!'"

To prepare for the writing, Ripley read Margaret's novel at least six times, looking for dates and studying the language. She hand copied two hundred pages of the book to experience Margaret's style. "My hand just won't write 'fiddle-dee-dee,'" she told *Life* magazine. "But I figure in my 1,000-page book I'll have to give them at least three and throw in 'God's nightgown!' 'Great balls of fire!' and 'As God is my witness!'"

The Morris Agency circulated among publishers an outline of the sequel and two sample chapters written by Ripley in advance of the novel's auction held in April 1988. Of the six publishing houses that participated in the spirited bidding, Warner Books came out on top with a bid of $4.94 million.

Over the next three years, publication postponements and plotline leaks plagued the project. Rumors swirled about a pregnancy for Scarlett, a move to Ireland, and involvement in a gun-running scheme. Unhappy with Ripley's initial draft, Warner Books ordered extensive rewrites then was forced to bring in a book doctor to salvage the sinking sequel.

Speculation that the sequel would end up as a television production rather than as a major motion picture caused Warner Books to state that the book's future on the small screen or the silver screen would be decided once the sequel was published. In early 1991, Warner Books announced that *Scarlett: The Sequel to Margaret Mitchell's* Gone With the Wind would be the publisher's lead title for the fall.

Life magazine won the exclusive right to publish nine pages of excerpts before the sequel's official release date. The cover of the magazine's September 1991 issue showed Clark Gable and Vivien Leigh in a close-up of the proposal embrace with the words: "Here it is at last—The Sequel to *GONE WITH THE WIND*" and "RHETT AND SCARLETT: The love story continues."

The sneak peek in *Life* added fuel to the *Scarlett* frenzy that gripped the country, fanned by a $600,000 national promotional campaign that Warner Books launched in major media markets. With the theme "Tomorrow Is Here, at Last . . . ," the campaign included bookstore preorder counter-display cards; newspaper and magazine print ads; television spots that aired during talk shows, soap operas, and nightly news broadcasts; and media coverage of and appearances by Ripley.

Prepublication demand for the 823-page, $24.95 book caused Warner Books to increase the sequel's first printing from 500,000 to 750,000 copies. The publisher ordered an additional 350,000 copies on publication day. To stoke book-buyer excitement, Warner Books declined to distribute advance copies. Instead, copies were express shipped to book-selling venues on publication day.

Bookstores across the nation were overwhelmed on September 25, 1991, with customers phoning to learn if book shipments had arrived and, if they had, lining up to buy their reserved copies. Clerks feverishly opened the white shipping cartons that bore the words "*Scarlett: The Sequel to Margaret Mitchell's Gone With the Wind*" in red lettering, and customers just as quickly grabbed the boxes as souvenirs.

Bookstores holding autograph sessions with Alexandra Ripley were mobbed. Rich's department store hosted Ripley for her first Atlanta signing session scheduled for September 28 from 1 p.m. to 4 p.m. Book buyers lined up four hours before the store even opened. When Ripley arrived at 12:30 p.m., the crowd went wild, screaming and clapping for the author. She graciously agreed to add extra time to her appearance, then diligently signed books throughout the afternoon, resting briefly twice and going to the ladies' room once. Women waiting in *that* line begged for autographs. "If you'll just hand your books over the wall, I'll sign them in here," an accommodating Ripley said.

Ripley returned to her autograph table and continued signing books until well after 7 p.m. Rich's had to turn away hundreds of people still waiting in line. The day's final tally? Ripley had signed five thousand copies of *Scarlett*.

Reader reaction to *Scarlett* was mixed, but critics were nearly unanimous in slamming the book. John Goodspeed provided a succinct summary in the title of his *Baltimore Sun* book review: "Frankly, my dear, it stinks." The kindest comments came from Celestine Sibley, a columnist for the *Atlanta Journal-Constitution* and an acquaintance of Margaret Mitchell. Sibley stated that *Scarlett* "is a lively book, prodigiously researched, meticulously written and a riveting read."

When asked about the criticism, Ripley told the *Richmond Times-Dispatch*: "I haven't read the reviews, but I understand that they are pretty awful. I don't think they would have liked a sequel written by Margaret Mitchell herself. I expected bad reviews, so why upset myself by reading them? I can't think of anything I could have done differently. I think I did a good job."

Defending *Scarlett*, president of Warner Books Laurence J. Kirshbaum told the *Baltimore Sun*: "The book's sale is going to be determined by the consumer and not the reviewer."

And the consumer spoke:

- On publication day in North American bookstores, book buyers purchased more than 250,000 copies of *Scarlett*. Sales hit 500,000 copies by the end of the first week.
- On the one-month anniversary of the book's debut, sales in the United States and Canada equaled 1.5 million copies, making *Scarlett* the year's best-selling book and the fastest selling novel of all time.
- *Scarlett* premiered as the number one best seller on the *New York Times* best-seller list for October 13, 1991, and remained there for sixteen consecutive weeks, falling to number two on the February 2, 1992, list.
- Warner Books announced foreign sales of at least four million copies. Among the forty countries where the book was released simultaneously, *Scarlett* was especially popular in Germany, France, the United Kingdom, Italy, and Spain.
- The Literary Guild and Doubleday Book Club both offered *Scarlett* as featured selections.
- Christmas purchases of *Scarlett* in the United States and Canada pushed total sales beyond two million copies.

Despite *Scarlett*'s stellar sales performance, *Entertainment Weekly* in a special year-end issue declared the sequel number six on its list of the ten worst books of 1991. But tomorrow is another day, and *Scarlett* had the last word regarding sales as the New Year dawned.

By the end of January 1992, Warner Books had issued thirteen printings of the sequel's North American hardcover edition for a combined total of 2,220,000 copies. Foreign sales were thriving. A six-hour, four-cassette audio version of *Scarlett* voiced by CBS-TV's *Designing Women* star Dixie Carter and released by Simon & Schuster Audio had hit the top of the best-seller lists with sales of more than 100,000 copies.

By May 1992, *Scarlett* was still on the *New York Times* best-seller list—ranked as number twelve—and had been on the list for thirty-one weeks.

For the novel's one-year anniversary, Warner Books released a deluxe, slipcased, hardcover edition limited to five thousand numbered copies signed by Ripley. Debuting on the one-year anniversary date was the paperback edition, which ranked number one on the *New York Times* best-seller list for three weeks.

By October 1992, *Scarlett* was still going strong. The paperback edition was in its fourth printing with a combined total of 4.2 million copies ordered by bookstores during its first month of publication. The hardcover edition— fourteen printings and counting—had sold 2.25 million copies.

SCARLETT: THE CRITICS HAVE SPOKEN

". . . I feel compelled by duty to join the herd of book reviewers who have concluded, after careful reading and consideration, that 'Scarlett' stinks. I know, of course, that frankly, the reading public doesn't give a damn about what book reviewers think. But fiddle-dee-dee, friends. We insist it's awful."

—*Baltimore Sun*

"The most unnecessary commercial product since the automatic card shuffler."

—*Columbus Dispatch*

"There is much thinking aloud in *Scarlett*, but little actual dialogue, maybe because most of this stuff is too embarrassing to say out loud."

—*Detroit Free Press*

"By the close of the book, no one could possibly care if Rhett and Scarlett end up together: In a cost-cutting coup, Ripley clearly junked the original, labour-consuming characters and replaced them with robots."

—*Globe & Mail* (Toronto)

"Ranks several miles below serious fiction and only a few inches above the cookie-cutter offerings from Harlequin."

—*Los Angeles Times*

"What is missing from Miss Ripley's two-and-a-half-pound doorstop, besides brains, heart, and guts, is any historical context, any psychological insight, any irony or tension."

—National Review

"Although Mammy is dying, she is the luckiest person here. In her delirium, she imagines she is back with the real Scarlett at the real Tara—back in the real book."

—New York Times

"Chewing, shopping and changing clothes do not a novel make."

—New York Newsday

"Alexandra Ripley don't know nothin' 'bout writin' no sequels. So what's wrong with *Scarlett?* Just plot, and characters, and prose."

—Richmond News Leader

"Oh fiddle-dee-dee. It's just ghastly."

—Sunday Oklahoman

"The world can be divided into two camps: those who consider any sequel to *Gone With the Wind* a sacrilege, and those who don't. The former will detest Alexandra Ripley's *Scarlett: The Sequel to Margaret Mitchell's* Gone With the Wind on principle. The latter will simply loathe the book itself."

—USA Today

"Damnable."

—Washington Post

SCARLETT: A NOVEL QUIZ

1. What three societal sins did Scarlett commit at Melanie's funeral?
2. When Scarlett arrived at Tara, who did she learn was dying?

3. What costume did Scarlett wear to Atlanta's Masked Ball?

4. What was the religious name taken by Scarlett's sister Carreen?

5. When Scarlett followed Rhett to Charleston, with whom did she stay?

6. What vegetable did Scarlett help Sally Brewton select at Charleston's Market?

7. How much money did Rhett offer to Scarlett for her to leave Charleston?

8. What flowers, grown on the Butler family's plantation, did Scarlett wear to the opening ball of Charleston's season?

9. Who was the gentleman in Charleston with whom Scarlett carried on a romance to make Rhett jealous?

10. On Charleston's Race Day, who did Scarlett realize was in love with Rhett?

11. What was Scarlett's plan to regain control of Tara?

12. How did Scarlett and Rhett celebrate their escape from the shipwreck?

13. Who burned the farewell letter to Rhett's mother that Scarlett wrote before leaving for Savannah?

14. Who offered Scarlett his entire estate if she would remain in his house and cater to his needs?

15. What life-changing realization hit Scarlett on her first day at sea on the voyage to Ireland?

16. What was the name of the O'Hara family's ancestral land in Ireland?

17. How much did Scarlett pay to the bishop to redeem Carreen's dowry?

18. What family title of honor did Scarlett earn because of her strength, courage, and determination?

19. When was Scarlett's child born?

20. What name did Scarlett give her daughter at baptism?

21. What nickname did Scarlett give her daughter because of her green eyes?

22. Since Rhett divorced her and remarried, whom did Scarlett agree to marry?

23. Who told Scarlett that Rhett's wife died in childbirth?

24. Who set fire to the arsenal in the church to avenge Colum O'Hara's death?

25. How did Scarlett, Rhett, and their daughter escape from the tower after the mob burned the rope ladder?

ALEXANDRA RIPLEY: BEFORE, DURING, AND AFTER *SCARLETT*

Once she was chosen to pick up where Margaret Mitchell left off, Alexandra Ripley steeled herself: "I'm trying to prepare myself for a universal hatred of what I'm going to do." She also acknowledged that the sequel "will never be mine. It's a foster mother kind of thing."

As a "foster mother," Ripley was well suited to the challenge. She was the best-selling author of "big fat, serious historicals" such as *Charleston, On Leaving Charleston, New Orleans Legacy*, and *The Time Returns*.

Ripley was also well connected to the world of Scarlett and Rhett. Born on January 8, 1934, she grew up in Charleston, South Carolina, the soul of the South and Rhett Butler's hometown. As a child, she took nickels from tourists in return for directions to Rhett Butler's grave.

She attended Ashley Hall, a Charleston finishing school, where she learned deportment by walking up stairs balancing a book on her head. "Because of Charleston's isolation and clannishness, I was fifty years out-of-date," Ripley said. "I feel as if I grew up in Margaret Mitchell's generation."

A scholarship from the United Daughters of the Confederacy allowed her to attend Vassar College in Poughkeepsie, New York. After graduation in 1955, she joined *Life* magazine's advertising department in New York City. She held a series of other jobs north of the Mason-Dixon Line and married and divorced before returning to Charleston with her daughters, Elizabeth and Merrill. Ripley settled in a house that had once been a home to slaves and began a career as a ghostwriter.

She returned to New York a few years later and accepted a job as a reader of unsolicited manuscripts at a publishing house. By the time she had become publicity director, she decided to try writing her own books. A mystery novel followed, then a joint venture involving a nonfiction account of a murder and a ghosted autobiography. By that time, her money was running low.

A 1975 visit to Virginia convinced Ripley that the modest standard of living there would allow her to write *and* to eat. So she moved south again and found a job as a bookstore stock clerk. In 1981, *Charleston* was published. Customers flocked to the bookstore to buy the book and to have the novel autographed by the author right in the stockroom. Set in the post–Civil War era, *Charleston* received outstanding reviews from critics, who compared the book to *GWTW*. Ripley's career was launched. *Charleston* and her subsequent books provided a body of work that boded well for her selection as the writer of the authorized sequel.

"I never considered not doing it," Ripley told the *Baltimore Sun*. "I just couldn't resist it. The book was going to be done. If I didn't do it, someone else would. And I thought that no one else could do it as well as I could."

After spending eighteen months researching the book, Ripley primed herself for writing the sequel by becoming immersed in Margaret's novel. Doing so, Ripley admitted, created "moments of absolute terror" because she realized "I couldn't write that well."

She also didn't like the main character. "When I began writing the sequel, I had a lot of trouble because Scarlett is not my kind of person. She's virtually illiterate, has no taste, never learns from her mistakes." Still, Ripley soldiered on and completed a first draft—written in longhand—in a year and a half.

Editorial disagreements abounded and delayed the book for about a year. Ripley's editor insisted on a manuscript "more in the style of contemporary best-sellers." Ripley refused. "When I started bellowing, 'It's not close to the spirit of Margaret Mitchell,' they listened," she said, and assigned a more like-minded editor to the project.

When *Scarlett* was published, Ripley undertook a grueling month-long, national promotional tour and became overwhelmed by the attention she and her book generated. "It [was] like going to Oz without the benefit of the tornado," she said. She contended with exuberant crowds clamoring for her book and the knowledge that her reviews were scathing. Although she ignored the caustic critical comments, she was hurt that her efforts were demeaned: "People can be so clever, but it's such an easy shot."

Another type of pain hit Ripley two months after the sequel's debut. She developed severe tendonitis and carpal tunnel syndrome in her right hand from having signed more than ten thousand copies of *Scarlett*. She had felt flattered that people had stood in line for hours, awaiting a chance to meet her and to have their books autographed. "Also, I figure[ed] the cover price is so immense, that I owed it to them to keep signing," she said. But she vowed that as soon as the *Scarlett* frenzy was over, "I'm going to dye my hair, put my right arm in a sling and go into seclusion."

Post-sequel, Ripley retreated to her home, Lafayette Hill Tavern, an eighteenth-century country farmhouse in central Virginia that she shared with her second husband, John Graham, a professor of rhetoric at the University of Virginia. The sequel and the money she earned from it allowed her to do what she loved to do: write.

When casting began for the *Scarlett* television miniseries, Ripley was asked about the actors and actresses she preferred to see in the lead roles. "I'm following in the footsteps of Margaret Mitchell who sold the movie rights and would have no more to do with it," she said, then went right back to her writing.

In 1994, Warner Books published her historical romance novel *From Fields of Gold*, a story about a tobacco baron and the woman who loves him. In 1996, Warner Books published her final work, the historical "biography" *A Love Divine*, about the life of Joseph of Arimathea, the man who gave his tomb to the crucified Jesus.

Ripley moved to Richmond, Virginia, in 2003 and was working on a novel whose setting was Lafayette Hill Tavern, her former home, when she died of natural causes on January 10, 2004—just two days after her seventieth birthday. Legally separated from her husband at the time of her death, Ripley was survived by her two daughters and one granddaughter.

HOW *SCARLETT* WAS SOLD TO TELEVISION

Once the fifty-five-year-old question—Do Scarlett and Rhett get back together?—was answered, *GWTW* fans wanted to know another: Would *Scarlett* have a future on the silver screen or on the small screen?

The man who had his sights set on bringing *Scarlett* to television was Robert Halmi Sr., chairman of RHI Entertainment Inc. and the producer of television movies and miniseries such as the award-winning 1989 blockbuster *Lonesome Dove*. Halmi offered Margaret Mitchell's estate $50,000 for the broadcast rights to *Scarlett*. (Interestingly, producer David O. Selznick paid the same amount for the film rights to *GWTW*.)

This opening bid for what turned out to be the fastest-selling novel of all time escalated as quickly as copies of *Scarlett* flew off bookstore shelves.

Halmi and three partners—a German company, an Italian firm, and CBS Television—finally shelled out the highest price ever paid to serialize a book for television: $9 million. On November 4, 1991, the William Morris Agency announced that the Stephens Mitchell Trusts and RHI Entertainment Inc. had struck a deal for the broadcast rights to *Scarlett*.

Halmi announced to the media that he planned to launch a worldwide search for an actress to play Scarlett and that he would seek "someone the audience roots for and that all men are in love with." He boasted that his search would rival the original 1930s actress-to-play-Scarlett quest. Casting himself as a modern-day David O. Selznick, Halmi stated: "It'll take a year to find her, about as long as it takes to write the screenplay." For the male roles, including Rhett Butler, he would cast already established actors.

Halmi planned to shoot the miniseries entirely on location in Atlanta, Charleston, Savannah, and Ireland. While the action of the novel ends in Ireland, Halmi promised that the television production would conclude the story in Atlanta. "That way we'll leave the story open for another sequel," he said.

Halmi expected the *Scarlett* miniseries to have a running time of eight hours and a production price tag of at least $30 million. As an investor in the deal, CBS Television agreed to pay two-thirds of that cost in return for exclusive rights to broadcast the miniseries in the United States. (In 1938, Metro-Goldwyn-Mayer contributed half of the projected $2.5 million production cost of *GWTW* in return for exclusive distribution rights to the film and other considerations.)

"We're pulling out all the stops," Halmi stated. "We want to do the story justice and make it a TV event."

THE NEW SEARCH FOR SCARLETT

On July 17, 1992, a bevy of women—many wearing bonnets and hoop-skirts—flounced into Atlanta's Civic Center hoping for a shot at the role of a lifetime. The open audition for the role of Scarlett O'Hara in the television miniseries attracted aspiring actresses from Georgia, neighboring states, and as far away as New York. At the end of the day, only two of the 410 women received callbacks for second readings.

Casting sessions for professional actresses recommended by agents were held in New York and Los Angeles and across the pond in London, Dublin, Munich, Paris, and Rome. But producer Robert Halmi and casting director Lynn Kressel had already heard from about twenty thousand would-be Scarletts from around the world.

"I had to change my phone number in New York seven times," Halmi complained during a news conference. "I had nothing but Scarlett messages 24 hours a day, and people came to the door dressed as Scarlett." (David O. Selznick was similarly pursued during his Scarlett search.)

The lengthy, costly, and well-publicized campaign to find an unknown actress culminated in plans for a live televised broadcast on Sunday, October 4, 1992, during which Halmi would announce his Scarlett choice.

As a lead-up to the much ballyhooed event, the producer invited twenty-three top contenders to Atlanta, where final auditions were held on Thursday, October 1. He chose nine semifinalists and scheduled screen tests that were filmed the next day by Academy Award–winning director Delbert Mann. Halmi viewed the tests and thought that three of the actresses were possibilities for the role. He reviewed the footage again on Saturday but had second thoughts.

A syndicated TV special, *The Search for Scarlett*, broadcast from the Georgia state Capitol, took a prime-time pratfall when, at the end of the hour, Halmi declared: "Unfortunately, none of the ladies that I have met, as wonderful as they are, is the Scarlett that I need, hope and must have." To counter the shock and disappointment, Halmi offered speaking roles in the miniseries as consolation prizes to the three finalists.

Afterward, he told the media that the search for Scarlett would go on: "The next thing to do is to look for actresses who are not stars but are marquee actresses."

HALMI FINDS HIS SCARLETT

After deciding to seek "marquee actresses" for the lead role in his miniseries, Robert Halmi found his Scarlett while watching television late one night. Joanne Whalley-Kilmer and her performance in *Scandal* (1989) mesmerized the producer. She portrayed Christine Keeler, a young exotic dancer whose affair with a senior politician rocks the British government.

Halmi's two-year search was over, and his selection of Whalley-Kilmer for the role of Scarlett was announced on November 8, 1993—the anniversary of Margaret Mitchell's birth.

"The most anticipated piece of casting has been the role of Scarlett O'Hara," Halmi said. "Scarlett . . . was the first feminist and independent lady who not only was strong of will but completely feminine—in other words, the ideal woman. I am very proud that we have found her in Joanne Whalley-Kilmer and can introduce her to the public."

"It's an honor to be chosen to play one of the great women's roles of all time," Whalley-Kilmer said, following the casting announcement.

In casting Whalley-Kilmer, Halmi followed in the footsteps of David O. Selznick. Both producers chose beautiful British actresses not yet well known to audiences of the day.

Born in Lancashire and raised in Cheshire, Joanne Whalley-Kilmer studied acting at the Braeside School of Speech and Drama. She gained prominence with roles in movies and television series for BBC Television. Her feature film work included roles in *Willow* (1988), where she met her husband, actor Val Kilmer; *Navy SEALS* (1990); *Shattered* (1991); *Storyville* (1992); and *The Secret Rapture* (1993).

HOW HALMI GOT HIS RHETT BUTLER

Like David O. Selznick before him, Robert Halmi sought his Rhett Butler from the constellation of established Hollywood stars. Halmi offered the part to Timothy Dalton, a British actor best known for portraying 007 in two James Bond films. Like Clark Gable before him, Dalton refused the role initially.

"I felt that Clark Gable's image as Rhett Butler was so indelible in everyone's mind that I couldn't possibly live up to it," Dalton explained to King Features Syndicate. "Of course, I had originally said no to becoming James Bond, too, and that would have been a horrible mistake since it boosted my career immeasurably."

Encouraged to meet with the director of the miniseries, Dalton was impressed by John Erman's vision of the character of Rhett Butler and of the relationship between Rhett and Scarlett. The director challenged the actor to consider the different ways Dalton could interpret such an iconic character. Erman kept up a steady drumbeat, hoping Dalton would reconsider his decision.

"I got to thinking," Dalton told *TV Guide*. "'How can you turn it down? If you walk away from Rhett, you may live to regret it forever. Take it on. Go for it.'"

To prepare for the role, Dalton studied *Gone with the Wind*, viewed the movie, and read *Scarlett* multiple times. That gave him insight about how Gable crafted Rhett. He did so, Dalton concluded, by taking on the character's essence. Dalton decided to use the same blueprint for developing his characterization.

While Gable eschewed a Southern accent in the film, Dalton and the director decided that Rhett would have one in the miniseries. Dalton developed and rehearsed a distinctive drawl then tried it out on Erman, who declared it too thick. The actor substituted a thinner version that Erman approved.

Dalton approved of the script, especially Rhett's reactions to Scarlett's attempts to get him to love her again. "He doesn't give in," Dalton said. "He was wounded deeply by his inability to make her love him in the past. Like all people who have been scalded by love, he is not eager to put his foot back in the water." Dalton was also happy that "both Scarlett and Rhett are actually better people by the time we've finished telling their story."

Born in North Wales and raised in England, Dalton made the decision to become an actor after seeing a production of *Macbeth* as a teenager. He studied at the Royal Academy of Dramatic Art but left after two years to join the Birmingham Repertory Theatre. His career included stage, television, and film roles, most notably as James Bond in *The Living Daylights* (1987) and *Licence to Kill* (1989).

A WHO'S WHO OF *SCARLETT*'S CAST

Ann-Margret—Belle Watling
Rakie Ayola—Pansy
Barbara Barrie—Pauline Robillard
Sean Bean—Lord Richard Fenton
Brian Bedford—Sir John Morland
Stephen Collins—Ashley Wilkes

Timothy Dalton—Rhett Butler
Rachel Dowling—Bridie O'Hara
John Gielgud—Pierre Robillard
Annabeth Gish—Anne Hampton Butler
George Grizzard—Henry Hamilton
Julie Hamilton—Old Katie Scarlett
Julie Harris—Eleanor Butler
Tina Kellegher—Mary Boyle
Delena Kidd—Lady Morland
Mark Lambert—Donnelly
Melissa Leo—Suellen O'Hara Benteen
Rosaleen Linehan—Mrs. Fitzpatrick
Ruth McCabe—Kathleen O'Hara
Ray McKinnon—Will Benteen
Colm Meaney—Father Colum O'Hara
Gary Raymond—Old Daniel O'Hara
Owen Roe—Tim O'Hara
Esther Rolle—Mammy
Jean Smart—Sally Brewton
Joanne Whalley-Kilmer—Scarlett O'Hara
Elizabeth Wilson—Eulalie Robillard
Paul Winfield—Big Sam

TROUBLE WITH *SCARLETT*

With casting underway, Robert Halmi's next challenge was transforming Alexandra Ripley's novel into a script suitable for a miniseries with six hours of action.

"If you interpret the book, it probably would have made four-and-a-half to five hours of entertaining television," Halmi said. "I think we had to carry it a bit further." For that, Halmi turned to Emmy Award–winning television scriptwriter William Hanley, who was tasked with cutting much of the book's Scarlett-in-Ireland story line. Numerous changes followed before the script was given the green light for filming.

The start of principal filming began in London in January 1994 and became a logistical nightmare for award-winning director John Erman, one of the directors of the wildly successful *Roots* (1977) and *Roots: The Next Generations* (1979), and director of photography Tony Imi. For *Scarlett*, Erman and Imi had a six-month shooting schedule involving fifty-three different locations in England, Ireland, and the United States and more than two thousand extras. "It was an intense shoot," Imi said.

Increasing the intensity was the manner in which interior and exterior scenes were filmed. Interior scenes of houses and rooms that appear to be in United States locations were actually filmed in England, while the exterior scenes of the "same" houses and rooms were filmed in the United States. "It was quite a challenge finding houses and rooms in England that looked like Atlanta or Savannah," Imi said.

Another issue was continuity. For example, when Joanne Whalley-Kilmer, on location in London, was filmed inside a house getting ready to leave, she had to look identical weeks later when, on location in Savannah, she was filmed walking down the stairs of the "same" house on her way to her carriage.

"This was the hardest job I've ever experienced in TV," director Erman said.

In no time at all, cost overruns ballooned the production budget to $45 million, putting even more pressure on the beleaguered director to run a tighter-than-usual ship. Fifteen-hour days, problems navigating London traffic, clashing egos, and fraying nerves made the set unbearable for some but apparently not for the stars.

"They were coddled," according to a unit production manager in Charleston. "Dalton was fine, but she [Whalley-Kilmer] could be pretty tough."

Whalley-Kilmer admitted to *TV Guide* that she found herself exhibiting some of her character's less-than-admirable qualities. "I didn't carry Scarlett around 24 hours a day, but sometimes the edges became blurred. I didn't know where I ended and she began," Whalley-Kilmer said.

Halmi pooh-poohed the turmoil on the set. "I had no problem with the logistics of the shoot," he stated. "My problem was, I had an airdate before I even began to shoot. Then I had the problem of a worldwide simultaneous broadcast and to dub it in seventeen languages. So I had to find seventeen Rhett and Scarletts. That's how it became tough."

Things were about to get even tougher, as Halmi soon discovered.

SCARLETT'S SNEAK-PEEK FIASCO

CBS-TV hosted a press conference and party event for *Scarlett* on July 19, 1994, as part of the Television Critics Association Summer Press Tour in Los Angeles. What a great way, the network thought, to screen a sneak peek of the much-anticipated miniseries for a large group of television reporters, representing media outlets from all across the country, and to spotlight producer Halmi and his stars.

That evening, Halmi primed the press by declaring: "When Margaret Mitchell ended her fantastic work with, 'Tomorrow is another day,' it left it completely for anybody to pick up tomorrow. We did tomorrow and the day after tomorrow."

The ten-minute compilation of *Scarlett* clips featured snippets of scenes: fingers unlacing a bodice, a hand fondling a breast, a boat capsizing in a storm-tossed sea, and events nowhere to be found in Ripley's novel: a rape, a murder, and a shocking trial. Watching this stew of potboiler ingredients caused reporters to groan, snicker, and laugh out loud.

"When you see the whole scene, you'll be so mesmerized and fascinated, you're not only not going to laugh, you're going to go completely with it," Halmi cajoled.

At the press conference that followed, Halmi, Whalley-Kilmer, and Dalton seemed stunned at the negative reaction their work had received.

Halmi fanned the flames further by stating that even if it were possible he would not have cast Vivien Leigh and Clark Gable in the miniseries because it's not *Gone With the Wind*: "It's a different story." Asked why the story strayed from Ripley's plotline, Halmi responded: "Anytime you dramatize a book, you have to be visual and interpret feelings that maybe are not in the written word."

Whalley-Kilmer described Scarlett's transformation in the miniseries: "She doesn't lose her drive and her power, and the admirable side of her nature, but she does become kinder and more compassionate." The actress called Scarlett "a great, great role."

In contrast, a question posed to Dalton unleashed a stream of invective uncharacteristic of a gentleman. The actor assailed *Scarlett*'s progenitor, *Gone With the Wind*, likening the film to "an extraordinary soap opera" and characterizing its heroine as "a bitch." In an attempt to explain himself, he stated: "I mean, she's a monster: I mean look at this woman. I mean: mean, selfish, ambitious, greedy, manipulative, marrying men for their money, you know. Come on."

Dalton didn't stop there. He characterized Scarlett as played by Whalley-Kilmer as "this four-letter word beginning with a [specific consonant]," an obscenity considered the worst English-language epithet for a woman. Reporter reactions ranged from "stunned silence to hisses of disapproval." It was all downhill from there, culminating in a woman reporter publicly calling out Dalton for his comments and the two exchanging icy glares until a CBS representative ended the press conference.

Later, Dalton told *TV Guide* he had been furious after seeing the press conference clip that he described as "bad cut after bad cut. It left the press baying for our blood." Halmi, on the other hand, remained effusively optimistic, telling *TV Guide*: "*Gone With the Wind* couldn't live up to this. My production is *beyond* the spectacle of the movie. I think this is *more* entertaining."

SCARLETT PREMIERES

GWTW fans tuned in to CBS for the debut of *Scarlett*, the most anticipated television event of the season, on Sunday, November 13, 1994. As a result, the two-hour premiere earned a 21.4 rating and a 32 share, according to Nielsen Media Research Company, and was crowned the highest-rated show of the week. The remaining two-hour episodes broadcast on November 15, 16, and 17 lost audience but were still ranked in the top ten of most-watched shows. Surprisingly, that added up to bad news for CBS.

The network had promised—and had failed to deliver—a 24 rating and a 36 share to advertisers that had spent $40 million for commercial time during the miniseries. To make it up to them, CBS gave free advertising time worth up to $5 million to sponsors such as Ford and Kmart for commercials placed in other prime-time programs.

Factors that sank CBS's lofty goals of delivering a blockbuster *Scarlett* for advertisers were viewers giving up on the saga after the first night plus reviews ranging from tepid to terrible:

"Scarlett O'Hara, whose independence and fortitude helped catapult Margaret Mitchell to fame in 1936 and made Vivien

Rhett and Scarlett in the proposal embrace. Turner Entertainment/New Line Cinema

Margaret Mitchell surrounded by Leigh, Gable, Selznick, and de Havilland in Atlanta. Photofest

The night of the Atlanta premiere. Photofest

Inside page of the 1939 program. From the author's collection

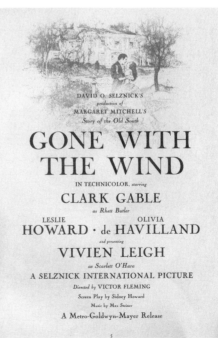

DAVID O. SELZNICK'S
production of
MARGARET MITCHELL'S
Story of the Old South

GONE WITH THE WIND

IN TECHNICOLOR, *starring*

CLARK GABLE

as Rhett Butler

LESLIE OLIVIA
HOWARD · de HAVILLAND

and presenting

VIVIEN LEIGH

as Scarlett O'Hara

A SELZNICK INTERNATIONAL PICTURE

Directed by VICTOR FLEMING

Screen Play by Sidney Howard

Music by Max Steiner

A Metro-Goldwyn-Mayer Release

5

The back cover of the 1939 program. From the author's collection

A German program for GWTW. From the author's collection

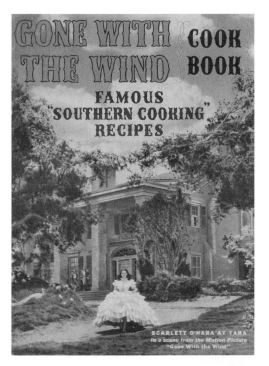

The GWTW *Cookbook.*
From the author's collection

Gone With the Wind
honored by the US Postal
Service. The Turner Store
Atlanta

Scarlett *Executive Producer Robert Halmi, Sr.*

Joanne Whalley-Kilmer as Scarlett.

Ashley and Scarlett.

*Anne Hampton accepts a
ride from Rhett.*

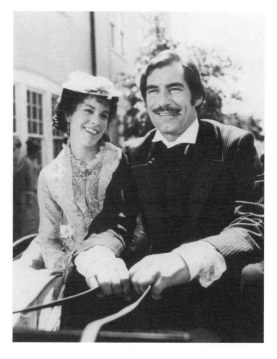

Rhett and Scarlett at Tara.

Exterior of Margaret Mitchell House, birthplace of Gone with the Wind. *Located at the Atlanta History Center's midtown campus. Courtesy of Atlanta History Center.*

Leigh a movie star in 1939, already has survived Alexandra Ripley's 1991 sequel to the novel. But she may not make it through this bilious, overblown sequel to the movie."

—Boston Globe

"Stuck with Ripley's inferior material [producer/director] Erman can't deliver a *Scarlett* that even begins to approach the grandeur of *Gone With the Wind*. The result is a flashy, trashy 19th century soap opera. . . . Those who appreciate rustic scenery, fancy period costumes and lusty bodice-ripping scenes may be entertained by this tempestuous melodrama, which is longer, raunchier but in no way better than its Oscar-winning forerunner."

—Chicago Sun-Times

"For a television industry enamored of sequels, soapish melodramas, sweeping mini-series and women in peril, *Scarlett* ought to be a dream come true. But it's more like a nightmare. A long, messy, costly nightmare."

—Chicago Tribune

"If *Gone With the Wind* is the slide trombone of the cinematic orchestra, *Scarlett* is the tuba of TV movies—ungainly and unsubtle."

—Entertainment Weekly

"The look of the miniseries is stunning, with sumptuous costuming and sets. But it's an essentially hollow and curiously dispassionate epic that forges relentlessly on without ever building up a head of steam."

—People

"On the whole, *Scarlett* is reasonably entertaining, an acceptable way to waste four long November evenings. It will not make you forget the original that supposedly 'inspired' this sequel."

—Seattle Times

". . . Whalley-Kilmer brings an unnecessary sophistication to a role that requires her to do little more than kiss in midsentence and appear alternately tortured and feisty. In fact, many cast members—including Sir John Gielgud (Scarlett's grandfather) and Julie Harris (Rhett's mother)—seem wasted on a story without much of a plot and a script devoid of sharp dialogue. Dalton is a sufficiently handsome Rhett, although he lacks the intelligence and wit of *Gone With the Wind*'s Clark Gable."

—Time

"[*Scarlett* is] twice as long as the original but delivers a fraction of the drama, with all its plot artificially injected, like the fake cream in Twinkies."

—TV Guide

". . . [N]ot much happens in the first few hours. Rhett and Scarlett go on a little boating jaunt, but a storm tosses her into the sea, and Scarlett passes out. Back on shore, they make love, and Scarlett passes out again. He files for divorce. So she goes to Ireland and dances a reel with her Irish relatives, but, since she's pregnant, Scarlett passes out. After she has the baby, she sees Rhett, who's now remarried, and they all go on a fox hunt, but Scarlett is thrown from her horse and passes out. In fact, Scarlett spends a lot of her time unconscious, and viewers are likely to follow her lead."

—Variety

"*Gone With the Wind* was a turbulent love story set against an even more turbulent historical background; *Scarlett* has virtually no context at all. It just kind of sits there in a puddle of its own tears."

—Washington Post

The last word about *Scarlett* came from *TV Guide* in June 1995 when it named Halmi's epic the worst miniseries of the 1994–1995 season: "It may have been the top-rated mini of the year, but frankly, *Scarlett*, we don't give a damn."

SCARLETT WHO SAID IT?

From the following list of characters, decide who spoke the lines of dialogue from the television miniseries.

Suellen O'Hara Benteen	Henry Hamilton
Will Benteen	Mammy
Big Sam	Sir John Morland
Mary Boyle	Lady Morland
Sally Brewton	Scarlett O'Hara
Anne Hampton Butler	Father Colum O'Hara
Eleanor Butler	Eulalie Robillard
Rhett Butler	Pauline Robillard
Lord Fenton	Belle Watling
Rosaleen Fitzpatrick	Ashley Wilkes

1. "Feelings are running real high against you here in Atlanta. Everybody seems determined to believe that you had your eye and your intentions set on Ashley Wilkes right up to the time Melanie passed on."

2. "I want you to take care of Miz Scarlett. She needs carin' so bad. Always needed carin' so bad Miz Scarlett did."

3. "The North just didn't suit me after a time, Miz Scarlett, but I did prosper. I did prosper. Enough so's I could come home here and establish my little business enterprise."

4. "I don't have to throw you out, Scarlett. Sooner or later you'll reveal yourself."

5. "She's a survivor. We need her kind in the South . . . even in Charleston. Especially in Charleston. I'm gonna sponsor her."

6. "Actually, I'm here on business, truth be told. . . . You might say I arrange social get togethers."

7. "Scarlett, this is Charleston, and you are ostensibly a lady. A lady does not accompany a man to his hotel room and certainly not in the broad light of day for anyone to behold and most certainly not in Charleston."

8. "Your mind's in too much turmoil to be thinking clearly now, Scarlett. For it's quite clear you won't be able to keep the truth from him once your baby's come."

9. I reckon we could buy enough whitewash to paint the entire house with what that fancy dress you're wearing cost."

10. "Maybe you don't want me, but I've got something now you do want . . . always wanted. The ace is up my sleeve now, and I'll play it when the time's right. When I'm good and ready."

11. "In absolutely certain knowledge that Scarlett will not make her own apologies no matter how deeply owed, may I beg your pardon in her stead, Father?"

12. "I suppose Father never was too very fond of Gerald O'Hara, if truth be told."

13. "I'm not accustomed to sudden onsets of chastity, Scarlett."

14. "A murderess? That enchanting creature? Ridiculous."

15. "You're well rid of him, Scarlett. He was never . . . never worthy of you."

16. "Are you thinkin' of selling up your share of Tara, Scarlett?"

17. "In your sleep one night you said her name. You said 'Scarlett' just like that."

18. "I must say. You sit that horse as though you've been riding to hounds all your life."

19. "No, she's not the one done it. She's not the one!"

20. "They're lovers. Her and Fenton. . . . What would you make of him comin' half dressed out of her bedroom in the middle of the night?"

THE TWISTS AND TURNS IN
THE SECOND SEQUEL'S SAGA, PART ONE

After the spectacular success yet critical castigation of Alexandra Ripley's sequel, the lawyers overseeing the Mitchell estate decided that the *next* continuation of Scarlett and Rhett's story would have "high literary quality." St. Martin's Press had high hopes of meeting that standard. In 1995, the publisher paid $4.5 million to the estate for the rights to publish a second sequel and then hired British novelist Emma Tennant for the project.

Tennant's body of work had been described by critic Gary Indiana, writing in the *Village Voice* in 1990, as "a startling progression of novels unlike anything else being written in England: wildly imaginative, risk-taking books inspired by dreams, fairy tales, fables, science fiction and detective stories, informed by a wicked Swiftian vision of the U.K. in decline."

Among her numerous novels was *Pemberley*, a continuation of Jane Austen's *Pride and Prejudice* published in 1993 that debuted to mixed reviews. *Booklist*, the review journal of the American Library Association, stated: "As a sequel to Austen's masterpiece, *Pemberley* is a very distant relation—one even the kindhearted Elizabeth [Bennet Darcy] would probably not deign to recognize."

Was Tennant the right writer to tackle the next sequel to *Gone with the Wind*? Her friend and fellow author Lady Antonia Fraser obviously thought so. She had recommended Tennant to one of the Mitchell estate's lawyers, who, by coincidence, had just read *Pemberley*, a book that had been published by St. Martin's Press.

"I was enormously flattered to be asked to further the adventures of Scarlett—and I loved the challenge," Tennant told London's *Mail on Sunday*. According to the author, her sixteen-page contract for the *GWTW* sequel required her to maintain the novel's characters, tone, and vision, and forbade her from including "any references to incest, lesbian affairs or sex between different racial groups." With those guidelines in mind, Tennant crafted her plot and then pounded out a 575-page manuscript on an inexpensive electric typewriter kept in the bedroom of her Notting Hill home.

In the book that Tennant titled *Tara*, Scarlett leaves Georgia for the high-society circles of Washington and New York and becomes the toast of the towns. In Washington, she attracts the attention of President Rutherford B. Hayes, who makes Scarlett his mistress. In New York, she learns that Rhett's business dealings have involved him with corrupt William "Boss" Tweed, head of Tammany Hall, and that Rhett's life is in peril. Scarlett infiltrates the criminal mob as a moll, rescues Rhett, but flees to Tara without him.

While restoring her plantation home, Scarlett learns that Rhett has been killed in South America. Grief-stricken, she marries Ashley Wilkes, despite the fact that she no longer loves him. Together they rebuild Twelve Oaks and make it their home. Time passes. One evening, while Ashley broods in the Twelve Oaks' library, Scarlett sits on the verandah and spots a bedraggled figure trudging toward her. She realizes the man is Rhett, and she rushes into his arms. With love thought lost found at last, Scarlett and Rhett pledge to remain together for all time—at Tara.

After submitting her manuscript to the publisher, Tennant was sacked from the project. She attributed the firing to "creative differences." What went wrong?

"It's hard to pin that down," Tennant said. "I was told the book was 'not in the style of Margaret Mitchell,' but I was hired specifically as a literary writer rather than an imitator." Tennant was also told that the book had too much of a British sensibility. Contractually, Tennant can never publish her manuscript.

"I felt a great responsibility in trying to recreate Scarlett's world, because I knew millions of people had their own strong views about how she ended up," Tennant said. "That is the quintessential ambiguity of Mitchell's original ending and, paradoxically, the perfect scene for setting off an intelligent but popular sequel. It is something that everyone wanted but now won't happen. Eventually, tomorrow may indeed be another day . . . but sadly, not from my pen."

THE TWISTS AND TURNS IN THE
SECOND SEQUEL'S SAGA, PART TWO

After firing Emma Tennant as the *GWTW* sequel author in May 1996, St. Martin's Press was faced with finding another writer to undertake the project. Imagine the delight in the publishing house when that writer, best-selling Southern novelist Pat Conroy, was found in the preface pages of *GWTW*'s sixtieth anniversary edition.

The stirring words Conroy had contributed about his connection to *GWTW* moved the editorial team at St. Martin's Press and the trustees in charge of the Mitchell estate. They agreed that Conroy possessed the *GWTW* passion and the Southern sensibilities necessary for writing a successful sequel. He'd be perfect, they decided, and set out to woo him for the project.

The wooing, done in secret for nearly three years, involved the trustees; Conroy; his agents; his book publisher, Doubleday, to whom he was under contract for another book; and St. Martin's Press. As they had with Emma Tennant, the trustees demanded that the sequel contain no references to homosexuality or to sex between people of different races.

"I told them that if they insisted on that," he said in an interview with the *New York Times*, "I'd write the novel with this first sentence: 'After they made love, Rhett turned to Ashley Wilkes and said, "Ashley, have I ever told you that my grandmother was black?"'"

Conroy refused to write the novel under the constraint of censorship, and the trustees gave in.

Conroy had a daring vision for the sequel that he shared with St. Martin's Press. His novel would not be a sequel at all. Instead, his book would tell Rhett's story in a first-person narrative titled *The Rules of Pride: The Autobiography of Capt. Rhett Butler, C.S.A.* The book would be "a companion" to *GWTW*, drawing characters and situations from the original. Conroy also mentioned to the publisher that he was thinking of possibly killing off Scarlett O'Hara, an idea that had been planted in his mind by his dying mother.

"She thought that Scarlett would be one of the great death scenes of literature," Conroy said.

When the trustees realized the implications of Scarlett's death, they balked, and Conroy threatened to walk, leaving on the table a deal that would have earned him a seven-figure advance. Negotiations stalled, but then the trustees had a change of heart. They would not prohibit a death scene, but they did want the final say on what would appear in print.

"I might have gone along with her not dying," Conroy said, "but they were also talking about editorial control, of their having final approval. That I couldn't go along with."

The deal was as dead as the Yankee deserter shot by Scarlett on Tara's staircase.

THE TWISTS AND TURNS IN THE
SECOND SEQUEL'S SAGA, PART THREE

In 1999, after the publishing deal with author Pat Conroy collapsed, St. Martin's Press had exhausted the second of its three contractual chances to find a writer for the second sequel. The publisher couldn't risk failure on the third try or else the Mitchell estate would be free to shop the sequel project to other publishers. With the clock ticking and with millions of dollars at stake, St. Martin's Press launched a third search for a sequel writer.

The long, laborious search for a capable candidate ended finally when executive editor Hope Dellon, while browsing in a bookstore, found

Donald McCaig's novel *Jacob's Ladder*. Impressed by this Civil War story of a slave-owning Virginia family, Dellon approached McCaig about taking on the sequel.

The award-winning author and Virginia sheep farmer admitted to Dellon that he hadn't read *GWTW*. After immersing himself in Margaret's masterpiece, he envisioned telling Rhett's story, "since he is enigmatic and disappears [from *GWTW*] for long periods of time. A conventional sequel was going to be pale by comparison. I had to take on the responsibility to find out about Rhett. I wanted to respect Margaret Mitchell's story and write in the spaces where she had not."

By January 2001, negotiations had culminated in a contract, stipulating that the deaths of Scarlett and Rhett were forbidden but that McCaig was not required to continue Ripley's story line, as would be the case with a typical sequel. The contract also approved "modernizing the treatment of the sensitive areas of race and sex to reflect the changes in public attitudes during the period of more than sixty years since the publication of the original novel."

During the six years McCaig spent researching and writing his book, he unearthed historical information in archives and libraries in Atlanta, Charleston, and New Orleans and in Kentucky, Tennessee, and Virginia. He even motored in a skiff in Charleston Harbor to replicate Rhett's efforts to evade federal naval blockades. His wife, Anne, prepared a one-hundred-page chapter-by-chapter synopsis of *GWTW* that allowed McCaig to stay true to the novel's timeline and to imagine actions Rhett might take or things he might say.

As the publication date neared, McCaig told the *New York Times*, "I'm almost certain that there's going to be people who really have a bone to pick with *Gone with the Wind* who are going to take it out on this. There's going to be adoring fans who find places where I distorted the true meaning of the original. And there's going to be some people who think it's a pretty good book."

THE SECOND SEQUEL PUBLISHED!

Traveling from his beloved sheep farm in Highland County, Virginia, Donald McCaig donned his signature white Stetson and hit the trail for a thirty-day, seventeen-city promotional tour for *Rhett Butler's People*, which was published on November 6, 2007.

The Margaret Mitchell House and Museum in Atlanta hosted a launch party for him on November 3, during which he inscribed 750 books in two hours. The following day he appeared at Jonesboro's Road to Tara Museum to sign books as the highlight of its annual Margaret Mitchell Birthday Weekend. Fans mobbed McCaig.

Expecting an enthusiastic response, St. Martin's Press had ordered a first printing of more than one million copies. Editor-in-Chief George Witte characterized *Rhett Butler's People* as a "reimagining, not a sequel." He told *USA Today*, "It's a wonderful retelling of *Gone with the Wind* from Rhett Butler's point of view."

McCaig's five-hundred-page book explores Rhett's life from 1843 to 1874, including his childhood on the Butler family's rice plantation, his connection to Belle Watling (and her son), his exploits as a blockade-runner, and his turbulent relationship with Scarlett O'Hara.

During its first month on bookstore shelves, *Rhett Butler's People* sold more than 100,000 copies, allowing the book to debut at number nine on *USA Today*'s best-seller list for November 16 and at number five on the *New York Times* best-seller list for November 25. The book stayed on the latter list for eight weeks.

Foreign publishing rights sold in more than fifteen countries, including Brazil, the Czech Republic, Denmark, England, Finland, France, Germany, Holland, Italy, Korea, Norway, Poland, Russia, Spain, and Sweden.

McCaig declined to reveal how much he was paid to write *Rhett Butler's People*, except to say that the deal allowed him to pay off his mortgage. But beyond the financial reward was the artistic gain for the author of previous books such as *The Butte Polka*, *Nop's Trial*, and *Nop's Hope*. Writing *Rhett Butler's People* "stretched me," according to McCaig. "It's the most difficult book I've ever written."

RHETT BUTLER'S PEOPLE: WHAT THE CRITICS SAID

"Most of *Rhett Butler's People* is a lively, entertaining read, but it bogs down somewhat in the postwar chapters, especially when McCaig tries to write from the point of view of his women characters."

—Diane White, *Boston Globe*

"Drawing Rhett's life before Scarlett enters, and taking their romance past their breakup while staying faithful to Mitchell's work, McCaig has written an earnest, competent, meticulously researched but unfortunately wooden novel."

—Kit Reed, *Chicago Sun-Times*

"McCaig's a decent writer, and the plot is better than middling. But he's missed the point about Scarlett: Nothing affected her indomitable spirit and innate selfishness . . . a docile, vapid Scarlett is worse than no Scarlett at all."

—Tina Jordan, *Entertainment Weekly*

"Donald McCaig's fine novel is not an homage. In reducing Rhett to a perplexed and worrying Everyman, McCaig reduces the power of Mitchell's original. Readers adore the enigma that is Rhett—because he is an enigma. . . . [A]fter finishing *Rhett Butler's People*, it may be impossible to read *Gone with the Wind* in quite the same way."

—Stephen L. Carter, *New York Times*

"McCaig is more persuasive on the battlefront than in the boudoir; one never feels the charge between the principals that [Margaret] Mitchell conjured. Still, this is a must-read for *GWTW* fans."

—Sue Corbett, *People*

"McCaig . . . imparts a Faulknerian tone to the saga that sharpens Mitchell's critique of Southern nostalgia without losing the epic sweep and romantic pathos. The result is an engrossing update of *GWTW* that fans of the original will definitely give a damn about."

—*Publishers Weekly*

"Well-drawn characters and a more nuanced view of history aside, the main attraction, of course, is the story. And what a story it is. With a sweep worthy of Mitchell, McCaig keeps the reader turning pages to find out the answer to the question all good fiction must answer: And then what happened?"

—Jay Strafford, *Richmond Times-Dispatch*

"*Rhett Butler's People* is faithful to Mitchell's lament for a vanished civilization, yet pleasingly updated in subtle ways, and it is an accurate portrayal of the time, mores, manners and thought to which the story unfolds. And McCaig's prose shows him to be a craftsman of the first rank."

—Michael J. Bonafield, *Minneapolis Star Tribune*

"This candid, self-doubting Rhett is too ordinary to be a romantic hero worthy of his setting; but then if there's no place for men like the old Rhett any more, that's not necessarily a bad thing. It takes a mighty writer to wrestle Captain Butler back from Clark Gable, and McCaig, by and large, proves himself equal to the task."

—Melissa Katsoulis, *Sunday Telegraph* (London)

"*Rhett* [*Butler's People*] comes across as two novels in one. There's the talented McCaig writing about un-gooey stuff: male rage, pride, despair, loyalty, the terror of the KKK, racial fury.... Then there's McCaig lacing himself into a *Gone With the Wind* romance corset trying to channel Margaret Mitchell and write domestic drama. This cross-dressing doesn't work. At all. By the end, the book dissolves into such a soap opera, you want to yell at Rhett to skip the Twelve Oaks barbecue."

—Deirdre Donahue, *USA Today*

RHETT BUTLER'S PEOPLE: A NOVEL QUIZ

1. What was the name of Rhett's favorite horse?
2. Who owned Broughton Plantation?
3. Who was the overseer of Broughton Plantation?
4. Whom did Rhett kill in a duel?
5. Who rescued young Rhett from the hurricane?

6. Who arranged Rhett's appointment to West Point?
7. How did Rhett's father disown him?
8. Who was Didi Gayerre?
9. Who invited Rhett to join him for the Twelve Oaks' barbecue?
10. What was the name of the blockade-running ship that Rhett sailed for Haynes & Son?
11. Whom did Rhett hire as the ship's pilot?
12. Who was Rhett's ward?
13. What was the name of Belle Watling's Atlanta sporting house in which Rhett owned a share?
14. What item did Rhett's sister give to him as a gift for Scarlett?
15. What incident convinced Rhett to join the Confederate Army?
16. Who was the wooden-legged ex-convict who befriended Rhett after he joined the Confederate Army?
17. Whom did Rhett shoot in the Jonesboro jail?
18. Who was the childhood friend and Connecticut senator to whom Rhett wrote letting him know he was in jail?
19. What was Belle Watling's first name?
20. What was Louis Valentine Ravanel's relationship to Rhett?
21. Who did Melanie Wilkes believe had made Rhett respectable?
22. What business transaction did Scarlett believe Rhett had tricked her to do?
23. Who was Tazewell Watling's father?
24. When Rhett's sister moved to Tara, how was she helpful to the household?
25. Who set fire to Tara?

MCCAIG PENS FIRST EVER *GWTW* PREQUEL

Writing about Rhett fueled Donald McCaig's fascination with Mammy. "We don't know where she was born, if she was ever married, if she ever had children," he told the *New York Times*. "Indeed, we don't even know her name." That changed in October 2014 when Atria Books, an imprint of Simon & Schuster, published *Ruth's Journey: The Story of Mammy from Gone with the Wind*. McCaig's authorized prequel tells Mammy's story, "from her days as a slave girl to the outbreak of the Civil War."

TWELVE

GWTW *Hits Fifty*

MACMILLAN CELEBRATES
GWTW'S FIFTIETH BIRTHDAY

In 1986, to celebrate the half-century birthday of its best-selling book, Macmillan published sixty thousand copies of a special *GWTW* golden anniversary edition: a facsimile of the first edition right down to a faithful reproduction of the original book-jacket artwork. The facsimile's prepublication price was set at $9.95; the price after June 30 was $16.95.

And fans of the novel rushed to buy copies. In fact, sales were so great that *GWTW* climbed back on the best-seller list again, just in time for its birthday.

Stamped into History

Even the United States Postal Service joined in the celebration of *GWTW's* fiftieth anniversary. On June 30, 1986, the Postal Service issued a one-cent Great American stamp bearing the likeness of Margaret Mitchell. The stamp was unveiled at a first-day-issue ceremony held at Atlanta's Omni International. Butterfly McQueen attended the event and was presented with an album of the new stamps. Following the festivities, Windies and stamp collectors alike besieged a nearby postal booth and cleaned out the stock of fifty thousand Margaret Mitchell stamps.

Other Golden Anniversary Celebrations

- The residents of Clark Gable's hometown, Cadiz, Ohio, kicked off *GWTW*'s golden anniversary year by honoring the "King of Hollywood" on the eighty-fifth anniversary of his birth. A seven-foot granite and bronze monument was dedicated to Gable on February 1, 1986, and placed at the site of his birth on Charleston Street.
- Collier Books, Macmillan's paperback division, reprinted *Margaret Mitchell's* Gone with the Wind *Letters, 1936–1949.*
- Dell re-released *Road to Tara: The Life of Margaret Mitchell* by Anne Edwards.
- Avon enlivened its *GWTW* paperback with a new anniversary cover.
- Outlet Books released *David O. Selznick's* Gone With the Wind by Ronald Haver.
- Book-of-the-Month Club offered a deluxe anniversary edition of *GWTW* with an introduction written by journalist Tom Wicker.
- The Madison-Morgan Cultural Center in Madison, Georgia, offered an exhibit from April 4 to May 25, 1986, called *The Big Book: Fifty Years of* Gone with the Wind. The exhibit featured American and foreign editions of the novel, photographs and stills from the movie, and letters written by Margaret Mitchell.
- A Norwegian magazine sponsored a *GWTW* Trivia Contest with the first prize a trip to Jonesboro, Georgia.
- Macmillan sponsored a raffle at the New Orleans convention of the American Booksellers Association. The prize was a first edition of *GWTW*.
- The Franklin Mint offered a Scarlett O'Hara porcelain doll for $195 and for $500 a coral replica of the necklace Scarlett wore at the Twelve Oaks barbecue.
- The Canfield Casino in Saratoga Springs, New York, was the place to be on August 1, 1986, as Mr. and Mrs. Cornelius Vanderbilt Whitney (Sonny and Marylou to their friends) threw a *Gone with the Wind* party. (Whitney and his cousin John "Jock" Whitney had financed

Selznick International.) Famous for her annual theme parties for the thoroughbred set, Mrs. Whitney arrived in a horse-drawn landau. She wore a replica of the green sprig silk muslin dress, complete with the picture hat that Scarlett wore to the Twelve Oaks barbecue. The *GWTW* theme was continued in the menu with barbecued chicken and ribs, steakburgers, and a salad bar.

TED TURNER ACQUIRES MGM LIBRARY

Turner Broadcasting System Inc. bought the MGM library of films, including *GWTW*, almost lock, stock, and barrel in 1986. Not part of the deal, though, were the television rights to *GWTW*, which CBS had acquired from MGM in 1976.

In 1987, however, the Atlanta-based Turner Broadcasting System announced that a deal had been struck with CBS for television rights. Specific terms of the arrangement were not released, but part of the negotiations gave CBS additional broadcasts of another 1939 MGM classic, *The Wizard of Oz*.

GWTW CHOSEN FOR NATIONAL FILM REGISTRY

In September 1989, the Library of Congress included *Gone With the Wind* on its National Film Registry, a list of twenty-five American films that are "culturally, historically or aesthetically significant" and that are "an enduring part of our national cultural heritage." Such a designation earmarks a film as worthy of preservation for future generations and requires the Library of Congress to maintain unaltered, archival-quality copies of all the films.

The National Film Preservation Act of 1988, authorized by Congress, established the National Film Preservation Board to select up to twenty-five films for inclusion on the National Film Registry. Composed of movie industry representatives and film scholars, the board chose these films for the first list:

1. *The Best Years of Our Lives* (1946)
2. *Casablanca* (1942)

3. *Citizen Kane* (1941)
4. *The Crowd* (1928)
5. *Dr. Strangelove or: How I Learned to Stop Worrying and Love the Bomb* (1964)
6. *The General* (1926)
7. *Gone With the Wind* (1939)
8. *The Grapes of Wrath* (1940)
9. *High Noon* (1952)
10. *Intolerance* (1916)
11. *The Learning Tree* (1969)
12. *The Maltese Falcon* (1941)
13. *Modern Times* (1936)
14. *Mr. Smith Goes to Washington* (1939)
15. *Nanook of the North* (1922)
16. *On the Waterfront* (1954)
17. *The Searchers* (1956)
18. *Singin' in the Rain* (1952)
19. *Snow White and the Seven Dwarfs* (1937)
20. *Some Like It Hot* (1959)
21. *Star Wars* (1977)
22. *Sunrise: A Song of Two Humans* (1927)
23. *Sunset Boulevard* (1950)
24. *Vertigo* (1958)
25. *The Wizard of Oz* (1939)

GWTW CITED AS ONE OF THE
MOST INFLUENTIAL BOOKS IN AMERICA

What book has made a difference in your life? That's what the Book-of-the-Month Club and the Library of Congress's Center for the Book wanted to know, so in 1991 they teamed up with the Information Analysis System Corporation to find out through a survey of lifetime reading habits. The survey was mailed to 5,000 Book-of-the-Month Club members. Of the 2,032 respondents, the majority chose the Bible as the most influential book and ranked *Gone with the Wind* at number six on the list of thirteen titles.

GWTW RESTORED

Through the last five decades, *GWTW* returned to theaters for several revivals, appeared on cable and network television, and even made it to videocassette. Turner Entertainment Company, owner of the film, called *GWTW* "the brightest jewel" in its library of 6,700 films.

But *GWTW* had been showing its age. Prints of the film made from second- and later-generation negatives had lost much of the vibrant colors. The soundtrack was plagued by clicks and pops and in some parts muffled dialogue. So in 1988, in preparation for *GWTW*'s golden anniversary, Turner Entertainment Company decided to polish "the brightest jewel" back to its original 1939 splendor. Through long and difficult processes, technicians created a fully color-corrected print directly from the original camera negatives and enhanced the soundtrack digitally using the original separate dialogue and music/effects tracks.

The newly restored *GWTW* debuted in Atlanta on December 15, 1989, at the gala fiftieth anniversary re-premiere, was subsequently shown in theaters and on television, and was available on a special fiftieth anniversary commemorative videocassette.

ATLANTA ROLLS OUT RED CARPET FOR *GWTW* AGAIN—FOR FIFTIETH ANNIVERSARY

In December 1989, the hottest ticket in town was for a seat in Atlanta's "Fabulous" Fox Theatre for the long-awaited re-premiere of the newly restored *GWTW* on Friday, December 15—fifty years to the day the film opened in Margaret Mitchell's hometown. As a prelude to the re-premiere, Turner Broadcasting System Inc., along with others, sponsored a week of special fiftieth anniversary events:

Kick-Off Reception: Festivities began on December 10 with an invitation-only reception at Stately Oaks Plantation, hosted by Historical Jonesboro/Clayton County Inc. The next day, an open-to-the-public event, "Plantation Christmas at Stately Oaks," featured a candlelight tour of the antebellum home, festooned for the occasion with period Christmas decorations.

Exhibits, Tours, Lectures: Each day during anniversary week, visitors enjoyed daily tours of city and metro-Atlanta historical societies, homes, and museums, plus exhibits and lectures on Margaret Mitchell and *GWTW*. For example, the Madison-Morgan Cultural Center hosted an exhibit, Gone With the Wind—*the Film After 50 Years*, featuring *GWTW* memorabilia related to the Atlanta premiere and the film's initial release. Noted experts and academics presented *GWTW* lectures at the Clayton County Library and the Atlanta-Fulton Library. The Atlanta Historical Society offered multiple screenings of the documentary *The Making of a Legend* and featured two exhibits, Gone With the Wind: *The Facts about the Fiction* and *The Premiere of* Gone With the Wind: *A Grand Event*, with displays of memorabilia, movie costumes, and collectibles.

Scarlett and Rhett Look-Alike Contest: On December 12 at the Hyatt Regency Atlanta, ten finalists from across the country competed for the coveted titles. Contestants fielded impromptu questions from a judging panel, modeled fashions based on the movie's costumes, and watched screen tests of themselves recreating key scenes from *GWTW*. And the winners were— Emily Jane Schapmann from Birmingham, Alabama, who sashayed herself into the title of "Scarlett O'Hara," and Robert Noll of Hudson, Ohio, whose roguish good looks captured the title of "Rhett Butler." The pair received a package of prizes, including designations as host and hostess for the *GWTW* ball and the re-premiere.

***GWTW* Cast Reunion Party and Personal Appearance:** Ten cast members gathered at Rich's downtown on December 13 for a reunion party that included Rand Brooks (Charles Hamilton), Patrick Curtis (infant Beau Wilkes), Cammie King Conlon (young Bonnie Butler), Fred Crane (Brent Tarleton), Greg Giese (infant Bonnie and Beau), Ric Holt (toddler Beau Wilkes), Evelyn Keyes (Suellen O'Hara), Mickey Kuhn (young Beau Wilkes), Butterfly McQueen (Prissy), and Ann Rutherford (Carreen O'Hara). Seated on a stage for a question-and-answer session, cast members shared memories of making the movie and discussed how appearing in *GWTW* had affected their lives. Patrick Curtis, who was five-weeks old when he played infant Beau Wilkes, said, "My epitaph, even though I was married to Raquel Welch and have done other things in the business, will read 'The Baby in *Gone With the Wind.*'" The following day cast members made personal appearances at Rich's Lenox Square.

***Gone With the Wind* Fiftieth Anniversary Ball:** More than 1,500 guests garbed in period costumes or black tie evening wear gathered at the

Georgia International Convention and Trade Center on December 14 for an event reminiscent of the 1939 Junior League Ball.

In the center of the massive ballroom was the framework of a re-created seventy-by-seventy-foot antebellum mansion. Around the mansion were spaced bazaar booths and buffet tables, the latter offering Southern delicacies such as "Gerald O'Hara's Venison Loin Roast," "The Tarleton Twins' Honey-Baked Ham," "Belle Watling's Bourbon Balls," and "Fiddle-Dee-Dee Fruit Cake Muffins."

The evening included a welcome from Turner Broadcasting System's chairman Ted Turner and a special appearance by *GWTW*'s remaining cast members, who shared behind-the-scenes stories from the making of the film. Greg Giese, who at less-than-two-weeks of age portrayed both Bonnie and Beau as infants, shared that he was paid ninety-five dollars for the roles and that he still had the contract to prove it.

What would a ball be without entertainment? The twenty-five-member Big Bethel AME Concert Choir sang nineteenth-century spirituals, and the Ray Bloch Orchestra provided music for dancing the night away. When leaving, each guest received a limited-edition lithograph of the iconic "Southern belle" ad that Delta Airlines used from 1959 until the early 1970s and a sample of the new perfume "*Gone With the Wind*—the Fragrance," courtesy of the Clayton County Chamber of Commerce.

GWTW **Re-premiere Events:** The day of the re-premiere, December 15, 1989, re-created all the excitement of the 1939 premiere. The hoopla started with a Pre-parade Party from 3:30 p.m. to 5:30 p.m. at CNN Center, featuring "spirited refreshments and commemorative giveaways in the Atrium," which attracted several hundred participants eager to see the stars. At 5:30 p.m., the Parade of Stars Motorcade left CNN Center for the Fox Theatre, escorted by Atlanta police on motorcycles with sirens blaring.

The limousines pulled up to the theater in pairs, the stars emerged from their cars in turn and amid cheers and applause from the crowd, and the celebrities walked the red carpet from curb to entrance. As befitting the occasion, the Fox Theatre was decked out with a columned-mansion façade, reminiscent of the one that graced the Loew's Grand Theatre for the 1939 premiere, and a banner high above the marquee of Scarlett and Rhett in flaming embrace. Across the street, giant searchlights swept the scene while on the porch of the Georgian Terrace a band played "Dixie," "Tara's Theme," and holiday favorites.

Inside the Fox, lucky one-hundred-dollar-ticket holders enjoyed drinks and hors d'oeuvres at a prescreening cocktail reception held in the Egyptian Ballroom. Guests mingled, chatted, and located the designated places throughout the room where celebrities signed autographs and posed for photographs. Adding to the festive atmosphere was a five-piece band that played period jazz.

After a towering cake made to resemble Tara had been cut, served, and enjoyed, the party moved to the main theater for the 7:30 p.m. welcoming ceremony. Master of ceremonies Larry King, host of CNN's *Larry King Live*, teased the four thousand audience members: "I have never been to the opening of a movie that opened 50 years ago." He shared film footage from the 1939 premiere, then invited honored guests to join him at center stage, including David O. Selznick's son, Daniel. King also welcomed Hattie McDaniel's great-nephew, Edgar Goff; Margaret Mitchell's two nephews, Joseph and Eugene Mitchell; and the man behind the fiftieth anniversary celebration, Ted Turner. After speaking briefly, Turner said, "Larry, you want to introduce the movie?"

King did. The curtain rose, Max Steiner's music soared, and the audience cheered.

By the end of the film, after Scarlett had vowed to find some way to get Rhett back, audience members were on their feet, applauding the magnificent return of *Gone With the Wind*. When the applause died down, most guests headed to the Fox's after-*GWTW* midnight champagne breakfast. There they basked in the afterglow of the fiftieth anniversary celebration of one of the most beloved films of all times.

GWTW LAUNCHES TURNER CLASSIC MOVIES

On April 14, 1994, at 6 p.m. in the Times Square district of New York City, cable television mogul Ted Turner presided over a ceremony that launched his sixth cable channel—Turner Classic Movies. With the flick of a switch, TCM was born.

The cable channel promised twenty-four-hour-a-day, uncut, uninterrupted, commercial-free broadcasting of classic movies from the massive Turner Entertainment film library. For the inaugural film, Turner chose *Gone With the Wind*. (*GWTW* had also launched a Turner sister channel, TNT, in October 1988.)

Robert Osborne, noted *Hollywood Reporter* columnist and film critic, debuted as the network host. As he told the *Chicago Sun-Times*, "I look forward to introducing classics like *Gone With the Wind* to a whole new world of people."

TCM has included *GWTW* in programming such as "31 Days of Oscar," "Star of the Month," and "Summer Under the Stars."

LOST LOVE AND *LOST LAYSEN*—FOUND!

In 1952, following his grandmother's death, Henry Love Angel Jr. inherited a deteriorating cache of letters, black-and-white photographs, and two blue-cover composition books that had once belonged to his late father. The materials, he was told, had something to do with *Gone with the Wind* author Margaret Mitchell, a family acquaintance, and might be valuable someday. Angel Jr. shoved everything into a pouch, stuck the small bag in a chest of drawers, and forgot about it.

He remembered the pouch in 1994 after hearing about an Atlanta museum dedicated to *Gone With the Wind*. Maybe his father's old papers might be worth something. The retired electronics salesman retrieved the small bag and brought the documents to the Road to Tara Museum for evaluation. In doing so, he turned *GWTW* history upside down.

An independent appraiser and Mitchell historian hired by the museum, Debra Freer, evaluated and authenticated the materials. She described them as "a meaningful historical discovery, their importance creating a necessity for portions of Mitchell's life story to be rewritten."

Among the treasure trove were fifty-seven never-before-seen photographs of Margaret and her friends taken by childhood pal and camera enthusiast Henry Love Angel during the late 1910s and early 1920s. Fifteen pieces of correspondence were also part of the cache and included handwritten letters from Margaret to Henry between 1920 and 1922. Addressing him as "my dear," "Angel, Mon Cher," and "Henry Dear," she shared thoughts and feelings both silly and serious that implied a more intimate relationship than mere friendship. In fact, in one 1922 letter, Margaret wrote, "I do love you, old timer, and feel you are my boy as long as you want to be my boy."

This was a revelation. Much like the suitors that had surrounded Scarlett at the barbecue, Henry was thought to be only one of a bevy of beaux who had buzzed around Margaret as a young woman. However, the same

1922 letter reveals the depth of their relationship: Henry and Margaret had discussed marriage. She wrote: "I want to see you happy, and Henry, for God's sake, if I ever say I care about you—or feel just the same toward you except that I can't marry you, please take my word for it."

While this insight into the early years of Margaret's adult life was surprising, the real stunner was contained in the two composition books. Handwritten in pencil on the ruled pages of the notebooks labeled "Book I" and "Book II" was a novella, *Lost Laysen*, that Margaret wrote when she was fifteen years old. She recorded her writing start date—July 10, 1916—and the date she finished the work—August 6, 1916—on an inside page. She pasted a twelve-chapter outline in the back of the book.

Gone with the Wind had been considered Margaret's only literary work. The discovery of a sophisticated novella that she wrote as a teenager and that foreshadowed *Gone with the Wind* rocked the literary world.

A romantic tale set in the South Pacific, *Lost Laysen* tells a story of honor and unrequited love, two themes Margaret would explore ten years later in writing *Gone with the Wind*. Rough-and-tumble first mate Bill Duncan is smitten by headstrong, independent Courtenay Ross, who sails to the island of Laysen in search of adventure as a missionary. Hot on her trail trying to convince her to return home is Douglas Steele, the man who wants to marry her. When the brutish Juan Mardo attacks Courtenay, the men who love her pursue the fiend until a volcanic eruption destroys the island and changes all their lives forever.

Finding *Lost Laysen* as well as the letters and photographs that revealed a lost love altered what had been known about the author of *Gone with the Wind*. The novella also confirmed one immutable fact about Margaret Mitchell: she was an extraordinary storyteller.

LOST LAYSEN—PUBLISHED!

In early 1995, Henry Love Angel Jr. sold the Mitchell-Angel materials for sixty thousand dollars to the Road to Tara Museum. News of the acquisition broke in the May 1995 issue of *Art & Antiques* magazine in an exclusive cover story, "Margaret Mitchell Has Not Gone with the Wind," written by Debra Freer. Soon after, according to Freer, "telephone calls and media inquiries poured in from around the world. From South Africa to Tokyo to London, people clamored to know more about the discovery."

Among the clamoring crowd were book publishers inquiring about the possibility of bringing to print the newly discovered collection. In a joint decision, the Mitchell Estate, the Henry Love Angel family, and the Road to Tara Museum agreed to have the materials published and, working with a literary agency, scheduled an auction of the work for May 31, 1995. The minimum auction bid reportedly was one million dollars.

"Wait one cotton-pickin' minute," or words to that effect, were no doubt heard in the hallowed halls of Scribner, the publisher-successor to Macmillan, which had issued the 1935 publishing contract for *Gone with the Wind*. Scribner produced a copy of the original contract, containing an option for the author's next book, and the auction was called off.

On May 1, 1996, Scribner published *Lost Laysen* as a companion to the sixtieth anniversary edition of *Gone with the Wind*. Foreign rights sold to at least twenty countries, including England, Finland, France, Germany, Japan, Portugal, and Sweden.

The slim volume presents the 13,000-word novella as Margaret Mitchell wrote her story except for minor changes, indicated by brackets, for clarity or punctuation. Included were photographs and letters from the Mitchell-Angel collection plus an introduction, "Margaret Mitchell and Henry Love Angel—a Lost Love," written by the book's editor, Debra Freer.

Lost Laysen debuted at number fourteen on the *New York Times* best-seller list for the week ending May 11, 1996, and jumped to number nine for the week ending May 18, 1996.

A reviewer for Margaret's hometown newspaper, the *Atlanta Journal-Constitution*, praised the book, writing, "Even at such a tender age Mitchell could spin a convincing yarn. She might call a volcanic eruption a storm and forget to develop a character or two, but already hers was a sashaying style." The reviewer concluded: "As the introduction says, this is no 'Gone With the Wind.' But then, nothing is."

MORE MARGARET MITCHELL
WRITINGS DISCOVERED

After *Lost Laysen* was published, wistful *GWTW* fans yearned to read more Margaret Mitchell writings. Imagine the delight of fans when these materials surfaced:

***Oh! Lady Godiva!*:** An eight-page skit written by Margaret Mitchell for the 1926 Atlanta Junior League Follies was found in the cinema/television library of the University of Southern California at Los Angeles. The one-act send-up depicts the efforts to find an Atlanta woman with long hair—in the days when bobbed hair was all the rage—to play the role of Lady Godiva in a Follies-style review. How did the typescript make its way from Atlanta to Los Angeles?

Margaret submitted the skit to the producer of the 1926 Atlanta Junior League Follies, Ned Wayburn, a prominent Broadway director, performer, producer, designer, choreographer, lyricist, and composer. He had staged New York's Ziegfeld Follies in the 1910s and 1920s and the Atlanta Junior League Follies in 1925. Some of Wayburn's papers—including Margaret's skit—were part of a collection donated to the University of Southern California at Los Angeles in the early 1970s. A research archivist discovered the skit in the collection a decade later. When *Lost Laysen* was published, the archivist remembered the Mitchell skit and contacted the Road to Tara Museum. The guest curator at that time was Debra Freer, editor of *Lost Laysen*, who subsequently evaluated the manuscript and authenticated it as Margaret's work.

***Before Scarlett: Girlhood Writings of Margaret Mitchell*:** In August 1993, Jane Eskridge and Wailes Thomas were cleaning out his late mother's Atlanta house. The house had also been the residence of Thomas's late aunt, Margueryte Reynolds Sharp. Her first husband was Glascock Reynolds whose sister, Carrie Lou, was the first wife of Stephens Mitchell, Margaret's brother. Eskridge and Thomas spent nearly a week sorting through belongings, furnishings, and papers that the family had accumulated over six decades.

From the basement, Thomas hauled up five filthy, battered cardboard boxes originally from his grandmother's Ansley Park house. The boxes contained, among other things, Reynolds's family items retrieved from the Mitchells' Peachtree Street house after Carrie Lou's death. Eskridge opened the first box and pulled out a moldy black shoe, discolored lace wound around a piece of cardboard, tubes of dried paint, and white envelopes containing letters signed "May Belle." (May Belle Stephens Mitchell was Margaret's mother.) After a long, hot morning of finding and tossing family flotsam, Eskridge was on the verge of chucking the rest of the contents.

"Then I pulled out something that looked like an address book," Eskridge remembered. "When I opened it up, on the inside flap it said Margaret Mitchell and her address, and it was dated 1913. Then I saw there were three story titles on the right, and when I flipped through it and realized there were stories, I just screamed."

Rummaging through the box, she and Thomas discovered a long-forgotten collection of letters, stories, a play, an essay, and journal jottings handwritten by Margaret Mitchell between the ages of nine and seventeen.

"Being a [middle-school] teacher, I was truly impressed that the stories and story fragments were all rough drafts with no erasures or cross-outs, that her sentence structure was excellent, that everything was fast-paced and had an energy to it, and that her use of dialogue between characters was remarkable," Eskridge said. "I have taught classes with [students] even more gifted than the normal 'Advanced Learners,' and I have never run across a student I thought could write stories as well as Margaret Mitchell as a young girl."

Impressed by the quality of Margaret's childhood writings, Eskridge decided that others should be able to read those early works, too. She transcribed Margaret's material, researched her subject, then wrote the preface, introduction, and chapter notes for *Before Scarlett: Girlhood Writings of Margaret Mitchell*. The book was published in May 2000 in time for the one-hundredth anniversary of Margaret's birth.

Margaret Mitchell, Reporter: From 1922 to 1926, Margaret Mitchell worked as a reporter for the *Atlanta Journal Sunday Magazine*. A collection of her favorite articles, interviews, sketches, and book reviews was published in fall 2000. Editor Patrick Allen categorized the sixty-four journalism reprints into eight topical chapters from "Mode and Manners" to "Bunko Gangs and Rum Runners."

According to the publisher, *Margaret Mitchell, Reporter* "present[s] a vivid portrait of a lively, far-ranging mind and an insightful observer well on the way to her full literary prowess long before the world even knew her name."

Letters from Margaret: The June 30, 1936, edition of the *New York Sun* carried an enthusiastic review of *Gone with the Wind* by literary critic Edwin Granberry, who wrote, "This novel has the strongest claim of any novel on the American scene to be bracketed with the work of the great from abroad—Tolstoi, Hardy, Dickens." On July 8, 1936, Margaret sent a thank-you letter to Granberry, expressing how grateful she was for his review and how overwhelmed she was by the upheaval *GWTW*'s publication had caused in her life. Sympathizing with her plight, Granberry invited Margaret to seek refuge at a Blowing Rock, North Carolina, writers conference at which he would appear. She attended, and the resulting friendship forged with Granberry lasted until the end of her life.

Following her death, John Marsh asked Granberry to destroy the letters Margaret had sent to him and to his wife, Mabel. Granberry respected the desire to protect Margaret's privacy, so he destroyed about forty highly personal letters. But he also believed in protecting her literary reputation, so he kept other letters that illuminated the authentic aspects of Margaret Mitchell as a person and as a writer in case those elements were ever questioned in the years to come. His wish was that Margaret's letters be published fiifty years after her death, but he died in 1988.

His son Julian compiled and edited *Letters from Margaret*, a book published in 2002 that contains almost sixty letters written by Margaret to Edwin and Mabel from 1936 to 1947.

SIXTIETH ANNIVERSARY
BEGINS NEW ERA FOR *GWTW*

Gone with the Wind's sixtieth anniversary in 1996 ushered in a new era. Macmillan, the novel's publishing home for six decades, was succeeded by Scribner, following a merger, and the Scribner name appeared for the first time on domestic editions of *GWTW*.

To mark the occasion, the publisher issued a collector's boxed edition of Margaret's novel with an introduction written by James Michener and a preface written by Pat Conroy, author of *The Great Santini*, *The Prince of Tides*, and *Beach Music*.

In the essay, Conroy shared his and his mother's deep, personal connection to Margaret's novel: "I became a novelist because of *Gone With the Wind*, or more precisely, my mother raised me up to be a 'Southern' novelist, with a strong emphasis on the word 'Southern,' because *Gone With the Wind* set my mother's imagination ablaze when she was a young girl growing up in Atlanta, and it was the one fire of her bruised, fragmented life that never went out."

On the same day as the release of the sixtieth anniversary edition, Scribner published *Lost Laysen*, the 13,000-word novella that Margaret handwrote as a gift to Henry Love Angel Jr. in 1916. The slim companion volume presented the story as Margaret wrote it except for minor bracketed changes for clarity or punctuation. The book also included photographs and letters from the Mitchell-Angel collection plus an introduction, "Margaret Mitchell and Henry Love Angel—a Lost Love," written by the book's editor, Debra Freer.

STAMPED INTO HISTORY—FIVE MORE TIMES!

Following the debut of the Margaret Mitchell one-cent stamp on June 30, 1986, *GWTW* was honored five more times by the United States Postal Service. In commemorative stamp series, the United States Postal Service:

- Honored four Oscar-nominated 1939 films—*Gone With the Wind*, *The Wizard of Oz*, *Stagecoach*, and *Beau Geste*—in its "Classic Films Series" stamps issued on March 23, 1990, in Hollywood in advance of the sixty-second Academy Awards. The twenty-five-cent *GWTW* commemorative stamp features a full-color illustration of Clark Gable as Rhett embracing Vivien Leigh as Scarlett with Tara visible in the background.
- Saluted *GWTW* as "1936 Bestseller" in its decade-by-decade stamp series "Celebrate the Century," commemorating the most notable people, places, things, events, and trends of the twentieth century. Among the other stamps in the 1930s decade fifteen-stamp panel were tributes to President Franklin D. Roosevelt, the Empire State Building, Superman's comic-book debut, Jesse Owens winning six world records, Walt Disney's *Snow White*, America Survives the Depression, and the Monopoly game. The thirty-two-cent stamps were issued on September 10, 1998, in Cleveland, Ohio. The one-and-a-quarter-inch square *GWTW* stamp portrays the novel in its yellow-and-brown dust jacket against a green velvet background. A white magnolia and a sword handle rest in the foreground.
- Recognized six Academy Award–winning composers, including the composer of *GWTW*'s musical score, Max Steiner, in its "Legends of American Music Series." The other honorees were Dimitri Tiomkin, Alfred Newman, Bernard Herrmann, Franz Waxman, and Erich Wolfgang Korngold, all of whom wrote memorable, much-loved music for Hollywood films from the 1930s through the 1960s. The

thirty-three-cent stamps were issued on September 16, 1999, in Los Angeles. The Max Steiner stamp shows the composer working at a desk.

- Acknowledged the skills and collaboration required by movie industry artisans to bring a story idea to the silver screen in its "American Filmmaking: Behind the Scenes" stamp series. In the ten-stamp series, "Screenwriting" is represented by a depiction of the Sidney Howard typewritten script page from *GWTW*'s final scene. Superimposed over Scarlett's last lines of dialogue is a hand holding a pen.

  The series offers two other nods to *GWTW*. The "Music" stamp depicts the right hand of Max Steiner as the composer works on a musical composition. The stamp pane selvage area recognizes "Producing" by including a quote from *GWTW* producer David O. Selznick: "Thousands and thousands of details . . . go into the making of a film. It is the sum total of all these things that either makes a great picture or destroys it."

  The eight other thirty-seven-cent stamps honor "Art Direction," "Cinematography," "Costume Design," "Directing," "Film Editing," "Makeup," "Sound," and "Special Effects." Each of the gray-green-and-silver stamps resembles a single frame of film.

  The stamp series was released on February 25, 2003, at an open-to-the-public special program at the Academy of Motion Picture Arts and Sciences' Samuel Goldwyn Theater in Beverly Hills, California, as part of the celebration of the academy's seventy-fifth anniversary. On that day, the academy used the "American Filmmaking: Behind the Scenes" stamps to mail to academy members the final ballots used for voting for the winners of the seventy-fifth Academy Awards. For most of the ballots, the subject of the stamp was matched with the award discipline. For example, envelopes containing ballots for directing were affixed with the "Directing" stamp.

- Hailed Hattie McDaniel, the first African American to win an Academy Award, as its twenty-ninth honoree in the long-running "Black Heritage" stamp series that recognizes outstanding African American achievers. The thirty-nine-cent commemorative stamp features a full-color portrait of McDaniel in the ensemble she wore—blue dress accented by a spray of gardenias and a dress clip—the night of February 29, 1940, when she won the Best Supporting Actress award for her role as Mammy.

The January 25, 2006, first-day-of-issue ceremony was held at the Academy of Motion Picture Arts and Sciences' Margaret Herrick Library, which is home to the Hattie McDaniel collection, in Beverly Hills, California. In attendance and applauding the recognition for McDaniel were family, friends, and five *GWTW* cast members: Fred Crane, Cammie King Conlon, Patrick Curtis, Mickey Kuhn, and Ann Rutherford.

WHAT BECAME OF THEIR OSCARS?

- Vivien Leigh's 1939 Best Actress Oscar for her portrayal of Scarlett O'Hara sold for a grand total of $563,500 to an anonymous telephone bidder at the December 15, 1993, auction at Sotheby's. The presale estimate had ranged from $100,000 to $150,000.
- Victor Fleming's 1939 Best Director Oscar for *GWTW* sold for a grand total of $244,500 to an anonymous bidder at a December 6, 1995, auction at Christie's East.
- Clark Gable's 1934 Best Actor Oscar for his portrayal of a wisecracking newspaper reporter in *It Happened One Night* sold for a grand total of $607,500 to an anonymous bidder at the December 15, 1996, auction at Christie's in Los Angeles. According to the auction house, the winning bid for Gable's Academy Award was two to three times the presale estimates and shattered the record auction price paid for Vivien Leigh's 1939 Best Actress Oscar for *GWTW*.
    The auction of Gable's Oscar had raised a ruckus with the Academy of Motion Picture Arts and Sciences. The organization had sued to block the sale on the grounds that the academy had the first right to buy any Oscar offered for sale. The issue became moot when, after the sale, director Steven Spielberg stepped forward as the mystery buyer of Gable's Oscar and donated the statuette to the academy.
- Producer David O. Selznick's 1939 Best Picture Oscar for *GWTW* sold for a grand total of $1,542,500 to singer Michael Jackson at the June 12, 1999, auction at Sotheby's. The presale estimate had ranged from $200,000 to $300,000. The winning bid by the King of Pop not only broke the previous record auction price paid for Clark Gable's 1934 Best Actor Oscar but also set a new record for the sale of Hollywood memorabilia.

WHERE IS HATTIE MCDANIEL'S ACADEMY AWARD?

On February 29, 1940, when she was honored with the Best Supporting Actress award for her role as Mammy in *Gone With the Wind*, Hattie McDaniel made history. She became the first African American performer to win an Academy Award.

The award that McDaniel received that night was not the iconic Oscar statuette but a plaque. Plaques were presented to best supporting actors and actresses from 1936 to 1942. Starting in 1943, winners in those categories received traditional Oscar statuettes. The Academy of Motion Picture Arts and Sciences allowed previous winners to exchange plaques for Oscars, but the academy does not have any record indicating that McDaniel made the swap.

In 1941, Howard University in Washington, DC, acknowledged McDaniel's cinematic achievement by hosting a celebratory luncheon for her. McDaniel probably held fond memories of that occasion through the years because she remembered the historically African American university in her will. Upon her death in 1952, McDaniel's Best Supporting Actress plaque was bequeathed to Howard University's drama department. That's where the mystery begins.

No official records in the university's archives show that the institution took possession of the award from McDaniel's estate. But students who attended Howard University in the 1960s recall seeing the award on display in a glass-enclosed case in the fine arts building. The award seems to have vanished in the late 1960s during a turbulent time of social unrest on campus.

Some speculate that the plaque was hidden to keep it safe from student protesters but then forgotten about once calm returned to the campus. Others think the award was stolen because of its historical significance or thrown away because of anger that McDaniel had won the prize for playing Mammy. Some have a simpler explanation: the plaque was simply removed from display, placed in a nondescript box, and stored somewhere in the bowels of the university. Over the years, efforts to find the award have been unsuccessful.

In 2006, Howard University petitioned the academy to issue a replacement for McDaniel's original award. The request was denied, citing official policy. The academy "rarely reissues statuettes when the actual recipient asks for a replacement. We have never replaced a statuette that has fallen out of the care of an inheriting individual or institution."

As the inheriting institution, Howard University remains haunted by the unanswered question asked by countless *Gone With the Wind* fans: where is Hattie McDaniel's Academy Award?

MO'NIQUE PAYS TRIBUTE TO
HATTIE MCDANIEL AT OSCAR CEREMONY

At the eighty-second annual awards presentation of the Academy of Motion Picture Arts and Sciences, Mo'Nique won the Best Supporting Actress award for her role as an abusive mother in *Precious*. In her acceptance speech, after thanking the academy, she stated, "I want to thank Miss Hattie McDaniel for enduring all that she had to, so that I would not have to."

In subsequent media interviews, Mo'Nique revealed that her ensemble was also a tribute to McDaniel. "The reason I have on this royal blue dress is because it's the color that Hattie McDaniel wore when she accepted her Oscar," Mo'Nique said. "The reason I have this gardenia in my hair? It is the flower that Hattie McDaniel wore when she accepted her Oscar. So, for you, Ms. Hattie McDaniel, I feel you all over me, and it's about time that the world feels you all over them."

Mo'Nique also revealed that the gardenia she wore was an unexpected gift from a stranger. "Something really strange happened—as I'm going through hair and make-up, someone knocked on our door. . . . There's a letter and there's the gardenia flower. The letter is from a woman I've never met before, who is friends with Hattie McDaniel's family members. It blew me away."

The Oscar winner also shared another secret from Academy Awards night: She felt McDaniel's spirit with her throughout the awards ceremony. "I could hear her whispering in my ear," Mo'Nique said.

THIRTEEN

The Wind *Roars On*

TED TURNER'S URGE TO
MERGE GIVES *GWTW* NEW OWNERSHIP

In 1995, Time Warner Inc. and Turner Broadcasting System Inc. announced a merger that created the world's largest media company and changed ownership of the film *Gone With the Wind*. When the $7.57 billion merger was finalized the following year, Ted Turner had sold his media empire to Time Warner.

As a result, Turner Broadcasting System became TBS Inc., a wholly owned subsidiary of Time Warner Inc. Ted Turner was named vice chairman and held status as the merged company's largest shareholder, and Time Warner became the new owner of *GWTW*.

THE MARGARET MITCHELL HOUSE REBORN

After their 1925 marriage, Margaret Mitchell and John Marsh were in debt because of John's recent medical bills. A tight budget prompted them to set up housekeeping at the Crescent Apartments, a three-story, Tudor Revival apartment building at the corner of Crescent Avenue and Tenth Street. Their ground-floor residence, apartment number one, offered two shabby rooms plus a kitchen and bath, so Margaret affectionately nicknamed their accommodations "The Dump."

Margaret was confined to the Dump in 1926 because of an injured ankle, and there she began writing her novel. She set up her mother's old sewing table in a living room alcove that boasted a triple set of tall, beveled-glass windows decorated on each side with panels of beveled mirrors. Pounding away on a Remington portable, she completed all but three chapters of *GWTW* during the seven years she lived on Crescent Avenue.

Since Margaret's days, the Crescent Apartments saw even harder times. Students, hippies, and vagrants called it home at various times through the years. A 1964 rehab reclaimed the building and transformed it into the Windsor House Apartments. But by 1978 a new owner had evicted all tenants, boarded up the structure, and began knocking down historic buildings in advance of a major redevelopment for the area.

The place where Margaret Mitchell gave birth to Scarlett O'Hara remained forlorn and forgotten until it, too, became a target of the developer's wrecking ball. Galvanized by this intolerable threat, a group of preservationists banded together in 1985 to rescue the house. They subsequently formed the Margaret Mitchell House Foundation. Through the organization's efforts, Mayor Andrew Young designated the building a city landmark in 1989, which protected the structure from the threat of demolition. The foundation, chaired by Mary Rose Taylor, commenced a campaign to raise funds to restore the structure.

That dream almost went up in smoke when an arson fire gutted the Margaret Mitchell House on September 17, 1994, and left standing only the structure's four brick walls. After Taylor arrived at the scene, she told reporters: "What stunned me, standing there, was that the house had not burned to the ground. The brick was still standing. It reminds me of the indomitable spirit of Margaret Mitchell. I think that spirit lives on in that house. It's refusing to fall down."

To the rescue came Daimler-Benz AG, the German industrial conglomerate that wished to make a significant contribution to the 1996 Summer Olympic Games in Atlanta. When the company weighed the options for boosting its image in the United States—underwriting an Olympic sponsorship versus restoring a cultural and historical landmark—the choice was clear. Daimler-Benz pledged $5 million to acquire the property, reconstruct the building, and transform the Margaret Mitchell House into a museum and education center in time for the Summer Olympics.

As work neared completion in late April 1996, an open house was scheduled for June 30 to coincide with the sixtieth anniversary of the publication of *GWTW* and to herald the July 19 opening of the Olympics. Those plans went down in flames when, on May 12, 1996, a second arson fire set the Margaret Mitchell House ablaze.

At the scene of the charred structure, Mary Rose Taylor vowed, "The phoenix is the symbol of Atlanta, and like the phoenix, we shall rise again, too."

Although the upper two floors of the building were gutted, Margaret and John's first-floor corner apartment suffered only water damage. Daimler-Benz came to the rescue again with a pledge to see the project through to completion.

On May 16, 1997, the Margaret Mitchell House, known as the "Birthplace of *Gone with the Wind*," finally opened. The restored structure featured two different facades: The one facing Peachtree Street evoked how the house looked in 1899 when it was built as a single-family residence by Cornelius J. Sheehan. The one facing Crescent Avenue was reminiscent of how the converted apartment building looked in 1926 when Margaret and John lived there.

Owned and operated since 2004 by the Atlanta History Center, the Margaret Mitchell House and Museum complex offers a visitor's center, an exhibit area, a sunken garden, and a gift shop. But the centerpiece that draws thousands of visitors from across the country and around the world is the renovated Mitchell-Marsh apartment. Decorated with period furnishings, the homey apartment gives visitors the impression that, when they enter, they might just find Margaret Mitchell sitting at her desk in the living room alcove, pounding away on her Remington typewriter.

HONORS FOR THE
MARGARET MITCHELL HOUSE AND MUSEUM

Added to the National Register of Historic Places in June 1996, the Margaret Mitchell House and Museum has since garnered other distinctions, including:

- Designation as a national "Literary Landmark" by Friends of Libraries USA in June 2002.
- Status as a "Living Landmark" by the Atlanta Preservation Center in 2003 in its inaugural celebration, "The Phoenix Flies: A Citywide Celebration of Living Landmarks."
- Inclusion as one of "25 Places to See in Georgia Before You . . . Well, You Know" by syndicated travel writer Mary Ann Anderson in 2008. For Anderson, the house "captures the heart, soul, and imagination" of the author of "the most famous book ever written about the South."

GWTW RESTORED TO ORIGINAL
GLORY FOR SIXTIETH ANNIVERSARY

Just in time for its return to theaters in 1998, *GWTW* was polished to near perfection in an extensive, $1 million restoration, involving a modern-day revival of Technicolor's original three-strip dye-transfer process. The process produced clear, vivid, color-drenched film images of Scarlett, Rhett, Tara, and Twelve Oaks.

"This is the way the picture was photographed and originally printed," said Roger L. Mayer, president of the Turner Entertainment Company. "This is the way the picture was intended to be seen."

Additionally, computer technicians and graphic artists examined and digitally repaired the original camera negative, restoring about twelve and a half minutes of damaged footage and eliminating imperfections such as scratches, spots, and smudges. For example, a hair visible on the print since 1939 was digitally erased. The film's aspect ratio was also restored from the wide-screen display introduced in 1967 to 1939's original 1.33:1 ratio of width to height. The restoration also featured a new multichannel stereo soundtrack that included Max Steiner's overture, intermission, and exit music.

This new, glorious Technicolor print of *GWTW* was set to return to theaters in 1998, and new movie-poster graphics were designed for the re-release. A larger-than-life proposal embrace replaced the "flaming embrace" image used for more than thirty years. A new tag line heralded: "For the First Time in Its Original Technicolor Glory and a Remastered Digital Soundtrack."

A benefit "premiere" for the film on June 24, 1998, at the Samuel Goldwyn Theater at the Academy of Motion Picture Arts and Sciences in Beverly Hills, California, brought out glittering guests such as Fred Crane, Patrick Curtis, Greg Giese, Evelyn Keyes, Mickey Kuhn, and Ann Rutherford, the largest reunion of *GWTW* family members since the fiftieth anniversary celebration.

In New York for a private viewing of the refurbished print, Olivia de Havilland granted multiple media interviews that were featured in newspapers across the country and on television shows such as *Entertainment Tonight*, *Good Morning America*, and *Today*. "I've now seen the film 27 times," de Havilland said, "and it never ceases to captivate and move me."

Radiant reviews of *GWTW* were enough to make a Southern belle blush. Roger Ebert of the *Chicago Sun-Times* proclaimed that "it is still a towering landmark of film, quite simply because it tells a good story, and tells it wonderfully well." Vincent Canby of the *New York Times* praised the "still ravishing performances" of Vivien Leigh, Clark Gable, and Hattie McDaniel. Eleanor Ringel of the *Atlanta Journal-Constitution* gushed, "After almost 60 years, *Gone With the Wind* remains the essential Hollywood movie . . . a superbly crafted apogee of Hollywood's Golden Age." Among the few dissenters was Stephen Hunter of the *Washington Post*, who declared, "It is overrated, overlong and overdue for oblivion."

The three-day opening weekend—June 26 to 28—had many sold-out screenings as fans flocked to theaters for *GWTW*'s limited release in just over two hundred theaters nationwide. Still, the film raked in nearly $1.2 million over Friday, Saturday, and Sunday. By the end of its first week, *GWTW* had grossed $1.9 million, earning the film fifteenth place on *Variety*'s weekly list of top movies. During its second week, *GWTW* added another $1.4 million to its earnings and moved to thirteenth place on *Variety*'s list.

Based on the boffo box office, the film's distributor, New Line Cinema, expanded *GWTW*'s release to theaters in smaller cities at the end of July and in early August. *Variety* later reported that in the first six weeks of limited release, *GWTW* had grossed nearly $6 million.

WHY *GWTW* RETURNED TO THEATERS IN 1998

GWTW fans scratched their heads, wondering why the beloved film had a theatrical re-release in 1998—a year *before* its sixtieth anniversary.

According to the distributor New Line Cinema, a subsidiary of Time Warner Inc., the early release ensured that *GWTW* would be the first film "to feature the reinstated Technicolor three-strip dyeing process for all prints." But other explanations soon surfaced.

Warner Home Video, a subsidiary of Time Warner Inc., wanted the summer theatrical release to tantalize fans for the new video of the restored print that would be on the market in the fall.

Another reason was floated for not releasing *GWTW* in December 1999—bad timing. With the world counting down to the year 2000, it was feared that the film's release on the cusp of the calendar change might be eclipsed by the hoopla surrounding the end of the 1990s.

Classic Hollywood one-upmanship also played a role. Roger L. Mayer, president of Turner Entertainment Company, told the *New York Times* that the 1997 mega success of James Cameron's *Titanic* was a factor. "There was all this talk about *Titanic* being the most successful picture of all time," Mayer said. "We knew if you updated the grosses to today's dollars, then *Gone With the Wind* would have, in fact, grossed more and been seen by more people than *Titanic*. We wanted to point that out. It was fun."

HOMETOWN RENOWN FOR CLARK GABLE

"There's no special light that shines inside me and makes me a star," Clark Gable once told a reporter. "I'm just a lucky slob from Ohio."

The future "King of Hollywood" was born in Cadiz, a small coal-mining town located about forty-two miles, as the crow flies, southeast of Canton, Ohio, on February 1, 1901. The birth took place at the home of his parents, William and Adeline Gable, who lived in the upstairs apartment of a two-family house on Charleston Street. Addie died before Clark reached his first birthday.

After her death, Will Gable and his son moved from Cadiz, eventually settling in nearby Hopedale when the elder Gable remarried. Clark grew up there, left the area as a young man to seek his fortune, and made his way to Hollywood and stardom.

Cadiz prided itself on being the birthplace of the "King of Hollywood." Yet the house on Charleston Street was torn down in the 1960s, and no marker existed to honor the town's most famous son. Embarrassed at the oversight and hoping to spark tourism, a group of Cadiz citizens established the Clark Gable Foundation in 1984 with the mission of preserving the actor's memory.

A local women's organization sponsored the first Clark Gable Birthday Celebration in Cadiz on February 1, 1985, and more than three hundred people attended. Guests clamored to know where Gable had been born. That inspired the Clark Gable Foundation to raise more than seven thousand dollars for a monument to the star that was erected on the site of his birth the following year. The foundation also took on responsibilities for the annual birthday event.

For the 1989 birthday celebration, the foundation invited actor Fred Crane and his wife, Anita, to attend. That Hollywood connection led to introductions to other *GWTW* cast members, who happily attended subsequent bashes for the King, held annually on the Saturday nearest his birthday. Their star power drew larger crowds to events. That momentum prompted the foundation to set a grand goal: building a replica of Gable's birthplace as a living museum.

A 1991 bequest to the foundation from the estate of a Gable contemporary who lived in the neighborhood where he was born served as seed money for the ambitious project and as a kick-starter for the fundraising campaign. The foundation spent more than $150,000 for the reconstruction.

To re-create the structure, the architect relied on historical photographs of the building to guide the drafting of blueprints. The interior design was based on photographs provided by a local woman who was a former resident of the house. Interior decoration of the second-floor apartment's three large and two small rooms included period furniture, carpeting, wallpaper, and window treatments.

For advice on the furnishings, the foundation's director, Nan Mattern, turned to the Ohio Historical Society and its collection specialist, Ellice Ronsheim. In choosing wallpaper, for example, Mattern and Ronsheim studied photographs of period home interiors and reviewed era-specific catalogs such as Sears & Roebuck and Montgomery Ward to determine the available wallpaper patterns.

"We found pieces that would work for wall and ceiling, that would give the feeling . . . the impression of the time rather than the exact duplication," Ronsheim said.

Period furniture included a bed with a high-back headboard in the bedroom and a baby's cradle in a small adjacent room thought to be Gable's nursery. Movie memorabilia and some of Gable's personal items decorated the apartment, including a pajama top, a boyhood sled, and a lamp from his California ranch. The foundation's gift shop occupies the first floor.

On January 31, 1998, the Clark Gable Birthplace and Museum was dedicated by the actor's son, John Clark Gable, who exclaimed, "I can't believe it's finally built. I'm just ecstatic." After cutting the ribbon and crossing the threshold, he made his way to the second-floor bedroom, no doubt thinking about the infant born there who became the father he never knew.

CLARK GABLE AND
LORETTA YOUNG'S LOVE-CHILD COVER-UP!

In 1935, Clark Gable and Loretta Young were on location with cast and crew at Mount Baker in Washington State for a ten-day shoot for *The Call of the Wild*. Fierce winter storms delayed filming, and ten days stretched into weeks of waiting in vain for the weather to break. During the delay, a love that could not be denied blossomed between star and leading lady. Gossip about the pair swirled like snow in the blizzard and continued even after location filming shut down and resumed on the back lot of Twentieth Century Pictures.

When Young discovered she was pregnant, the circumstance jeopardized her career and Gable's. Movie contracts included morals clauses that bound stars to good behavior. If a scandal broke—such as an out-of-wedlock pregnancy—the studio could use the clause to terminate the contracts of the actress and actor involved.

Although illegal, abortions were often arranged by studios for actresses who found themselves "in trouble." Yet the Catholic Church forbade abortion, and the devout Young would not go against her faith. After telling Gable about the baby, Young swore him to secrecy and then devised a plan she hoped would save both of their hides.

Young's meticulous plan unraveled almost immediately. Newshounds sniffed a story in Young's sudden "vacation," sailing with her mother to England on June 30, 1935. Reporters dogged her New York departure, her London arrival, and her summer stay.

Toward fall, a visibly pregnant Young, accompanied by her mother, secretly returned to Los Angeles; and the star hid out in a Venice rental property her mother owned. *The Call of the Wild* had opened in August without Young participating in the film's promotion. After her absence dragged on through autumn, both fans and studio bosses demanded to know: where is Loretta?

Young's personal physician notified the studio "that her physical condition required respite from work." When the studio announced it had delayed her next picture because Young had a "serious illness," rumors resurfaced that she was pregnant with Gable's child.

In an effort to quell the fever-pitch gossip, Young granted an exclusive interview to a friendly reporter from *Photoplay* magazine, Dorothy Manners. At her Bel Air mansion, Young disguised her pregnancy with quilts and gave the performance of a lifetime. She portrayed an ailing actress valiantly conserving her strength so she can eventually have a health-restoring operation. Manners fell for the fish tale hook, line, and sinker.

In October, Gable left on a cross-country promotional tour for *Mutiny on the Bounty*. On the evening of November 6, 1935, the star was in his suite at New York's Waldorf-Astoria when a bellhop arrived with a telegram. Gable opened the envelope and read the unsigned message—"Beautiful, blue-eyed, blond baby girl born, 8:15 this morning." Walking to the bathroom, he tore the telegram to shreds and then flushed the pieces down the toilet, probably realizing that this marked the end of only the latest scene in his and Loretta's love-child cover-up.

GABLE AND YOUNG'S LOVE CHILD: THE BEST-KEPT SECRET IN HOLLYWOOD

Loretta Young returned to work in January 1936, leaving her two-month-old child—named Judith but called Judy—at the Venice house in the care of a nurse. Young was on loan to MGM for a film, putting her in proximity to Gable, who was filming *San Francisco*.

The more Young saw Gable, the guiltier she felt that her fears of exposure as an unwed mother had kept him from seeing his child. Attending a Hollywood gala in late January 1936 and watching Gable and actress Carole Lombard dance and snuggle convinced Young to do the right thing.

Soon after, under cover of darkness, Gable drove to the Venice house and saw his daughter for the first time, asleep in a bureau drawer. Appalled, he pulled out a wad of cash from his pocket, peeled off four one-hundred-dollar bills, and handed them to Young, telling her: "The least you can do is buy her a decent bed." He spent the next few hours cradling the baby, rocking her gently, kissing her, and cuddling her.

Young loved her child and rejected the idea of putting her up for adoption. Instead, Young devised a scheme she hoped would allow her to keep both her child and her reputation. She left her infant daughter in a Catholic orphanage in San Francisco, claimed the child five months later, kept her hidden until she was nearly two, then concocted a phony story for the press.

In June 1937, Young gave an exclusive to Hearst gossip columnist and personal friend Louella Parsons. Parsons's column heralded the news: "Loretta Young, film star, admitted to me today she is a mother—by adoption."

Young had hoped the "adoption" story would suppress the rumors that still swirled around her and Gable. Instead it only stirred speculation, especially since Judy Young had inherited her father's prominent ears and her mother's charming overbite.

Judy wore bonnets to hide her ears until Young had them surgically corrected. She also had her daughter's baby teeth and then her adult teeth straightened to blot out traces of resemblance. Despite these efforts, many in Hollywood guessed the truth but maintained a conspiracy of silence amid the rumors.

One rumor Young welcomed was the talk that she was in contention for the role of Scarlett in *GWTW*. Another role for which she secretly yearned was that of Mrs. Clark Gable, especially after Ria Gable filed for divorce in January 1939. Yet by the end of March 1939, Gable had married Carole Lombard, and Young's dream died. The following year she married producer Tom Lewis, who gave Judy his surname but didn't adopt her.

Young and Gable reunited for their second film, 1950's *Key to the City*, providing a natural opportunity for the father to see his now fifteen-year-old daughter. Gable spent an afternoon in Young's living room, chatting with Judy about her interests, activities, and school studies.

"He was warm and considerate and caring," Judy wrote in her autobiography, *Uncommon Knowledge*. "I answered his questions freely because something told me that he needed to know everything I could tell him about myself." When the visit ended, Gable cupped Judy's face in his hands, kissed her on the forehead, and walked out of her life forever.

Meeting Gable was another piece of the identity puzzle that Judy Lewis had grappled with for years. She couldn't understand why, if she was adopted, she looked so much like her mother. Young always sidestepped Judy's questions about her parentage.

Judy learned the truth finally in 1958 from her fiancé a month before their June wedding. She confessed that she couldn't marry him because she didn't know anything about herself or her biological parents. "I know everything about you," he told her. "Your father is Clark Gable."

Eight years passed before Judy found the courage to confront her mother. After throwing up in the bathroom, Young admitted that Gable, who had died in 1960, was Judy's father and that Young was her mother. Wistfully, Young said, "I think the biggest regret that I have in my life is that I didn't get your father to marry me."

The admission of long-kept secrets drove a wedge between mother and daughter. After Young refused to acknowledge publically the circumstances of her daughter's conception, considering it a "mortal sin," they became estranged.

Judy claimed her parentage in her 1994 autobiography; Young confirmed her daughter's parentage in the authorized biography *Forever Young*, but the book was published only after she died on August 12, 2000, at the age of eighty-seven.

Before Young's death, Judy and her mother reconciled. But Judy never had the chance to know her father and to ask him: Did he want her? Why didn't he marry her mother? Did he want to tell Judy he was her father the day he visited?

Since learning that Gable was her father, every time Judy watched scenes in *GWTW* between him and his on-screen daughter, she cried. "I like to pretend that he was thinking of me when he was playing his scenes with her."

Judy Lewis died on November 25, 2011. She was seventy-six.

THE WIND DONE GONE VS. *GONE WITH THE WIND*

Detroit native Alice Randall first read *Gone with the Wind* at the age of twelve. While she loved "the ambitious, resilient, hardworking, hard-loving character who is Scarlett," Randall hated the "racist stereotyping and Klan whitewashing." Of mixed-race ancestry, Randall believed that Margaret Mitchell's novel portrayed Southern history inaccurately.

"Then one day, rereading the novel, an enormous question arose for me from the center of the text," Randall said. "Where are the mulattos on Tara? Where is Scarlett's half-sister? Almost immediately I knew I had to tell *her* story, tell the story that hadn't been told. Tell it because the silence injured me."

Randall wrote *The Wind Done Gone* as the diary of Cynara, a former slave also called Cindy or Cinnamon, who is the green-eyed daughter of Mammy and the owner of the plantation. Introductory notes explained that the diary "was among the effects of an elderly colored lady who had been in an assisted-living center just outside Atlanta."

As *GWTW* fans know, the name "Cynara" comes from the Ernest Dowson poem "Non Sum Qualis Eram Bonae Sub Regno Cynarae," from which Margaret Mitchell found the title for her novel in the first line of the third stanza: "I have forgotten much, Cynara! Gone with the wind."

Other elements of Randall's book ringing familiar literary bells include the characters:

- Other, who "was the belle of five counties. She was not beautiful, but men seldom recognized this." The daughter of Planter and his wife, Lady, Other was married to R.
- R., who has just left Other following the death of their daughter, Precious, who "was afraid of the dark." Cynara, his longtime lover, learns that R. told Other "he didn't give a tinker's damn what happened to her."
- Beauty, the owner of an Atlanta brothel, loves R. and has a son she sent away to school. Cynara describes Beauty's hair as "the same shade of burgundy as the velvet of her front room chairs."
- Mammy, who was Cynara's mother by Planter, the owner of Cotton Farm also called Tata, located "just outside Atlanta."

Randall also included characters named Dreamy Gentleman, who "had made up his mind to marry his cousin Mealy Mouth" and live together at the family home, Twelve Slaves Strong as Trees; his sister, China; Planter's valet Garlic, who is the father of Miss Priss; Jeems and his former masters the Twins, S. and B.; and Aunt Pattypit.

The Harvard-educated Randall expected the Houghton Mifflin Company to publish her book in spring 2001, but the Margaret Mitchell estate had other ideas. A $10 million lawsuit filed in March 2001 on behalf of the

Stephens Mitchell Trusts argued that *The Wind Done Gone* was an "unauthorized sequel" that violated *GWTW*'s copyright. Houghton Mifflin and Randall countered that *The Wind Done Gone* was a "classic parody" of the original work and protected as "fair use" under the First Amendment.

Randall's declaration to the court asserted that her book was a parody: "a book that uses characteristic elements of *Gone With the Wind* and imitates them in a way that makes them appear ridiculous. I made *Gone With the Wind* the target of my parody because that book, more than any other work I know, has presented and helped perpetuate an image of the south that I, as an African-American woman living in the south, felt compelled to comment upon and criticize."

In April 2001, the U.S. District Court for the Northern District of Georgia issued a preliminary injunction, prohibiting Houghton Mifflin from publishing the book, on the grounds that *The Wind Done Gone* was a sequel that represented "unabated piracy of *Gone With the Wind*." The publisher appealed, bolstered by letters of support sent to the court from nearly two dozen writers, scholars, and activists.

In May 2001, a three-judge panel of the Eleventh U.S. Circuit Court of Appeals lifted the injunction and characterized the prior ruling as an "extraordinary and drastic remedy" that "represents an unlawful prior restraint in violation of the First Amendment." Like a hurricane, copies of *The Wind Done Gone* blew into the nation's bookstores, and the book made the *New York Times* best-seller list. The work received mixed reviews from critics.

In the meantime, the copyright infringement suit headed toward trial until May 2002, when the Stephens Mitchell Trusts issued a joint statement with Houghton Mifflin, indicating the two sides had reached a confidential out-of-court settlement. The Trusts agreed to drop the suit; the publisher agreed to make an undisclosed charitable contribution to Atlanta's Morehouse College. Both sides maintained "the correctness of their respective legal positions," and copies of *The Wind Done Gone* would continue bearing the label "The Unauthorized Parody."

MARGARET MITCHELL'S NEPHEW ENDOWS A CHAIR IN HER NAME AT ATLANTA'S MOREHOUSE COLLEGE

In March 2002, as the copyright infringement case against Alice Randall was reaching crescendo, one of Margaret Mitchell's nephews presented a $1.5

million donation to Morehouse College to endow the Margaret Mitchell Chair in the Division of Humanities and Social Sciences. One of the largest individual gifts in the history of the private, all-male, liberal arts, historically African American college, the endowment honors the author for her dedication to literature, scholarship, and humanity.

"I thought it might be a good idea to take it up again as a family charity," Eugene Mitchell said. "I hope it helps race relations and that they don't go to the other extreme to have some radical saying Morehouse sold out."

The connection between Morehouse College and Margaret Mitchell was forged in 1942 when Dr. Benjamin E. Mays, the college's sixth president, asked Margaret Mitchell to assist financially strapped Morehouse students who wished to go to medical school. Margaret was spurred to help after the family's longtime maid, Carrie Holbrook, was refused medical treatment at Atlanta hospitals because she was African American. For the next seven years, Margaret was the anonymous donor who paid the tuition of at least twenty Morehouse students in Holbrook's memory.

One of those Margaret helped was Otis Smith, a Morehouse graduate in his second semester at Nashville's Meharry Medical College. His bank account drained, he was about to drop out when, through Mays, Margaret took care of his tuition. Smith completed medical school and became the first licensed African American pediatrician in Georgia. Only decades later did Smith learn about his benefactor.

"When Dr. Mays told me Margaret Mitchell had paid for my education, I was flabbergasted," Smith said. "Margaret Mitchell had a great impact on my life, and we, as a race, need to be grateful to her."

CELEBRATING SELZNICK'S CENTENNIAL BIRTHDAY

The one-hundredth anniversary of legendary producer David O. Selznick's birth on May 10, 1902, was commemorated in style in 2002:

- Hollywood's historic El Capitan Theatre hosted a "David O. Selznick Film Festival" during May, screening *Duel in the Sun, Portrait of Jennie*, and *The Adventures of Tom Sawyer*.

- The Producers Guild of America's quarterly magazine, *Produced By*, featured the five-page article "Selznick at 100: A Master Showman Remembered" by Hollywood writer Tom Heyes. Accompanying the article were black-and-white photographs of Selznick on the set of *GWTW* and with Vivien Leigh and her Best Actress Oscar at the 1940 Academy Awards ceremony; a color reproduction of a one-sheet from *GWTW*'s 1939 release; and color photographs of movie promotional materials from other Selznick productions, including *Intermezzo* and *Anna Karenina*.
- Cable TV channel Turner Classic Movies showcased more than forty Selznick films during Monday and Wednesday nights in October. *GWTW* was broadcast on October 23.

SELZNICK RECEIVES STAR ON
THE HOLLYWOOD WALK OF FAME

For his work on *GWTW* alone, David O. Selznick would be counted among the luminaries of Hollywood. Yet on the Hollywood Walk of Fame, the producer had no star.

"David Selznick should have been among the first 1,500 names when the Walk of Fame was started in 1960," said Johnny Grant, Hollywood's ceremonial mayor. The October 26, 2004, star ceremony sponsored by the Producers Guild of America "remedied that unbelievable omission," according to Grant.

"My father's feelings were hurt that he wasn't included," Daniel Selznick told more than one hundred attendees that had gathered to see his father's star unveiled at 7000 Hollywood Boulevard. That spot is in front of the historic Hollywood Roosevelt Hotel, the site of the first Academy Awards banquet held in 1929. On behalf of his father, Selznick expressed appreciation for the belated honor.

Among those applauding the recognition during the sidewalk ceremony were Selznick's two stepsons from his marriage to Jennifer Jones, several Selznick biographers, Ann Rutherford, and Cammie King Conlon. Rutherford shared written greetings from those unable to attend, including Olivia de Havilland, whose letter read, "I am with you in spirit and with all those who have gathered with you to honor this giant among creators, who, through his films, has enriched the lives of generation after generation and will continue to enrich the lives of many generations to come."

Following the ceremony, invited guests enjoyed a lavish reception in the Hollywood Roosevelt Hotel. There among photographs of Selznick International Pictures studio, of the producer and the players he made stars, memories of David O. Selznick bubbled like uncorked champagne, and guests remembered and saluted many of his cinematic triumphs—*Dinner at Eight, David Copperfield, Anna Karenina, A Tale of Two Cities, A Star Is Born, The Prisoner of Zenda,* and *Gone With the Wind.*

GOING ONCE . . . GOING TWICE . . . *GWTW* MEMORABILIA SOLD!

The excited bidding at Christie's New York auction house rivaled the bidding to lead the opening reel at Atlanta's Monster Bazaar. This July 24, 2002, auction marked the first time that Christie's had held a full auction dedicated to one film—*Gone With the Wind*—and the first time that thousands of items from the Herb Bridges *Gone With the Wind* Collection were offered for sale.

The auction included 348 lots of memorabilia ranging from movie posters and publicity materials, scripts, call sheets, programs, playbills, photographs, dolls, figurines, jewelry, first and foreign editions of the novel, and costumes from the film. When the gavel came down on the final bid—$14,000—for Melanie's hand-knitted gray-and-rose woolen sweater, the crowd's reaction matched that of the Atlanta crowd shocked at Rhett's $150 bid in gold for Mrs. Charles Hamilton. Expected to sell for between $4,000 and $6,000, Melanie's garment had a total price tag of $16,730 (including a 19.5 percent buyer's premium), making the costume the auction's highest-priced single item. Auction sales totaled $334,588.

The items in the public sale represented only part of what was considered the world's largest collection of *GWTW* memorabilia owned by Joseph Herbert Bridges, a retired mail carrier from Sharpsburg, Georgia. His passion for collecting memorabilia related to the book and the film began in the early 1960s with a friendly disagreement over which actress portrayed Belle Watling. Bridges found a motion picture edition of *GWTW* in an Atlanta bookstore and proved to his friend that Ona Munson had played the on-screen madam. That purchase triggered a lifelong fervor for collecting anything related to *GWTW*, and the collection he amassed for more than forty years made him famous.

A noted *GWTW* author and historian, Bridges died unexpectedly at his Newnan, Georgia, home on September 24, 2013, at the age of eighty-three. He left behind his wife, family, and legions of friends and fans who mourned the passing of a true Southern gentleman and an extraordinary *GWTW* collector.

KEEP TYPING AND PASS THE PEANUTS:
MOONLIGHT AND MAGNOLIAS PREMIERES

In February 1939, after shutting down production and hiring Victor Fleming to take over directorial duties on *GWTW*, David O. Selznick realized that his script had morphed into a mess. He turned to noted script doctor Ben Hecht to whip the mess into a masterpiece. But Selznick was shocked when he learned that neither Hecht nor Fleming had read Margaret's book.

In the producer's office for five days and nights and starting from scratch with Sidney Howard's treatment, Hecht attacked the script mercilessly in eighteen- to twenty-four-hour stretches. Since Hecht was unfamiliar with the characters, Selznick and Fleming acted out each scene as Hecht wrote and edited on a typewriter. The trio ate only bananas and salted peanuts to keep up their strength. At the end of the marathon scriptwriting session, Hecht had saved *GWTW*.

This real-life scenario inspired playwright and screenwriter Ron Hutchinson's three-act play *Moonlight and Magnolias*, which premiered in May 2004 at Chicago's Goodman Theatre.

"As a rewrite guy myself for the past 20-plus years in Hollywood, I was instinctively drawn to the tangled tale of how this iconic movie script got written, unwritten, and re-written," said Hutchinson, a Ben Hecht fan since youth.

Moonlight and Magnolias imagines what took place behind closed doors when a determined producer, a disdainful director, and a dubious writer—"Does it have to be set during the Civil War?"—hammered out a script while Selznick's long-suffering secretary, Miss Poppenghul, guarded the door and fielded phone calls from Louis B. Mayer. Transcending farce, the play illustrates the egocentric perspectives and biases of producer, director, and writer and re-creates the painful process of creative collaboration.

According to *Daily Variety*, "There's a delicious preponderance of juicy insider gags that should allow this show to snag mucho guffaws in L.A. or New York." Since opening, the play has been a hit with theatergoers, especially *GWTW* fans, on national and foreign stages.

Hutchinson described *Moonlight and Magnolias* as a "kind of screwball comedy of the period. It's a way to examine a lot of things—how this film, through a series of accidents and happenstance, became one of the greatest films of all time. It's celebrating the glory days of Hollywood . . . and the dynamics of these three men."

HALL OF FAME HONOR
FOR *GWTW*'S PRODUCTION DESIGNER

In 2005, *GWTW*'s production designer, William Cameron Menzies, was one of seven initial inductees to the Art Directors Guild Hall of Fame, which recognizes "the many contributions and achievements of those artists who created and evolved our unique craft of design and art direction for the moving image."

Born on July 29, 1896, in New Haven, Connecticut, Menzies brought his own brand of visual style to the film industry in 1919, working in film design and special effects for silent films. His exceptional work in *The Dove* (1927) and *Tempest* (1928) earned him an Academy Award for Best Art Direction at the first Academy Awards ceremony in 1929.

Studios and independent producers, such as David O. Selznick, hired Menzies to craft the look of a story on film through elements such as color, composition, and lighting. Impressed with the cave sequence Menzies created for *The Adventures of Tom Sawyer*, Selznick tapped Menzies's talents for *Gone With the Wind*.

In a September 1, 1937, memo Selznick wrote: "In short it is my plan to have the whole physical side of this picture . . . personally handled by one man who has little or nothing else to do—and that man, Menzies. Menzies may turn out to be one of the most valuable factors in properly producing this picture." Such a pivotal role demanded a special title, and Selznick decided on "production designer" for Menzies.

In his role, Menzies and his staff created at least 1,500 color storyboard sketches that established camera and lighting angles and character interactions for *GWTW*'s sets and scenes from first to last shot even before filming started. Menzies also directed the escape from Atlanta fire scene filmed on December 10, 1938; several montages; and the scenes of Atlanta citizens grimly awaiting the Gettysburg casualty lists and of Scarlett running through the panic-gripped city streets.

Selznick acknowledged Menzies's importance to *GWTW* in the film's opening credits. The producer included "This production designed by William Cameron Menzies" on a card separate from the other technical credits. Menzies's credit also stayed on the screen for six seconds and matched the six seconds for the credit "Produced by David O. Selznick."

Menzies died at the age of sixty on March 5, 1957, in Beverly Hills.

STEINER'S *GWTW* SCORE HONORED BY AFI

In 2005, the American Film Institute (AFI) saluted Max Steiner's *Gone With the Wind* score as the second greatest film score in a century of movie music, behind *Star Wars*. More than five hundred film artists, composers, musicians, critics, and historians chose the top twenty-five film scores of all time that were included in *The Big Picture—AFI's 100 Years of Film Scores.*

Called "the father of film music," Steiner died at the age of eighty-three on December 28, 1971. He was honored in 1975 with a star on the Hollywood Walk of Fame at 1559 Vine Street for his contributions to film.

TCM DECLARES *GWTW* ONE OF THE ESSENTIALS

On July 1, 2006, Turner Classic Movies saluted *Gone With the Wind* as one of "The Essentials," films that are considered must-see masterworks. TCM emcee Robert Osborne and film critic Molly Haskell provided a special introduction to *GWTW*'s broadcast and a post-film discussion.

Haskell called the character of Scarlett O'Hara "fantastically modern." Osborne praised Vivien Leigh as "the linchpin that makes it all work and stay modern." For Haskell, the heart of *GWTW* "is the family, the love of these people . . . the love of the land." She called *GWTW* a "great movie" and declared that "it stands the test of time. . . . An absolute essential."

NEW *GWTW* MUSICAL DEBUTS ON LONDON STAGE

Thirty-six years after the first *GWTW* musical opened at London's Theatre Royal, Drury Lane, a new musical version of Margaret Mitchell's novel debuted on April 22, 2008, at the West End's New London Theatre. Directed by Sir Trevor Nunn, *Gone with the Wind* featured music and lyrics by novice composer and playwright Margaret Martin, making her own theatrical debut.

Martin had dabbled in songwriting for years but had not considered writing a musical until 1998, when she completed her dissertation for a public health doctorate. Needing a diversion from scholarly work, she decided the most fun, creative thing she could do was write a stage musical based on a book she loved: *Gone with the Wind*.

She worked on the project for two years before she approached representatives of the Stephens Mitchell Trusts with the book, lyrics, and demo CD and requested the rights to make a musical adaptation of the novel. Despite Martin's theatrical inexperience, the representatives liked her take on the story and granted her request. "This show is largely an homage to the things that women do and the capacity of women to get through difficult times," Martin told the Associated Press.

Subsequently, Martin read an interview with British theatrical director Trevor Nunn of *Cats*, *Les Miserables*, and *Nicholas Nickleby* fame, who discussed his passion for American history and for the American Civil War. Martin sent Nunn her materials. Before she knew it, Nunn had agreed to collaborate in adapting her book and then to direct *Gone with the Wind* as a West End production. Nunn told Playbill.com, "I am drawn to the challenge of telling Margaret Mitchell's epic story through words, music, and the imaginative resources of the theatre."

Casting for the $9.5 million production included:

- American actress Jill Paice (*Curtains*) as Scarlett.
- Scottish pop singer Darius Danesh (*Guys and Dolls*) as Rhett.
- British actress Madeleine Worrall (*Cinderella* at the Old Vic) as Melanie.

- South African actor Edward Baker-Duly (*De-Lovely*) as Ashley.
- American actress NaTasha Yvette Williams (*The Color Purple*) as Mammy.

Although audiences praised the musical—the cast received a standing ovation on opening night—critics were cruel. Karen Fricker of *Daily Variety* opined, "It's not for a lack of talent among the cast and A-list design and musical teams, but neither the material nor the production offers persuasive evidence as to why this well-known story needed transposing into a new form." Charles Spencer of the *Daily Telegraph* wrote, "This soullessly efficient show merely feels like one damn thing after another." Michael Billington in the *Guardian* queried, "How do you cram a 1,000-page novel into three-and-a-half hours of stage time? With great difficulty."

On May 30, 2008, executive producer Aldo Scrofani pulled the plug on the production. *Gone with the Wind* closed on June 14, 2008, after seventy-nine performances.

THREE ATLANTA ANNIVERSARIES CONVERGED INTO GRAND *GWTW* CELEBRATION

Atlanta had much to celebrate in 2009. *Gone With the Wind* turned seventy. The Fox Theatre, which had hosted *GWTW*'s fiftieth anniversary re-premiere, hit eighty. Atlanta-based Turner Classic Movies (TCM) marked fifteen years of broadcasting classic films, including the one that launched the channel: *Gone With the Wind*.

Spearheaded by the Fox and cosponsored by TCM, the Literary Center at Margaret Mitchell House, and the Atlanta Film Festival, events of this anniversary convergence included:

- The broadcast of *GWTW* at 8 p.m. on Tuesday, April 14, on TCM— the date of the movie channel's fifteenth anniversary—an event that was billed as "The 70th Anniversary of the Atlanta Premiere of *Gone With the Wind*."
- A discussion hosted by the Literary Center at Margaret Mitchell House on Saturday, April 18, at 4 p.m. Led by TCM host Robert Osborne, the discussion featured Michael Sragow, author and movie

critic at the *Baltimore Sun*, and Molly Haskell, author and critic, who discussed *GWTW*'s legacy, its director Victor Fleming, and Hollywood's golden year of 1939.

- A Southern Breakfast buffet hosted by Scott Benson, director of *The Race to Save 100 Years*, as a fundraiser for the Atlanta Film Festival on Saturday, April 19, at 10 a.m., which was attended by Osborne, Sragow, and Haskell.
- A "Scarlett and Rhett Reception" hosted by the Fox Theatre in its Egyptian Ballroom on Sunday, April 19, at 10:30 a.m., which featured elegant continental breakfast items.
- The screening of *GWTW* at the Fox Theatre on Sunday, April 19— twice. The first showing in the 4,674-seat theater sold out so quickly a second screening was added to accommodate demand. Before the show, Robert Osborne held an audience Q&A about the importance of the film.

"Its survival message strikes people," Osborne said. "It always seems like we're going through some sort of crisis, so it's very meaningful to realize you have to learn how to survive."

HOORAY FOR HOLLYWOOD'S GREATEST YEAR!

The Academy of Motion Picture Arts and Sciences kicked off a ten-week seventieth anniversary cinematic salute to "Hollywood's Greatest Year: Best Picture Nominees of 1939" with a sold-out showing of *Gone With the Wind* on May 18, 2009, at the Samuel Goldwyn Theatre.

The event started with the screening of newsreel footage of the Atlanta premiere and then the first episode of the 1939 serial *Buck Rogers*. Afterward, special guests—Patrick Curtis (infant Beau); Cammie King Conlon (Bonnie Butler); Mickey Kuhn (young Beau); Ann Rutherford (Carreen O'Hara); and Daniel Selznick, son of the film's producer—were invited onstage to share their *GWTW* memories.

A recorded message from Olivia de Havilland welcomed the thousand-plus audience members and introduced the film. She said, in part: "In 1939 the war in Asia had already begun, late in that year the Second World War began in Europe, and two years later our own country was engaged in both great conflicts. *Gone With the Wind*, with its universal theme of struggle, devastation and rebirth, touched the lives of people the world over, and the vitality of its characters gave hope to the most despairing. In one way or another the film goes on doing both."

The other nine Best Picture nominees were screened on successive weeks of the retrospective, preceded by an animated 1939 short and a *Buck Rogers* episode. The seventieth anniversary celebration concluded on August 3, 2009, with *The Wizard of Oz*.

GWTW PARODY "CURTAIN ROD DRESS" GIVEN TO SMITHSONIAN

In 2009, designer Bob Mackie and comedienne Carol Burnett donated to the Smithsonian Institution the costume he created and she wore for *The Carol Burnett Show*'s famous 1976 *GWTW* parody *Went With the Wind*.

For the now-iconic costume, Mackie imagined a funny version of the green velvet gown Mammy fashioned for Scarlett from Tara's draperies. The result was hilarious.

In the sketch, Burnett's "Miss Starlett" descended a staircase with the green velvet drapes of her gown still attached to a brass-plated curtain rod balanced on her shoulders. On her head, she wore a fringed valance made to resemble a hat. Responding to a compliment about the dress, "Miss Starlett" quipped, "I saw it in a window, and I just couldn't resist it." The audience roared.

TV Guide included this spoof on its 2004 list of "100 Most Memorable TV Moments," where it was ranked as number forty-seven.

The costume is housed in the Smithsonian's National Museum of American History, which is dedicated to collecting, preserving, and displaying American heritage in the areas of social, political, cultural, scientific, and military history.

NEW COLLECTOR'S EDITION OF *GWTW* RELEASED FOR SEVENTIETH ANNIVERSARY

The November 17, 2009, release of a deluxe seventieth anniversary video of *Gone With the Wind*, in both Blu-ray and DVD formats, capped off the anniversary-year celebration. Packaged in a numbered, limited-edition red velvet box, the "70th Anniversary Ultimate Collector's Edition" included oodles of new extras:

- The documentary *Gone With the Wind: The Legend Lives On*.
- The 1980 Emmy Award–winning made-for-TV movie *Moviola: The Scarlett O'Hara Wars* about the search for an actress to play Scarlett.
- The documentary *1939: Hollywood's Greatest Year*.
- A reproduction of the 1939 original movie program.
- A commemorative fifty-two-page photo and production art book.
- Ten five-by-seven watercolor reproduction art prints of the film's scenes and characters.
- Archival correspondence from producer David O. Selznick.
- CD soundtrack sampler.

The Blu-ray version offered an extra bonus: a DVD of the six-hour 1992 documentary *MGM: When the Lion Roars*, including a section about the making of *GWTW*.

CONNECTICUT LIBRARY REDISCOVERS RARE PIECES OF *GWTW* MANUSCRIPT

Most libraries have copies of *GWTW* in their collections. Pequot Library in Southport, Connecticut, tops that. This Fairfield County public library has in its collection the last four chapters of Margaret's *GWTW* typescript. Those chapters include some of the novel's most famous lines—"My dear, I don't give a damn" and "After all, tomorrow is another day." How did a library in a Yankee seaport town come to own such a Southern literary treasure?

The link is George Brett Jr., who was president of Macmillan when the company published *GWTW*. A Southport resident, Brett served as president of the Pequot Library's board of trustees in the 1950s and donated more than ninety foreign editions of *GWTW*, most inscribed to him by Margaret, to the library. The manuscript chapters were included in this Brett Collection, which the library cataloged and safeguarded.

Through the years, the library displayed some of the *GWTW* manuscript pages twice—in 1979 for an exhibition devoted to Macmillan first editions and in 1991 for a salute to *Scarlett*, the authorized *GWTW* sequel. Then the pages were returned to storage.

The typescript remained tucked away until 2010, when the library received a research request about the Brett Collection from writer Ellen F. Brown, who with coauthor John Wiley Jr. was preparing *Margaret Mitchell's Gone with the Wind: A Bestseller's Odyssey from Atlanta to Hollywood*. In researching the inquiry—Do any of the foreign editions have author inscriptions?—library staff stumbled upon the manuscript pages. Subsequently, the find was authenticated and appraised by New York's Christie's auction house, which declared the partial manuscript "a precious literary artifact."

Typed on a Royal portable, the typescript pages bear handwritten changes made by Margaret and her husband, John Marsh. So experts believe this manuscript represents the second draft of *GWTW* written by Margaret Mitchell.

Margaret wrote her novel over a ten-year period during which she stored her rough-draft chapters in manila envelopes. When Macmillan vice president Harold Latham coaxed the manuscript from Margaret during his literary tour in 1935, he received a stack of those manila envelopes. Some contained different versions of the same chapter. Other chapters were missing, including the first chapter. Yet the writing was compelling enough that Macmillan offered Margaret a book contract in July 1935, with the stipulation that she deliver a complete manuscript.

In August, Macmillan returned the manila-envelope rough draft to Margaret. From then until January 1936, she revised her story; added missing content; verified for historical accuracy; and corrected spelling, grammar, and punctuation problems. With the help of her husband and typists hired to produce the final typescript, Margaret sent the manuscript to Macmillan in sections that were typeset as they were received.

After *GWTW* was published, Margaret asked Macmillan's George Brett to return the final typescript to her. The company located the manuscript in a vault, insured the document for one thousand dollars, and shipped it to the author.

After her death, John Marsh burned most of the typescript as well as most of the manila-envelope rough draft. He saved enough material to confirm Margaret's authorship of *GWTW*, should it ever be questioned, and entrusted the sealed envelope to an Atlanta bank.

How, then, did George Brett happen to have the last four chapters of *GWTW*'s typescript? Experts aren't sure but agree on one possibility: Margaret gave those chapters to him as a gift in gratitude for bringing her story of the Old South to life.

GWTW FANS SAVE SCARLETT'S COSTUMES

The fates of five original *Gone With the Wind* costumes were hanging by a thread at the Harry Ransom Center at the University of Texas at Austin in 2010. That's when the Center issued an appeal for thirty thousand dollars to rescue Scarlett's wedding gown, the green velvet drapery dress, the green-and-gold dressing gown, the burgundy velvet gown, and the blue velvet peignoir with fox-fur trim. In just three weeks, more than six hundred donors from forty-four states and thirteen countries contributed funds that exceeded the goal.

The conservation work required 180-plus hours to complete from fall 2010 to spring 2012. As a result, the Ransom Center rescued three of the five costumes. Textile experts had deemed the fabrics of the wedding gown and veil and the blue peignoir too fragile, so these costumes were returned to storage to prevent additional damage.

Designed by Walter Plunkett, the costumes are part of the David O. Selznick Collection—five thousand boxes of materials—housed at the center since the 1980s. Before that, the costumes were exhibited widely for promotional purposes in the years after *GWTW* premiered. They spent decades traveling to theaters and had even been displayed at New York's Metropolitan Museum of Art. Wear and tear took a toll.

"Most costumes are not constructed to last beyond the production of the film nor are they finished in the same way as a ready-to-wear garment," said Jill Morena, assistant curator for costumes and personal effects at the Ransom Center. "We've taken steps to prevent further damage, but we want to be able to safely display and share the dresses."

Get a behind-the-scenes view of the conservation work at www.hrc. utexas.edu/conservedresses.

The costume conservation was completed in time for the Ransom Center to lend the green velvet drapery dress and the burgundy velvet gown to the Victoria and Albert Museum in London for the *Hollywood Costume* exhibition that ran from October 2012 through January 2013. Spotlighting more than one hundred iconic movie costumes, the exhibition explored the integral role of costume design in film storytelling.

THE NOVEL AT SEVENTY-FIVE:
CELEBRATING MARGARET MITCHELL

Celebrating the woman behind the book seemed fitting for *Gone with the Wind*'s seventy-fifth anniversary in 2011, and eleven events did just that:

1. The Atlanta-Fulton Public Library offered a three-exhibit series with items drawn from the author's personal collection. *The Book* exhibit focused on the writing and publishing of *GWTW* and featured Margaret's portable Remington typewriter, three facsimile pages from her original manuscript, and the one-millionth copy of *GWTW* that Macmillan presented to her. *The Movie* exhibit focused on the making of the Academy Award–winning film based on Margaret's novel and featured the leather-bound presentation script of *GWTW* given to her by David O. Selznick, invitations to premiere events, and original newspapers that reported on the premiere. *The Writer* exhibit focused on the personal life of the author and featured family photographs, her honorary degree from Smith College, and books from her personal library.
2. The University of Georgia's Hargrett Rare Book and Manuscript Library offered the exhibit *In a Weak Moment, I Have Written a Book* that featured photographs of the author, samples of childhood writings, foreign editions of *GWTW*, and letters that detailed her copyright battles with foreign publishers.
3. Scribner published a seventy-fifth anniversary edition of *Gone with the Wind* in both hardcover and trade paperback that featured a preface by Pat Conroy. The hardcover version was the 126th printing of the Pulitzer Prize–winning novel.
4. The Margaret Mitchell House offered a one-day *"Gone With the Wind*: 75th Anniversary Celebration" that focused on daily life for Civil War soldiers, life in Atlanta in the 1920s, and *GWTW*'s enduring legacy.
5. Georgia Public Broadcasting offered the premiere of its production *Margaret Mitchell: American Rebel* at a black-tie benefit dinner in honor of GPB's fiftieth anniversary.

6. The Marietta *Gone With the Wind* Museum: Scarlett on the Square offered *A Tribute to Margaret Mitchell: The Book That Touched the World*, that featured events with movie cast members and a panel discussion with authors of books about *GWTW*.

7. The Clayton County Conventions and Visitors Bureau offered *Legendary Tales . . . 75 Years of History in the Official Home of* Gone With the Wind, which featured a self-guided, six-stop living history tour through Jonesboro. Costumed storytellers paralleled *GWTW*'s literary setting and events with locations and episodes in Jonesboro's history.

8. Atlanta's Oakland Cemetery hosted a reception on the Bell Tower veranda, a guided walking tour, and a champagne toast at Margaret Mitchell's gravesite.

9. The Mary G. Hardin Center for Cultural Arts in Gadsden, Alabama, offered Gone With the Wind *at 75: A Diamond Jubilee*, the largest exhibit of *GWTW* items ever displayed in the United States, drawn from the nation's leading collectors. Highlights included *GWTW*'s original 1936 dust jacket printing plate, the original Paris hat, and copies of the novel from every country in which the book has been published.

10. The Pequot Library in Southport, Connecticut, offered *With Best Regards: The George P. Brett, Jr.,* Gone With the Wind *Collection*, an exhibit that featured material donated to the library by the former Macmillan president and Southport resident, including pages from the original *GWTW* typescript.

11. The Atlanta History Center offered *Atlanta's Book: The Lost* Gone With the Wind *Manuscript*, an exhibit of sections of the original *GWTW* typescript, on loan from Connecticut's Pequot Library. Individual pages of the final chapter were wall mounted for ease of visitor reading. The exhibit also included the desk used by the author while writing her book.

MITCHELL NEPHEW'S BEQUEST
BENEFITS ATLANTA ARCHDIOCESE

The Catholic Archdiocese of Atlanta inherited a *Gone with the Wind*–fall from the estate of the author's nephew, Joseph Mitchell, who died on October 11, 2011, at the age of seventy-six. The younger son of Margaret's brother Stephens Mitchell left a multimillion-dollar bequest to the Archdiocese that included a collection of family artifacts and his half share of the literary and trademark rights to *GWTW*. (His brother's widow inherited the other half share when Eugene Mitchell died on August 8, 2007, at the age of seventy-six.)

The family artifacts included signed first and foreign editions of his aunt's novel; personal effects such as her wallet, driver's license, and press card; her bed and her dining room table; her silver; and an unpublished history of the Mitchell family, handwritten by her father.

The literary legacy includes revenue from book royalties, merchandise sales, and movie rights along with an obligation to help protect *GWTW*'s copyright, which expires in the United States in 2031, from infringement. To manage the legacy, the archdiocese turned to the trust committee of the Stephens Mitchell Trusts, which has safeguarded *GWTW* for decades.

"This gift is a reservoir of the funds earned through the genius of Margaret Mitchell and her depiction of the harsh struggles of Southern life during and after the Civil War," Archbishop Wilton D. Gregory said. "The Mitchell family has a proud Catholic legacy, and this gift will allow that legacy and that pride to be shared with many others in the archdiocese."

A longtime parishioner of Atlanta's Cathedral of Christ the King, Joseph Mitchell was Margaret Mitchell's last direct descendant.

FIND YOUR WAY ON THE *GWTW* TRAIL

For decades, *GWTW* fans have journeyed to Georgia on personal pilgrimages, seeking sites in and around Atlanta connected to Margaret Mitchell, her novel, and the film. In 2012, the Peach State made it easier to find those key locations with its designation of the official *GWTW* Trail. Stops along the trail, starting in Marietta, going through Atlanta, and ending in Jonesboro, include:

- Marietta *Gone With the Wind* Museum: Scarlett on the Square, where fans can tour an extensive collection of novel- and film-related memorabilia.

- Margaret Mitchell House and Museum, where fans can see the apartment where the author wrote her novel, first and foreign editions of the book, and exhibits related to the film.
- Atlanta-Fulton Public Library System's Central Library, where fans can explore one of the largest collections of Margaret Mitchell's personal items, including photographs, books, awards, and the Remington typewriter she used to write her novel.
- Historic Oakland Cemetery, where fans can visit Margaret Mitchell's gravesite in Atlanta's Victorian cemetery.
- Road to Tara Museum in Jonesboro, where fans can glimpse original film props and costumes, a library of foreign editions, a photo gallery, and plate and doll collections.

Off the trail, fans can visit Kennesaw Mountain National Battlefield for exhibits related to the Atlanta Campaign; the Atlanta History Center for one of the nation's largest Civil War exhibits; the Atlanta Cyclorama for a three-dimensional, panoramic experience of the Battle of Atlanta; and Stately Oaks Plantation for the experience of the life and times in a Greek Revival antebellum home.

MORE RECOGNITION FOR MARGARET MITCHELL

In October 2013, the Atlanta Press Club inducted five Georgia journalists into its third Hall of Fame class. Among the honorees was Margaret Mitchell, about whom it was noted: "Her investigative skills and descriptive writing style earned her merit as one of the South's pioneer female journalists even before writing *Gone with the Wind*."

The Atlanta Press Club's Hall of Fame "recognizes journalists for their lifetime achievements and high standards of journalistic integrity."

HAPPY ONE-HUNDREDTH BIRTHDAY, VIVIEN LEIGH!

The year 2013 marked the one-hundredth anniversary of Vivien Leigh's birth, and celebrations of her life and career dotted the year, including:

- On April 16, the Royal Mail honored Leigh with a commemorative stamp in its "Great Britons" series.

- From August 3 to October 31, Topsham Museum in Devon hosted the exhibit *Vivien Leigh: A Century of Fame*, which included movie and stage memorabilia; letters and photographs; and personal items and clothing owned by Leigh, including a gift from David O. Selznick: the nightdress Leigh wore during the scene in which Rhett asks for a divorce.
- On October 15, the coffee table book *Vivien Leigh: An Intimate Portrait* by film historian Kendra Bean was published, and the volume was featured as that month's Turner Classic Movies Book Corner Selection.
- On November 5—Leigh's birthday:
  - Turner Classic Movies hosted a twenty-four-hour film tribute to her. Among the movies presented were *Storm in a Teacup, Fire Over England, Waterloo Bridge, That Hamilton Woman, Anna Karenina, A Streetcar Named Desire, Roman Spring of Mrs. Stone, Ship of Fools*, and *Gone With the Wind*.
  - London's Victoria and Albert Museum opened an exhibit of items from the Vivien Leigh Archive, including some of her love letters to Olivier.
- On November 6, the British Film Institute Southbank opened a season devoted to Vivien Leigh that featured lectures and a retrospective of her films, including multiple showings of *GWTW* in a new 4K digital restoration. Made from the original negative, the high-resolution digital print offered spectacular color, sharp images, and perfect contrast.
- On November 19, the "Vivien Leigh Anniversary Collection" debuted on DVD and Blu-ray and included restorations of *Fire Over England, Dark Journey, Storm in a Teacup*, and *Sidewalks of London*.
- On November 30, London's National Portrait Gallery opened an eight-month photographic and ephemera exhibition, *Starring Vivien Leigh: A Centenary Celebration*, that explored the luminous Leigh's career and image as one of the twentieth century's most famous British women.

SCARLETT COSTUME—THOUGHT LOST— SOLD AT AUCTION

Scarlett is resting on the Butler terrace, recuperating from her miscarriage, when Rhett comes from the house to discuss their marital future. Bonnie interrupts their conversation, demanding that her parents watch as she and her pony jump a hurdle in the garden.

For this poignant scene, Vivien Leigh wore a black-fox-trimmed, blue velvet peignoir. Beneath this she had on a pale blue, accordion-pleated silk negligee, a costume that was long thought lost. But the gown surfaced in 2013 in an extraordinary public sale.

The November 25 event—"What Dreams Are Made Of: A Century of Movie Magic at Auction, as Curated by Turner Classic Movies"—combined the talents of TCM and fine art auction house Bonhams. According to TCM, the auction featured "a stunning array of costumes, props, scripts, production designs, production memos, movie posters, and other rare treasures from some of the greatest films of all time."

Items from *GWTW* included a group of seven manuscripts that detailed the evolution of the novel from synopsis to screenplay, sets of scene stills, a signed poster from the 1989 *GWTW* cast reunion, a Vivien Leigh photograph owned by Hattie McDaniel, a typed letter signed by Vivien Leigh, and her negligee from the scene in which Bonnie takes her fatal ride.

Where has the gown been since 1939? After *GWTW*'s filming wrapped, the costume was returned to the Western Costume Company. This coincided with the marriage of one of the seamstresses who had worked on *GWTW*'s wardrobe, so the company gave the negligee to her as a wedding gift. It remained with her family until the 1980s, when she sold the costume to a private collector who arranged the gown's auction through Bonhams.

The ankle-length gown has angel sleeves, a hook-and-eye bodice closure with blue satin ribbon detail, and a Selznick International Pictures label with a black-ink inscription: "Name Scarlett / No. 108-W.W. 381." The negligee sold for $56,250 (including a 25 percent buyer's premium).

THE FILM AT SEVENTY-FIVE: CELEBRATING A CINEMATIC MASTERPIECE

Twelve months just weren't enough for celebrating *Gone With the Wind*'s seventy-fifth anniversary in 2014. The festivities started early and included these highlights:

On November 8, 2013—Margaret Mitchell's birthday—the Road to Tara Museum in Jonesboro launched a yearlong series of anniversary events with "Rhett and Scarlett Reunited . . . for the Evening." During the reception, where guests were greeted by Scarlett and Rhett look-alikes, the museum opened two permanent exhibits.

The first exhibit was a set of four sixty-four-inch roundel portraits of *GWTW*'s main stars that were displayed on the building across the street from the Loew's Grand Theatre for the 1939 premiere. Part of the Herb Bridges Collection, the roundels were salvaged from the theater by Bridges several years before the movie palace was destroyed by fire in 1978. The museum renamed its exhibit of *GWTW* memorabilia—most of it from the late collector—in his memory: *Herb Bridges: A Gentleman's Legacy*.

The second exhibit expanded the museum's salute to actress Ann Rutherford, who played Carreen. Some of the items were donated by her daughter; others were on loan from a private collector.

From April 10 to 13, 2014, Turner Classic Movies hosted its fifth-annual Classic Film Festival in Hollywood with the theme "Family in the Movies: The Ties that Bind." The festival showcased two films celebrating seventy-fifth anniversaries: the digitally restored *Gone With the Wind* and the IMAX 3D version of *The Wizard of Oz*.

From June 6 to 8, 2014, the Marietta *Gone With the Wind* Museum: Scarlett on the Square celebrated in style with a "Bazaar Ball," an authors' panel discussion, and a memorabilia auction.

From September 9, 2014, through January 4, 2015, the Harry Ransom Center at the University of Texas at Austin presented *The Making of* Gone With the Wind. The exhibit featured more than three hundred items from the David O. Selznick Collection, including original and reproduction film costumes, photographs, storyboards, production records, audition footage, correspondence, and fan mail that provided multiple behind-the-camera perspectives about the film's creation and its legacy as a quintessential American film. The Ransom Center celebrated the exhibit with an illustrated book and a companion web-based exhibition.

SCARLETT, CONTROL THAT BALL GOWN

Would-be Scarletts will no doubt receive a number of invitations to *GWTW*-dress parties honoring the film's seventy-fifth anniversary. But how do you fit a hoopskirt into a MINI Cooper?

Actually, antebellum-style gowns are quite smooshable. So it is possible to dress like a Southern belle and still remain a lady.

Sitting in a crinoline gown is perhaps the number-one problem. Do it incorrectly and you'll look like a giant bell, and no Southern lady wants her legs confused with a clapper. So just before you sit down, pick up the back of the hoop. Keep the hoop in the middle of your back and arrange the fullness of the skirt around you.

Moving around in a *GWTW* ball gown can be equally as tricky. When walking, take small steps and maintain good posture. Otherwise, the hoop will sway.

When you want to go through a doorway, push the sides of the dress in. The same rule applies when you enter a car. When exiting the car, just hold the gown down around you.

Why fiddle-dee-dee, it's as easy as can be! And no Rhett Butler will be able to resist you!

FOURTEEN

Look What They've Said

MEMORABLE QUOTES ABOUT *GWTW*

"Forget it, Louis. No Civil War picture ever made a nickel."

During a conference with Louis B. Mayer, MGM's production chief, Irving Thalberg, listened to a story synopsis of an about-to-be-published Civil War novel. Thalberg's comment prompted the studio head to turn down movie rights to *GWTW*.

"I beg, urge, coax, and plead with you to read this at once. I know that after you read the book you will drop everything and buy it."

Katherine (Kay) Brown, story editor of Selznick International Pictures' New York office, was excited after reading *GWTW*, which had been submitted to her by agent Annie Laurie Williams. Along with the novel and a synopsis, Brown sent this enthusiastic message to David O. Selznick.

"Scarlett is going to be a difficult and thankless role. The one I'd like to play is Rhett Butler."

After her fans reacted negatively to rumors of her playing Scarlett, Norma Shearer explained to the *New York Times* why she withdrew from contention for the role.

> "Oh, you don't want to be in *Gone With the Wind*, it's going to be the biggest bust in town."

Jack Warner tried to dissuade Olivia de Havilland when she expressed an interest in playing Melanie.

> "I guess we're stuck with you."

At a Hollywood party, George Cukor's comment to Vivien Leigh was her first hint that she had captured the role of Scarlett O'Hara.

> "Yesterday I put on my Confederate uniform for the first time and looked like a fairy doorman at the Beverly Wiltshire [*sic*]—a fine thing at my age."

A disgruntled Leslie Howard shared his feelings about playing Ashley in a letter to his family.

> "At noon, I think it's divine; at midnight, I think it's lousy. Sometimes I think it's the greatest picture ever made. But if it's only a great picture, I'll still be satisfied."

David O. Selznick commented on the film to reporters the night before *GWTW*'s Hollywood press preview, held on December 12, 1939, at the Four Star Theatre on Wilshire Blvd.

> "No movie has a right to be that long!"

President Franklin Delano Roosevelt fell asleep during a screening of *GWTW* at the White House and awoke with critical comments about the film.

> "Oh, dear, do you realize that poor Melanie will not be in it?"

Olivia de Havilland reacts upon hearing that producers Richard Zanuck and David Brown were planning a sequel to *GWTW*.

"I'm quite sure that Clark Gable, Vivien Leigh, and Leslie Howard are up there somewhere right now incensed over the proceedings."

Olivia de Havilland was angered that *GWTW*'s network television premiere would be marred by numerous commercial interruptions.

"One of my favorite scenes was the burning of Schenectady, New York, just before Grant surrendered to Robert E. Lee."

President Jimmy Carter's joke caused peals of audience laughter at a 1977 reception honoring the American Film Institute's tenth anniversary and an AFI membership poll that declared *GWTW* the number-one most popular film.

"This is terrific. We now have the television rights to the greatest movie ever made."

Ted Turner was thrilled after Turner Broadcasting System Inc. bought from CBS all the television rights to *GWTW*.

"Yes, Margaret Mitchell writes better than I do—but she's dead."

Alexandra Braid Ripley acknowledged the tough act she had to follow in writing the sequel to *GWTW*.

"We wanted to be the first to know what happened to Rhett and Scarlett."

Laurence J. Kirshbaum, president of Warner Books, quipped about his company's $4.94 million bid for the right to publish the sequel to *GWTW*.

"I have nothing against trashy books—I'm quite fond of good trash—but this is dreadful."

In her October 27, 1991, review of *Scarlett*, Molly Ivins recommended to *New York Times Book Review* readers that they borrow—not buy—the book and then "skim the early chapters, read the Charleston part and flip through the pages of the Irish section until you find Rhett again."

"My Scarlett is very different from the character that Vivien Leigh played. This is a mature lady. At the end of *Gone With the Wind*, she winds up with no friends, just money. What kind of ending is that? I had to create somebody who starts there. Vivien Leigh started gorgeous and young and perky and ended up completely broken. I had to find somebody who could start out broken and end up being gorgeous and fulfilled and in love."

Executive producer Robert Halmi Sr. explained his vision for the heroine of his television miniseries *Scarlett*.

"Margaret Mitchell's Rhett Butler is unlike any Southerner of his generation. He's not only indifferent to his reputation, he glories in being misunderstood."

Southern novelist Donald McCaig commented to the *Roanoke Times* that *Rhett Butler's People* is his answer to the question, "What would make somebody turn out that way?"

"I would never write a sequel to *Gone with the Wind*. I'm not a romance novelist. I didn't seek to exploit her characters but explode them."

After a preliminary injunction prohibited publisher Houghton Mifflin from publishing *The Wind Done Gone*, author Alice Randall explained to the media why her book is a parody of *Gone with the Wind*.

"Scarlett would admire *The Wind Done Gone* as a great way of making money, and Rhett would admire it as a great way of stirring things up."

Southern novelist Pat Conroy commented on the copyright infringement lawsuit against writer Alice Randall and publisher Houghton Mifflin.

"Randall doesn't unearth anything fresh. . . . *Gone With the Wind* is still the impregnable fortress. *The Wind Done Gone* a shack."

Lisa Schwarzbaum reviewed *The Wind Done Gone* for the May 15, 2001, issue of *Entertainment Weekly*.

"They made other movies after *Gone With the Wind*?"

When asked why she didn't make other movies after *GWTW*, Alicia Rhett, who played India Wilkes, responded with a question of her own, according to the *Charleston Post and Courier*.

> "Their world having been turned upside down, they saw a parallel between their plight and the story of the disappearance of the antebellum South. Hence their embrace of Mitchell's epic about a society pulverized to human dust that is blown about by history's leveling wind."

In noting the seventieth anniversary of *GWTW*'s publication, columnist George F. Will opined in his June 25, 2006, column for the *Washington Post* why Depression-era Americans were drawn to the novel.

> "The presence of these chapters in the Pequot Library's collection is not only remarkable but is of national importance. These are among the most memorable pages in the entire book . . . those last pages in the book (which she actually wrote first) are right here."

Library Director Dan Snydacker reveled in the rediscovery of the last four chapters of *GWTW*'s typescript in the special collections section of Connecticut's Pequot Library.

> "[*Gone With the Wind* is] a magnificently flamboyant film about love and desertion, ambition and survival, despair and courage. And best of all it contains the greatest unresolved love story in movies."

British film critic, writer, and media personality Barry Norman, CBE, of *Radio Times* explained why *GWTW* is more than a "glorified chick flick."

Answers to Quizzes

GWTW: A NOVEL QUIZ, PAGES 10 TO 12

1. He had killed an English absentee landlord's rent agent
2. James and Andrew O'Hara
3. In poker games
4. Pork
5. Mammy
6. Robillard
7. Philippe Robillard
8. In a barroom brawl in New Orleans
9. Sixteen
10. Katie
11. Lemon verbena
12. Fayetteville Female Academy
13. Susan Elinor and Caroline Irene
14. Three. They died in infancy.
15. Frank Kennedy
16. Brent Tarleton
17. To buy Pork's wife, Dilcey, from John Wilkes
18. Prissy

19. Honey and India Wilkes
20. Charles Hamilton favored Honey; Stuart Tarleton courted India.
21. Beatrice
22. A horse-breeding farm
23. They all had red hair.
24. Tom, Boyd, and twins Stuart and Brent
25. Jeems
26. After his wife's death, he married his children's Yankee governess.
27. After the death of her fiancé, Cathleen Calvert married her family's Yankee overseer.
28. Wade Hampton Hamilton, Ella Lorena Kennedy, and Bonnie Blue Butler
29. Atlanta received its name the same year Scarlett was born.
30. Sarah Jane Hamilton
31. Uncle Peter
32. Henry Hamilton
33. Five hundred dollars
34. K.
35. Rhett Butler
36. Rock Island, Illinois
37. John Wilkes
38. September 1
39. A radish
40. Mimosa
41. In the diaper of Melanie's son
42. The kitchen
43. Will Benteen
44. Suellen O'Hara
45. He was accused of having killed a black man who had insulted a white woman.
46. Tony Fontaine
47. Carreen entered a convent.
48. Archie
49. Mr. Butler
50. Twenty-eight

THE MOVIE MOGULS SELZNICK BESTED
WITH HIS *GWTW* BUY, PAGE 18

1. e
2. f
3. d
4. a
5. c
6. b

THE GREATEST MOVIE OF
ALL TIME, PAGES 93 TO 95

1. Brent and Stuart Tarleton
2. Ashley Wilkes was engaged to marry his cousin, Melanie Hamilton.
3. Tell Ashley she loved him so he wouldn't marry Melanie
4. Whether Scarlett will eat and which gown she will wear to the barbecue
5. Cathleen Calvert
6. West Point
7. A vase; Rhett Butler
8. Charles Hamilton (Melanie's brother)
9. Pneumonia following an attack of measles
10. $150 in gold
11. Aunt Pittypat
12. A hat
13. Three days
14. Major
15. Scarlett promised to look after Melanie.
16. $50 in gold wrapped in Rhett Butler's handkerchief
17. Above the Red Horse Saloon
18. Dr. Meade; Melanie was in labor.
19. Prissy
20. Ashley's picture and Charles's sword
21. He wanted to join the Confederate Army.
22. Ellen O'Hara (Scarlett's mother)

23. That she will never be hungry again
24. A Yankee deserter
25. $300
26. Jonas Wilkerson
27. Emmy Slattery
28. From Ellen O'Hara's draperies
29. Rhett Butler
30. The condition of her hands
31. Frank Kennedy; her sister Suellen
32. At the counter of the Wilkes and Kennedy store
33. The lumber business
34. Shantytown; Big Sam
35. Melanie, Scarlett, Mammy, India Wilkes, and Mrs. Meade
36. *David Copperfield*
37. Ashley
38. He proposed marriage.
39. A red silk petticoat
40. Twenty inches
41. India Wilkes and Mrs. Meade
42. Ashley's birthday party
43. London
44. Bonnie missed her mother. She was terrorized by nightmares in the dark.
45. Scarlett fell down the staircase in her Atlanta home.
46. Bonnie had just learned to ride sidesaddle.
47. Melanie
48. A mateless glove
49. Charleston
50. Scarlett decided to return to Tara and to think of a way to get Rhett back.

THE PLAYERS WHO'S WHO, PAGE 97

1. h	4. i	7. m
2. e	5. n	8. q
3. p	6. a	9. r

10. c	15. b	20. k
11. o	16. j	21. d
12. f	17. g	22. u
13. s	18. t	
14. l	19. v	

WHO SAID IT? (#1), PAGES 97 TO 99

1. Rhett (in the library of Twelve Oaks after Scarlett smashed the vase against the mantle)
2. Scarlett (stirring a kettle of soap and greeting Pork returning from town, where he had learned that the taxes on Tara were going up)
3. Ashley (during the scene of Melanie's death)
4. Rhett (as he was about to walk out on Scarlett)
5. Melanie (after Scarlett's shooting of the Yankee deserter)
6. Rhett (in the wagon after rescuing Scarlett from the fleeing crowds in the Atlanta streets)
7. Ashley (as he said goodbye to Scarlett at the end of his Christmas leave)
8. Rhett (warning Scarlett what would happen if she didn't have Bonnie's things packed for the trip to London)
9. Melanie (after giving Ashley the tunic she had made for him as a Christmas present)
10. Scarlett (after telling Frank Kennedy that Suellen was engaged to marry one of the County boys)
11. Ashley (after Scarlett's declaration of love in the library at Twelve Oaks)
12. Rhett (as he left Scarlett at Melanie's front door on the night of Ashley's birthday party)
13. Ashley (following Scarlett's declaration of love in the library at Twelve Oaks)
14. Scarlett (speaking to a drunken Rhett in their Atlanta dining room following Ashley's birthday party)
15. Rhett (after presenting the Paris hat to Scarlett)
16. Scarlett to Ashley (during the scene of Melanie's death)
17. Scarlett (after she was attacked at Shantytown)
18. Ashley (during the discussion of the possibility of war as the gentlemen enjoyed brandy and cigars at Twelve Oaks)

19. Rhett (speaking to Mammy after Bonnie's birth)
20. Rhett (during the escape from Atlanta)
21. Scarlett (her plea to Mammy, who caught her trying on a colorful bonnet while in mourning for Charles)
22. Melanie (meeting Scarlett at Twelve Oaks)
23. Rhett (while dancing with Scarlett at the Atlanta Bazaar)
24. Ashley (speaking to Melanie during the barbecue at Twelve Oaks)
25. Rhett (as he walked out on Scarlett)
26. Scarlett (speaking to Rhett before she drove to the lumber mill via Shantytown)
27. Rhett (speaking to his card-playing Yankee major in the Atlanta jail)
28. Scarlett (speaking to Ashley in the lumber mill office on the afternoon of his birthday party)
29. Melanie (speaking to Mammy following Bonnie's birth)
30. Ashley (after Scarlett's declaration of love in the library at Twelve Oaks)
31. Scarlett (following Rhett's walking out on her)
32. Melanie (when Melanie thanks Belle Watling for saving Ashley's life)
33. Rhett (speaking to Scarlett on the road to Tara before leaving her to join the army)
34. Scarlett (on Tara's front porch with Brent and Stuart Tarleton)
35. Rhett (following Prissy's pleas outside Belle's establishment for Rhett to bring his carriage for Scarlett)
36. Scarlett (following her declaration of love to Ashley in the library at Twelve Oaks)
37. Scarlett (after Rhett bid for her to lead the opening reel at the Atlanta Bazaar)
38. Rhett (at Twelve Oaks with the gentlemen enjoying brandy and cigars)
39. Scarlett (after her declaration of love to Ashley in the library at Twelve Oaks)
40. Scarlett (during various episodes of her life)
41. Rhett (during the discussion of the possibility of war as the gentlemen were enjoying brandy and cigars at Twelve Oaks)
42. Scarlett (in her bedroom at Tara following Charles's death)

THE MASTER'S *GWTW* GAME:
MINOR CHARACTERS MATCH, PAGES 99 TO 100

1. e	5. h	9. j
2. i	6. k	10. l
3. b	7. g	11. d
4. f	8. a	12. c

WHO SAID IT? (#2), PAGES 100 TO 101

1. Gerald O'Hara (speaking to Scarlett in the fields of Tara on his return from a visit to Twelve Oaks)
2. Suellen O'Hara (during nap time after the barbecue)
3. Charles Hamilton (during the discussion of the possibility of war as the gentlemen were enjoying brandy and cigars at Twelve Oaks)
4. Gerald O'Hara (speaking to Scarlett in the fields of Tara on his return from a visit to Twelve Oaks)
5. Suellen O'Hara (reacting to Scarlett's marriage to Rhett Butler)
6. Ellen O'Hara (comforting Scarlett, who has objected to wearing black mourning garments)
7. India (pleading to Doctor Meade about Melanie, who is on her deathbed)
8. Cathleen Calvert (speaking to Scarlett on the staircase of Twelve Oaks on the day of the barbecue)
9. Frank Kennedy (following Scarlett's outburst at the mill to stop bothering her and not to call her Sugar)
10. India Wilkes (speaking to Scarlett during the evening sewing circle)
11. Gerald O'Hara (speaking to Scarlett following her return to Tara)
12. India Wilkes (during the evening sewing circle)
13. Carreen O'Hara (picking cotton with Suellen in Tara's field)
14. Frank Kennedy (asking Scarlett for Suellen's hand in marriage)
15. Charles Hamilton (comforting his weeping bride on their wedding day)
16. Frank Kennedy (to Scarlett following her tour of his Atlanta store and lumber mill and her invitation for dinner and a visit)
17. Carreen O'Hara (speaking to Suellen, who reacted badly to Scarlett's plans to restore Tara and to build a house in Atlanta)

WHO SAID IT? (#3), PAGE 102

1. Uncle Peter (chasing Belle Watling from the steps of the Atlanta hospital)
2. Beau Wilkes (during the scene of Melanie's death)
3. Dr. Meade (speaking to Aunt Pittypat, who has questioned the propriety of Scarlett and Melanie remaining in Atlanta unchaperoned)
4. Bonnie Butler (speaking to Rhett before her fatal pony ride)
5. Uncle Peter (stalking the rooster that would become Christmas dinner in honor of Ashley's holiday homecoming)
6. Aunt Pittypat Hamilton (at the Atlanta Bazaar)
7. Bonnie Butler (her exclamation of delight as Rhett announced he will take her on a trip to London)
8. Mrs. Meade (questioning Dr. Meade as he searched for a probe with which to treat Ashley's wound)
9. Beau Wilkes (during the scene of Melanie's death)
10. Mrs. Merriwether (speaking to Mrs. Meade of Rhett's love for his daughter, Bonnie)
11. Aunt Pittypat Hamilton (before fleeing Sherman's cannonballs that were raining on Atlanta)

WHO SAID IT? (#4), PAGES 107 TO 108

1. Jonas Wilkerson (the evening Mrs. O'Hara returned home from the bedside of Emmy Slattery)
2. Mammy (announcing to Scarlett the arrival of Rhett Butler after Frank Kennedy's funeral)
3. Belle Watling (referring to Scarlett, when Melanie thanks Belle for saving Ashley's life)
4. Mammy (holding back Scarlett as Ashley returned home from the war)
5. Belle Watling (outside the Atlanta hospital)
6. Mammy (after Scarlett sees Belle Watling going to visit Rhett in the Atlanta jail)
7. Yankee major (while playing cards with Rhett in the Atlanta jail)
8. Mammy (after Scarlett refused to eat before going to the barbecue)
9. Prissy (during Melanie's labor)

10. Yankee deserter (to Scarlett at Tara)
11. Mammy (after Mrs. O'Hara decided to send Scarlett to Atlanta to visit Melanie and Aunt Pittypat)
12. Mammy (putting Frank Kennedy's pants into the boiling pot)
13. Belle Watling (when Melanie thanked Belle for saving Ashley's life)
14. Prissy (during Melanie's labor)
15. Pork (following Scarlett's return to Tara)
16. Jonas Wilkerson (while visiting Tara with his wife, Emmy Slattery Wilkerson)
17. Johnnie Gallegher (showing off the prisoners who will work in the lumber mill)
18. Scarlett's attacker at Shantytown
19. Big Sam (while rescuing Scarlett from her attacker at Shantytown)
20. Tom, a Yankee captain (interrupting the evening sewing circle)

SCARLETT: A NOVEL QUIZ, PAGES 186 TO 188

1. In public she made a scene, laid her hands on a man who wasn't her husband, and raised a ruckus that interrupted Melanie's burial.
2. Mammy
3. Queen of Hearts
4. Sister Mary Joseph
5. Her aunts Pauline and Eulalie
6. Onions
7. A half-million dollars in gold
8. White camellias
9. Middleton Courtney
10. Anne Hampton
11. To buy Carreen's third share of Tara from the convent
12. They made love.
13. Rhett's sister Rosemary
14. Her grandfather Pierre Robillard
15. She was pregnant.
16. Ballyhara
17. Five thousand dollars
18. The O'Hara
19. October 31 (Halloween)

20. Katie Colum O'Hara
21. Cat
22. The Earl of Fenton
23. John Morland
24. Rosaleen Fitzpatrick
25. They used the old rope ladder hidden under Cat's quilts.

SCARLETT WHO SAID IT?, PAGES 201 TO 202

1. Henry Hamilton
2. Mammy
3. Big Sam
4. Rhett Butler
5. Sally Brewton
6. Belle Watling
7. Eleanor Butler
8. Father Colum O'Hara
9. Suellen O'Hara Benteen
10. Scarlett O'Hara
11. Eulalie Robillard
12. Pauline Robillard
13. Lord Fenton
14. Sir John Morland
15. Ashley Wilkes
16. Will Benteen
17. Anne Hampton Butler
18. Lady Morland
19. Mary Boyle
20. Rosaleen Fitzpatrick

RHETT BUTLER'S PEOPLE: A NOVEL QUIZ, PAGES 209 TO 210

1. Tecumseh
2. Langston Butler
3. Isaiah Watling
4. Shad Watling
5. Thomas Bonneau
6. Senator Wade Hampton
7. Langston Butler struck Rhett's name from the family Bible.
8. Rhett's New Orleans Creole mistress
9. Frank Kennedy
10. *Merry Widow*
11. Tunis Bonneau
12. Tazewell Watling
13. Chapeau Rouge
14. A yellow silk scarf
15. Seeing the boy soldier collapse on the road
16. Archie Flytte
17. Tunis Bonneau
18. Edgar Puryear
19. Ruth
20. He was Rhett's nephew.
21. Bonnie
22. Selling the sawmills
23. Andrew Ravanel
24. She became the schoolmarm for the children.
25. Isaiah Watling

Bibliography

The author thanks the following sources, which were invaluable during the writing of *The Complete* Gone With the Wind *Trivia Book.*

BOOKS

Allen, Patrick, ed. *Margaret Mitchell: Reporter.* Columbia: University of South Carolina Press, 2010.

Anderson, Joan Wester. *Forever Young: The Life, Loves, and Enduring Faith of a Hollywood Legend.* Allen, TX: Thomas More, 2000.

Behlmer, Rudy, ed. *Memo from David O. Selznick.* New York: Viking, 1972.

Brown, Ellen F., and John Wiley Jr. *Margaret Mitchell's* Gone with the Wind*: A Bestseller's Odyssey from Atlanta to Hollywood.* Lanham, MD: Taylor Trade, 2011.

Cameron, Judy, and Paul Christman. *The Art of* Gone With the Wind*: The Making of a Legend.* Upper Saddle River, NJ: Prentice Hall Editions, 1989.

Edwards, Anne. *Road to Tara.* New Haven, CT: Ticknor and Fields, 1983.

———. *Vivien Leigh: A Biography.* New York: Simon and Schuster, 1977.

Eskridge, Jane, ed. *Before Scarlett: Girlhood Writings of Margaret Mitchell.* Columbia: University of South Carolina Press, 2011.

Farr, Finis. *Margaret Mitchell of Atlanta: The Author of* Gone with the Wind. New York: William Morrow & Company, 1965.

Flamini, Roland. *Scarlett, Rhett, and a Cast of Thousands*. New York: Macmillan, 1975.

Gardner, Gerald, and Harriet Modell Gardner. *Pictorial History of* Gone With the Wind. New York: Bonanza Books, 1983.

Harmetz, Aljean. *On the Road to Tara*. New York: Harry N. Abrams, 1996.

Harris, Warren G. *Clark Gable: A Biography*. New York: Harmony Books, 2002.

Harwell, Richard, ed. *Margaret Mitchell's* Gone with the Wind *Letters, 1936–1949*. New York: Macmillan, 1976.

Haver, Ronald. *David O. Selznick's* Gone With the Wind. New York: Bonanza Books, 1986.

Hecht, Ben. *A Child of the Century*. New York: Simon and Schuster, 1954.

Higham, Charles. *Sisters: The Story of Olivia de Havilland and Joan Fontaine*. New York: Coward-McCann, 1984.

Howard, Leslie Ruth. *A Quite Remarkable Father*. New York: Harcourt, Brace and Company, 1959.

Howard, Ronald. *In Search of My Father*. New York: St. Martin's Press, 1981.

Katz, Ephraim. *The Film Encyclopedia*. New York: Thomas Y. Crowell, Publishers, 1979.

Lambert, Gavin. *GWTW: The Making of* Gone With the Wind. Boston: Little, Brown and Company, 1973.

——. *On Cukor*. New York: G. P. Putnam's Sons, 1972.

Leff, Leonard J., and Jerold L. Simmons. *The Dame in the Kimono: Hollywood, Censorship, and the Production Code*. Lexington: University Press of Kentucky, 2001.

Levy, Emanuel. *And the Winner Is . . . : The History and Politics of the Oscar Awards*. New York: Ungar, 1987.

Lewis, Judy. *Uncommon Knowledge*. New York: Pocket Books, 1994.

McCaig, Donald. *Rhett Butler's People*. New York: St. Martin's Press, 2008.

Mitchell, Margaret. *Gone with the Wind*. New York: Macmillan, 1936.

——. *Lost Laysen*. Edited by Debra Freer. New York: Scribner, 1996.

Myrick, Susan. *White Columns in Hollywood: Reports from the* Gone With the Wind *Sets*. Macon, GA: Mercer University Press, 1994.

Pratt, William. *Scarlett Fever: The Ultimate Pictorial Treasury of* Gone With the Wind. New York: Macmillan, 1977.

Ragan, David. *Who's Who in Hollywood, 1900–1976*. New Rochelle, NY: Arlington House, 1976.

Randall, Alice. *The Wind Done Gone*. New York: Houghton Mifflin, 2001.

Ripley, Alexandra. *Scarlett: The Sequel to Margaret Mitchell's* Gone with the Wind. New York: Warner Books, 1991.

Sragow, Michael. *Victor Fleming: An American Movie Master*. New York: Pantheon Books, 2008.

Steinberg, Cobbett. *Film Facts*. New York: Facts on File, 1980.

Thomas, Bob. *Selznick*. New York: Doubleday and Company, 1950.

Thomson, David. *Showman: The Life of David O. Selznick*. New York: Alfred A. Knopf, 1992.

Tornabene, Lyn. *Long Live the King: A Biography of Clark Gable*. New York: G. P. Putnam's Sons, 1976.

Truitt, Evelyn Mack. *Who Was Who on Screen*. New York: R. R. Bowker, 1983.

Walker, Alexander. *The Life of Vivien Leigh*. New York: Weidenfeld & Nicholson, 1987.

Wiley, Mason, and Damien Bona. *Inside Oscar*. New York: Ballantine Books, 1986.

WEBSITES / INTERNET SOURCES

American Film Institute (www.afi.com)

American National Biography Online (www.anb.org)

Atlanta History Center (www.atlantahistorycenter.com)

Atlanta Press Club (www.atlantapressclub.org)

Box Office Mojo (www.boxofficemojo.com)

British Film Institute (www.bfi.org.uk)

Catholic News Service (www.catholicnews.com)

Christie's (www.christies.com)

Clark Gable Foundation (www.clarkgablefoundation.com)

Clayton News Daily (www.news-daily.com)

CNN (www.cnn.com)

Daily Beast / Newsweek (www.thedailybeast.com)

Daily Mail (www.dailymail.co.uk)

Georgia Bulletin (www.georgiabulletin.org)

Greg Giese (www.gwtwgreg.8m.com)

Harry Ransom Center (www.hrc.utexas.edu)

Hollywood Walk of Fame (www.walkoffame.com)

Houghton Mifflin Harcourt (www.houghtonmifflinbooks.com)

Internet Broadway Database (www.ibdb.com)

Internet Movie Database (www.imdb.com)

Kendra Bean (http://kendrabean.com and www.vivandlarry.com)

Motion Picture Association of America (www.mpaa.org)

National Portrait Gallery (www.npg.org.uk)

National Register of Historic Places (www.nps.gov)

Playbill (www.playbill.com)

Royal Mail (www.royalmail.com)

Smithsonian Institution (http://newsdesk.si.edu)
Turner Classic Movies (www.tcm.com)
United States Postal Service (www.usps.com)
University of South Carolina Press (www.sc.edu/uscpress)
Victoria and Albert Museum (www.vam.ac.uk)

PERIODICALS

Albany Times Union
American Film
Art & Antiques
Atlanta Journal-Constitution
Bergen City (NJ) Record
Black Issues in Higher Education
Boston Globe
Charleston Magazine
Chicago Sun-Times
Chicago Tribune
Charleston Post and Courier
Cosmopolitan
Daily Telegraph
Daily Variety
Desert Sun
Detroit Free Press
Entertainment Weekly
Frankly My Dear . . . Fans! (newsletter of the Clark Gable Foundation)
Guardian (London)
Herald
Independent (London)
Irish Examiner
Knickerbocker News
Knight Ridder / Tribune Business News
Life
Los Angeles Times
Mail Tribune (OR)
Milwaukee Journal
Minneapolis Star Tribune
National Observer
New York Daily News

New York Times
New York Times Book Review
Newsweek
Parade
People magazine
Piedmont Triad (NC) News & Record
Poughkeepsie Journal
Publishers Weekly
Richmond Times-Dispatch
Roanoke Times
Rome (GA) News-Tribune
Scarlett Letter
Seattle Times
Sunday Telegraph (London)
Sun Sentinel
Time
Times Record
TV Guide
Under the Arches (Pequot Library Newsletter, spring 2011 and fall 2011)
USA Today
Vancouver (WA) Columbian
Variety
Wall Street Journal
Washington Post
Winston-Salem Journal

OTHER SOURCES

Associated Press
BBC America
Bonhams / Turner Classic Movies auction catalog
Cox News Service
King Features Syndicate
McClatchy-Tribune News Service
NPR *Morning Edition*
State News Service
Turner Home Entertainment, *GWTW* 50th Anniversary Press Kit

Index

Note: Names of the fictional characters are alphabetized by first name (e.g., "Scarlett O'Hara" rather than "O'Hara, Scarlett").